Mental Health
Consultation in Early Childhood

Mental Health
Consultation in Early Childhood

by

Paul J. Donahue, Ph.D.
The Center for Preventive Psychiatry
White Plains, New York

Beth Falk, Ph.D.
Byram Hills School District
Armonk, New York

and

Anne Gersony Provet, Ph.D.
The Center for Preventive Psychiatry
White Plains, New York

·P·A·U·L·H·
BROOKES
PUBLISHING Cº

Baltimore • London • Toronto • Sydney

Paul H. Brookes Publishing Co.
Post Office Box 10624
Baltimore, Maryland 21285-0624

www.brookespublishing.com

Typeset by Barton Matheson Willse and Worthington, Baltimore, Maryland.
Manufactured in the United States of America by
The Maple Press Co., York, Pennsylvania.

All of the vignettes in this book are based on the authors' experiences. In all
instances, names have been changed; in some instances, identifying details
have been altered to protect confidentiality.

Library of Congress Cataloging-in-Publication Data
Donahue, Paul J.
    Mental health consultation in early childhood / by Paul J. Donahue,
  Beth Falk, and Anne Gersony Provet.
        p.   cm.
    Includes bibliographical references and index.
    ISBN 1-55766-449-8 (pbk.)
    1. Child psychiatry.   2. Mental health consultation.   3. Child mental
  health services.   I. Falk, Beth.   II. Provet, Anne Gersony.   III. Title.
  RJ499.D595   2000
618.92'89—dc21   99-37494
                                                                                         CIP

British Library Cataloguing in Publication data are available from the British
Library.

Contents

The Changing Role of Early Childhood Education
New Demands in the Classroom
Integrating Mental Health and Early Childhood
  Education
  A New Model of Partnership
Developing a Shared Vision:
  Precursors to an Effective Collaboration

I   **THE COLLABORATIVE PROCESS**
Establishing Collaborative Relationships
  Working with the Program Director
  Connecting with Staff
Potential Pitfalls in the Entry Process
Assessing the Early Childhood Program
  Readiness to Collaborate
  An Assessment Tool
Initial Plan of Intervention

Staff Alliances and Conflicts
Maintaining an Ongoing Dialogue Between the
  Consultant and the Program Director
Consultation and Educational Planning
Consultation and Social Work
Liaisons with Community Agencies

Developing and Maintaining Rapport
  Race, Class, Culture, and Profession
  Past Experience with Mental Health and
  Related Services

About the Authors

Paul J. Donahue, Ph.D., is the Director of Early Childhood Consultation at The Center for Preventive Psychiatry in White Plains, New York. He has written and lectured widely on the impact of trauma on children and the assessment and treatment of young children and their parents. Dr. Donahue has been active in designing mental health services for Head Start and has served on a national committee charged with rewriting the federal definition of mental health in childhood. Dr. Donahue is in private practice in Scarsdale, New York.

Beth Falk, Ph.D., is a school psychologist in the Byram Hills School District in Armonk, New York. Dr. Falk began her career as a special education teacher in New York City. As a school psychologist, she continues to promote effective partnerships among families, educators, and mental health professionals. While on the staff of The Center for Preventive Psychiatry, Dr. Falk provided consultation to local Head Start centers and clinical services to children and families affected by human immunodeficiency virus/acquired immunodeficiency syndrome (HIV/AIDS). Dr. Falk is in private practice in Mount Kisco, New York.

Anne Gersony Provet, Ph.D., is a supervising psychologist and the Coordinator for Early Intervention Services at The Center for Preventive Psychiatry in White Plains, New York. Dr. Provet began her career as an early childhood educator. Her current clinical interests include building resilience and reducing stress in young children and their families. Dr. Provet has investigated the long-term effects of risk and protective factors first identified in early childhood. Her work has been published in academic journals and edited volumes. Dr. Provet is in private practice in Yorktown Heights, New York.

Foreword

Mental Health Consultation in Early Childhood is a timely and important book. Throughout the United States, staff and directors working in Head Start, Early Head Start, preschool, and child care programs are asking for help. Reports are consistent from all parts of the country. Too many young children are showing behaviors that are troubling, some so provocative and challenging that they are asked to leave their programs because staff do not know how to help them. Families are experiencing greater and greater stress levels, and early childhood staff report feeling burdened despite the enormous dedication and commitment of many. This book can help.

The insights and wisdom that Dr. Paul Donahue and his colleagues Drs. Beth Falk and Anne Gersony Provet have amassed in *Mental Health Consultation in Early Childhood* provide a framework for enhancing the quality of early childhood programs, particularly center-based ones, and for helping staff as well as children and families. The book is about how to use clinical mental health perspectives and skills in the service of promoting healthy emotional development in young children, including those who are already scarred by harsh early experiences, who participate in early childhood programs. It provides an insider's view of the consultation process, highlighting the central importance of building mutually respectful collaborations between consultants and administrators and consultants and teachers. It also articulates clearly the many roles that mental health consultants can play. These include problem solving with staff about individual children and families or classroom management issues; guiding staff to solve collective problems; helping staff members recognize and celebrate their hard work and importance to the children; modeling alternative approaches and behaviors for caregivers; offering guidance to families; facilitating referrals if necessary; helping staff respond to crises, such as community violence or family disasters; and, most important, helping to restart the healthy growth process for young children who have experienced damaging early relationships and experiences.

The authors bring a unique perspective to the task of getting inside the consultation process. They are grounded in the daily realities of the kinds of pressures that pervade the lives of early childhood program administrators and staff, as well as the children and families in the programs. From this knowledge, they have built a rich resource for others—a book filled with a sophisticated blend of clinical insights and common sense, organized in a way that is useful for practitioners and students seeking to master the complexities and possibilities of effective consultation. Theirs is not a "cookbook approach," a behavior management curriculum for all children or a set of guidelines for workshops. Rather, what the authors describe is a form of ethnographic and psychological consultation. It is ethnographic in that the consultants enter into the life of the center, viewing it as a culture, and psychological in that the role of the consultant is to try to assess and understand not just the dynamics of individual children, caregivers, and families, but the program culture and dynamics as well. The aim is to understand and intervene respectfully to enhance the caregiving context for all staff, children, and families involved.

Key to the vision of consultation espoused in this book, and underscored in virtually every chapter, is the importance of building relationships with the staff and the directors—trying to walk, as it were, in their shoes. This book does not offer a quick-fix set of tools, although it is rich with ideas and specific activities that consultants can undertake. The point is also clear that to do their job well, early childhood mental health consultants must make a sustained investment in the many (and sometimes tangled) relationships in a particular setting. They must be strategic about how to enter into an ongoing context; to develop interventions that work for the culture of each program; to respond with sensitivity and openness to issues of class, race, and ethnicity; and to help staff cope with the varied challenges they face. Yet mental health consultants also get to share in the victories, small or large.

The authors are well aware that mental health consultation is no substitute for having staff trained in early childhood development and quality child care and early education practices. But they also recognize that training in these basics is often woefully inadequate and that it is even less adequate in equipping staff to address the widespread—indeed, virtually predictable—stresses and even trauma that so many young children and families experience. Hence, the authors pay particular attention to coping with trauma in young children in the context of early childhood environments.

This book fills a gap in the early childhood and mental health literature, which offers relatively few resources for enhancing mental health in the context of early childhood settings. But it also signals a larger societal challenge, that of paying more attention to the emotional well-being and development of young children. Although this is not a new perspective, it is one that often gets lost in the efforts to promote the cognitive and physical well-being of young children, particularly by funders and policy makers. Yet, as recent research on early brain development has reconfirmed, the emotional pathways and patterns established in early childhood are key to the later success of young children. This gives special significance to the authors' view that early childhood programs provide an opportunity to check the "wellness" of young children.

This book is targeted to practitioners, both new and experienced. (It would, for instance, be especially useful for those supervising new consultants.) But it is my hope that the message of this book will also reach two other very important audiences. The first audience is those studying early childhood education, early intervention, social work, and psychology. For these students, this book offers a gold mine of real-life experiences to discuss and role play, drawing on the many vignettes illustrating both successful and unsuccessful strategies.

But even more important, it is my hope that the message of this book will be translated back to a second group, policy makers. We face a policy context that is inhospitable to strengthening and expanding early childhood mental health consultation. Too often, there seems to be no way to pay for the kind of work that is described in this book. Many of the children are at risk of developing behavior and emotional disorders, especially if they do not have access to ecological and supportive interventions. Yet current mental health reimbursement and other policies typically require children to have a diagnosable disorder in order to receive treatment or consultation. Even for young children, being at risk of developing a disorder is not a sufficient gateway to services.

Perhaps this book will inspire a rethinking about the need to target more mental health resources toward young children and to use them in ways that support the kind of consultation strategies highlighted throughout this book, as well as to provide treatment to the young children and families facing the greatest difficulties. Perhaps it will also spur the increased use of Head Start and Early Head Start dollars for this kind of on-site mental health consultation. Equally important, it may stimulate the still too small but growing initiatives to use child care quality enhancement dollars to support efforts like these. This book is a practical, grounded guide to helping those who work directly with young children and families. Yet it is also a wake-up call to include program and case consultation as a routine part of efforts to promote the well-being of young children and families, particularly those burdened by poverty, disability, and other risk factors that have potentially and—sadly—often predictable deleterious effects. In short, this book is a call to reinvent a societal commitment to strengthening the tools, strategies, and policies that will allow every child to enter school emotionally ready to succeed.

Jane Knitzer, Ed.D.
National Center for Children in Poverty
Columbia University Joseph L. Mailman School of Public Health

Preface

The model presented in this book reflects our experiences as consulting psychologists in a variety of preschool and child care settings. We were introduced to early childhood consultation through our affiliation with The Center for Preventive Psychiatry (the Center), a community mental health center in White Plains, New York. We have drawn extensively from our clinical work at the Center and from the seminal work of many of our colleagues there as well as from our experiences in school systems and in private practice as consultants. A number of researchers, clinicians, and educators have made considerable strides in developing school-based consultation and prevention models (Alpert, 1982; Cowen et al., 1996; Gutkin & Curtis, 1990) and on-site interventions in early childhood programs (Edlefsen & Baird, 1994). This book should be viewed as an extension of previous school-based efforts to reach out to young children and their families, with a particular emphasis on building collaborations between mental health professionals and early childhood educators.

We are often contacted by program directors who want their staff to learn more about child development and to gain strategies in dealing with children who pose challenges in the classroom. Sometimes there is a particular crisis in the school that warrants our immediate intervention. In other cases, we are asked to address long-standing conflicts between staff members or to make suggestions for improving specific program areas, such as parent outreach. Usually we contract to be on site on a weekly basis for at least 1 academic year and spend anywhere from 3 hours to 3 days per week on site.

In our initial meetings with the preschool staff, we emphasize three features of our work. First, we talk of possible roles that we might play as consultants and try to define the initial parameters of our work based on the individual program's needs. Second, we emphasize that although we strive to enhance the workings of the entire system, we can best accomplish this goal by developing trusting relationships with the individuals in the program, including teachers, families, and children. To do this we must have the freedom as clinicians to respect the confidentiality of our clients and to define the boundaries of our communication with administration and other staff members (see Tobias, 1990). Last, we encourage the school staff to view our work as an ongoing process that may not lead to immediate change or a "quick fix" but, given time, should influence the system in positive ways.

We expand on these themes throughout the book and try to bear in mind the opportunities and perils present at each step in the collaborative process. The book is arranged in three sections. First, we explore ways of establishing a collaborative relationship between the consultant and the staff of the school, focusing initially on the entry process and then proceeding with specific suggestions and techniques for working with administrative staff and teachers. Second, we examine the consultant's on-site work with children and parents, including classroom-based prevention strategies and therapeutic group activities. This section also focuses on dealing with crises in the school and designing interventions for individual children and families who experience trauma. Finally, we reflect on the challenges we have faced in this work and the rewards, for both the consultants and the early childhood centers, of developing a strong partnership. We also discuss practical ways of establishing and maintaining a collaborative relationship and end with a review of the broader implications of this model.

This book is intended to enhance the working relationship between mental health professionals (also referred to as consultants, therapists, and clinicians throughout this book) and early childhood educators. It is designed for individuals from traditional clinical settings as well as administrators, directors, and special needs professionals from early childhood programs who share the goal of meeting the mental health needs of young children. We also expect the book to be of interest to graduate students in clinical and school psychology, social work, and education. The book may also be a useful resource for policy makers and community activists looking to build more effective community-based programs for young children.

Although many of our case illustrations and substantive clinical discussions emerged from our work in Head Start and other programs serving disadvantaged children in urban environments, we have selected examples and themes with relevance for diverse ethnic, cultural, and programmatic contexts. Early childhood environments include full-day child care centers, school-based prekindergarten programs, Head Start centers, and private nursery schools. Child care programs are sometimes less structured and academic than preschools that offer more formalized education, but the central issues and educational goals for these programs are quite similar. We therefore expect that the majority of the material will be applicable to both environments. Although we do not specifically address the concerns of in-home child care providers, we believe that some of the material will be relevant to them.

There are salient differences that can be expected across program settings, geographic location, and population served, but a central feature of our collaborative model is the absence of a simplistic blueprint that rigidly prescribes the activities and roles of the mental health professional or presumes to predetermine the needs of the preschool program. Rather, the model emphasizes the transactional relationship between the consultant and the child care center: Both parties work together to determine goals and select from a multitude of possible roles, activities, and structures whereby the mental health professional strives to meet the early childhood program's needs. Although there are a number of general principles—as well as philosophical and ethical beliefs—that remained fixed, the form and content of the partnership is indeed fluid so that a wide range of collaborators can work effectively with diverse populations in a variety of environments.

Our goal is to provide both a conceptual framework and concrete guidance for mental health professionals and educators who may find themselves in situations and settings for which their training has not adequately prepared them. By highlighting the difficult but extremely rewarding nature of this work, we hope this book encourages partnerships that foster children's development and ultimately strengthens the resilience and coping abilities of young children and their families.

Acknowledgments

This book's model emerged from a longstanding mental health–early childhood education partnership. For several years, large numbers of teachers, social workers, and directors in early childhood programs in our region, Westchester County, New York, had been reporting increases in challenging behaviors and family problems. Many directors stated that adding on-site mental health services was their number one priority. As a result of these requests, the social service agency overseeing many of the Head Start and child care programs, the Westchester Community Opportunity Program (WestCop), decided to expand its contract for consultation services with The Center for Preventive Psychiatry (the Center), where all of this book's authors have served on staff. Funding for the program came primarily from Head Start, which in 1998 changed its program mandate to include a goal of on-site mental health services in all Head Start centers. In addition, the Center secured a grant from the Community Development Block Grant program of the U.S. Department of Housing and Urban Development to support its efforts in child care and preschool programs. We are perhaps proudest of this source of funds, with its symbolic recognition that quality child care and preventive mental health services are essential building blocks of a community.

The Center for Preventive Psychiatry is an outpatient mental health clinic that for more than 30 years has emphasized prevention and early intervention services for young children and their families, with a particular focus on childhood trauma. Clinicians from the Center have been consulting to nursery schools, child care centers, and Head Start programs almost from its inception. Since the early 1990s, the Center has greatly expanded its community-based projects, and its staff have focused a good deal of time and energy on developing its early childhood consultation service as a cornerstone of these programs. As of 1999, the Center provided on-site mental health services to more than 20 nursery schools, Head Start programs, and child care centers in Westchester County and offered professional training to child care staff and educators throughout the region.

We owe our gratitude to many of our colleagues at the Center. A number of current and former staff members have imparted their clinical wisdom to us and allowed us to tap into a deep reservoir of early childhood experiences. We would especially like to cite the work of Arthur Zelman, Medical Director of the Center; Ann Kliman, Director of the Situational Crisis Service; and Tom Lopez, Director of the Cornerstone Nursery. All were forerunners in providing community-based mental health services to young children and their families, and they continue to train and inspire the next generation of clinicians regarding the value of prevention and early intervention. We also want to thank Karen Roser, who made a substantial contribution to the conceptual development of this book and the early stages of the manuscript and always approached her consultation work in a thoughtful and compassionate manner. We are indebted to Monica Morton, whose ability to connect with families having multiple stressors and commitment to treating young children affected by trauma served as benchmarks for our own clinical and training endeavors. Our colleagues in the Early Childhood Consultation service deserve special mention for their efforts on behalf of young children and families, their collective clinical wisdom, and the *esprit de corps* that they brought to our group discussions. In particular, we thank Susan Davis, Amy Resnick, Ann Spiegel, and Rita Stewart. We also appreciate the administrative support of Sylvia Bloom, Jonathan Cohen, Harvey Newman, and Rosetta Rhodes at the Center.

Without the help of many of our colleagues in early childhood education this book would not have come to fruition. We thank all the administrative and teaching staff in the nursery schools, Head Start programs, and child care centers in Westchester County and New York City with whom we have worked, as well as the administrators and teachers in the Byram Hills School District. We acknowledge Jodie Greenbaum, Coordinator of Disabilities and Mental Health Services for WestCop, for her unwavering support and efforts to bring mental health services to young children. We also express our gratitude to Lois Alterman, Ellen Ferrar, Denise Gilman, Rita Hulkower, and all the staff, past and present, at St. Bernard's Center for Learning, where all of the authors served as consultants and therapists. Jane Knitzer deserves a special note of thanks for her kind words and encouragement and her willingness to challenge us to see our work in broader terms and to complete this book before the end of the millennium.

To my wife, Jennifer, my partner in love and work;
to our children, Sean and Nora, who are a constant
source of wonder and joy in my life
(PJD)

To my husband, Daniel Herman, and our children,
Matthew and Rachel, my wellsprings of love and learning
(BF)

To my husband, Peter, and our sons, Jeremy, Jackson,
and Samuel, who are the center of my life; also to
the memory of my mother, Toby Braverman,
for her love and dedication to young children
(AGP)

chapter one

Introduction

More young children in the United States are spending a significant amount of time in preschools and child care centers than ever before. In 1965, only 6% of children younger than 5 were cared for in centers. By 1995, the number had risen to 31% (Scarr, 1998). For many families, these early childhood programs provide an essential service, as most women (nearly 60%) with children younger than 6 are now in the labor force and need child care for at least part of the work week (Zigler, Finn-Stevenson, & Stern, 1997). New changes in welfare and workfare legislation will likely increase the demand for out-of-home child care, as more mothers on public assistance are required to enter the work force while their children are in preschool.

THE CHANGING ROLE OF EARLY CHILDHOOD EDUCATION

Early childhood programs fill important educational and child care demands and are no longer viewed as optional opportunities for casual play. With the advances in the study of brain development in infants and toddlers and research on the early acquisition of learning skills, preschool education has taken on a new significance. It is now widely

1

accepted that early childhood educators play a major role in shaping children's emotional, social, and cognitive development and help lay the foundation for future academic success. Many early childhood centers have also become cornerstones of their communities, offering parenting workshops, recreational programs, and health and education classes as well as extended child care hours for working families.

In many instances, early childhood programs have taken on these additional roles out of necessity. Hospitals, clinics, mental health agencies, child welfare agencies, and other institutions that traditionally supported families have been forced to cut back on early intervention and treatment programs. The dwindling supply of resources has often resulted in funding of only the more cost-effective programs, high-profile causes, or those that feature biologically based interventions of the most current academic interest. Although there are many model programs that emphasize prevention, community-based services, or more intensive long-term relationships with young children and families, they are not easily replicated because funding generally remains project driven and does not typically lead to policy changes at the local or state level. More and more preschools must function on their own as there is only limited support for collaborative efforts with health, mental health, and social services providers.

With their increasing prominence, early childhood programs are typically the first to feel the impact of family stresses. In many urban and some rural communities, Head Start centers and child care programs serve large numbers of disadvantaged families. Nearly a quarter of all children younger than age 6 in the United States, or 5.5 million children, live below the poverty line (National Center for Children in Poverty, 1998). Many of these children, affected by their parents' struggle to provide for their families' basic needs and to maintain adequate housing and employment, come to their centers bringing their concerns with them.

As of 2000, fewer young children live in two-parent households than at any other time. Across all socioeconomic groups in the late 1990s, a large percentage of marriages that have produced children will end in divorce, and 40%–50% of children born in the United States between 1989 and 1999 will reside in single-parent homes at some point in their childhood (Dubow, Roecker, & D'Imperio, 1997). Though intended to preserve the rights of children, legal custody and financial agreements do not always translate into equitable and amicable arrangements in which both parents remain actively involved in their children's lives (Dion, Braver, Wolchick, & Sandler, 1997). With these developments, early childhood education programs are often implicitly or explicitly asked to take a more primary role in child rearing.

The increase in the reported incidence of trauma in families has raised new concerns about the psychological development and educational needs of young children. Violence, both in the community and within the home in the form of domestic violence and child abuse, has been shown to have a profound impact on children's emotional adjustment and cognitive development (Aber & Allen, 1987; Pynoos & Eth, 1986; ZERO TO THREE: National Center for Infants, Toddlers, and Families, 1994a). In families affected by substance abuse, human immunodeficiency virus (HIV)/acquired immunodeficiency syndrome (AIDS), mental illness, and other debilitating diseases, young children have been forced to cope with the loss or potential loss of parenting figures, often obligating them to take on caregiving responsibilities. Research has also shown that children with multiple risk factors are most likely to show signs of emotional difficulties or behavior problems (Rutter & Quintin, 1977).

Young children are especially vulnerable to the disruptions caused by traumatic events because they do not have well-developed physical or psychological resources to defend against them. They depend on adults to help them make sense of the trauma, heighten their resilience, and shield them from its ill effects. Yet primary caregivers may also be affected, making them less available to provide reassurance and a sense of security and safety to their young children. As a result, the burden of care for these children often shifts, at least in part, to caregivers outside their home. The child care center frequently takes on added significance for children contending with trauma, who crave consistency, nurturance, and a safe haven where they can play and learn and focus on more age-appropriate tasks of development.

NEW DEMANDS IN THE CLASSROOM

Children who have had disruptions in their early development and attachments often present challenging behaviors in the classroom. They may appear to be fearful, disorganized, inattentive, and unresponsive to learning (Koplow, 1996). Head Start teachers have reported that their students are displaying more symptoms of emotional distress, including withdrawal and depression as well as acting-out and aggressive behaviors (Yoshikawa & Knitzer, 1997). This trend mirrors findings from epidemiological research suggesting an increased prevalence of psychiatric disorders in children, with onset at younger ages (Cohen, Provet, & Jones, 1996). In addition, many of the disturbances that emerge in older children can be traced to risk factors present in infancy and early childhood (Werner, 1989).

Many early childhood programs are struggling to adapt to this added responsibility. Preschool teachers and other staff are often overwhelmed by the extent of their children's disturbance or distress and do not believe they have received adequate training to respond to their students' needs (Knitzer, 1996). They fear that opening up discussion of traumatic or stressful events might lead to unpredictable emotional reactions in the children that the staff cannot control. Teachers also frequently feel pressured to maintain a formal academic curriculum, with an emphasis on the mastery of cognitive concepts, and do not consider it appropriate to use classroom time to deal with their children's emotional turmoil (Hyson, 1994).

The heightened concern around child abuse has also, understandably, made teachers more cautious about providing emotional or physical comfort to young children. Even experienced educators sometimes fear that their actions might be misinterpreted, especially in light of highly publicized accusations that have been aimed at the staff of child care centers in many parts of the United States. Some schools have explicit policies on what kind of touching is appropriate and have set limits on the amount of affection and hugs that children can receive from teachers. Many schools are concerned about safety and liability issues during boisterous, active play and discourage physically challenging pursuits. Teachers often express anxiety about how to handle aggressive children and are not sure how much physical intervention is appropriate. They may refrain from confronting acting-out behavior for fear of exacerbating a conflict or having to restrain or hold a child.

Despite these challenges, numerous educators now recognize that the preschool classroom presents a unique opportunity to provide a reparative milieu for children in distress (Koplow, 1996). They are urging nursery schools to return to their roots as centers of play, open emotional expression, and close adult–child relationships (Hyson, 1994). The expanded model of early childhood education that they embrace allows for a wide range of feelings in children, does not shy away from conflicts or trauma, and does not always impose a happy face on the children's experiences. This model also recognizes that children benefit from open and honest dialogue with adults and can best resolve their insecurities and gain access to their abilities in a warm, consistent school environment where they can develop strong attachments to their teachers.

INTEGRATING MENTAL HEALTH AND EARLY CHILDHOOD EDUCATION

As preschools have had to adapt to this changing climate, so too have mental health practitioners. Drawing from work pioneered with older children and adolescents, researchers and clinicians working with young children are recommending that mental health providers expand their focus beyond the traditional model of office- or clinic-based services (Knitzer, 1993, 1996). Children at high risk and their families are often unresponsive to these services as treatment can be derailed by logistical difficulties, including transportation or child care; by financial constraints; or by psychological factors, including family disorganization and a fear or mistrust of mental health agencies. In a typical clinic model, intervention occurs only when a child's behavior or emotional distress reaches clinically significant levels. Symptoms often escalate, and behavior becomes more entrenched in the intervening period between the first detection of emotional problems and referral for treatment. It is also not uncommon for educational and mental health agencies to have an "all or none" threshold for psychological intervention in which children not diagnosed with specific mental illnesses receive few or no services. In the process, opportunities for prevention or early intervention are lost.

In addition, traditional therapies are often poorly integrated with the rest of children's lives because other professionals involved rarely get or give regular feedback on their progress. Nor do they have a chance to plan interventions together. Young children instead tend to be segmented into functional components (e.g., speech-language, cognitive, emotional), with each specialist devising his or her own treatment plan, perhaps ignoring the underlying developmental struggles and stressors that a more holistic approach might uncover. Mental health services often still emanate from a child-focused rather than a family or systems approach. In this framework, clinicians spend much time and energy on a child's specific presenting difficulty, with relatively little examination of the family as a key contributor to the problem as well as a central player in its resolution. As young children are so dependent and emotionally engaged with their caregivers, clinicians who fail to involve parents, teachers, and other significant adults in treatment can miss critical opportunities for change.

A New Model of Partnership
Given the changes in early childhood education and mental health, the preschool has become, in many ways, the ideal setting for integrating the work of professionals in both disciplines (see Knitzer, in press, for examples of current preschool–mental health partnerships). Forging a real partnership between mental health professionals and educators allows schools to provide a comprehensive approach to the emotional and cognitive development of the children they serve and lessens the risk of specialists seeking piecemeal solutions in their own areas of expertise. On-site psychological services with joint treatment and educational planning by team members offer the best possibility for children and families to benefit from the diverse training and perspectives of clinical and educational staff. These partnerships are essential in both developing a working curriculum and therapeutic plan for children ex-

periencing multiple stressors and in helping staff cope with their own stresses by sharing the challenges of intervention.

The preschool is also a logical place for clinicians to reach out and involve parents in their children's development and to support them in cultivating their own coping strategies. Unlike the clinic or office, the school provides ample opportunities for informal and brief interactions between a mental health consultant and parents. In this way, parents and other family members can come to know the clinicians at their own pace in a familiar environment and before any crises arise. As Fantuzzo, Coolahan, and Weiss (1995) pointed out, it is essential that mental health providers support parents as the principal agents of change in their children's lives. On-site meetings give clinicians the chance to offer their impressions and ask parents for advice and insights on how to enhance their children's adjustment to and enjoyment of preschool. Parents then have the opportunity to engage with the mental health consultant as an interactive participant in the school team. Formal workshops on child development topics as well as individual parent conferences can also be effective, but they must be approached in the same spirit of cooperation and collaboration.

Another advantage of these preschool partnerships is the opportunity to develop true community-based interventions. Early childhood programs are often mainstays in their neighborhoods, respected and trusted by the local population. Joining together with these programs gives clinicians sanction to practice without the same stigma or skepticism that might be applied in the less familiar office environment. The clinician must, of course, respect the ethnic and cultural traditions of the families and seek to learn about the customs of the program and the community. The adept clinician must also aim to foster a "resiliency partnership" (Fantuzzo et al., 1995) with the community, drawing on its strengths to promote the adaptive functioning of its children rather than focusing solely on remediating delays or impairments. This approach emphasizes the protective factors (Rutter, 1979) that can mitigate the impact of stress on children and maintains hope that the community has the ability and resources to solve its problems.

The preschool–mental health partnership presents the opportunity to provide interventions that respond to the needs of all the children in the center, not just those with identifiable symptoms of emotional disturbance or those deemed most at risk. In this relationship, the consultant's primary role should be to foster the behavioral, emotional, and cognitive development of all children; the clinician should be available to consult on issues of any magnitude. This prevention model includes "checkups" of all of the classrooms, through observations and sitting in on team meetings, and "wellness" visits with those children who are responding nicely to the school environment. This allows the clinician to not only respond to crises and dire situations, but in some instances, to anticipate them and to provide early intervention to children at risk. In addition, the consultant has the opportunity to acknowledge and enhance the everyday workings of the teachers and staff in the school that create a welcoming and supportive environment for all the children.

DEVELOPING A SHARED VISION: PRECURSORS TO AN EFFECTIVE COLLABORATION

Developing an effective collaboration between mental health providers and preschool staff requires a good deal of enthusiasm, respect, and support from both parties. The mental health consultant must be careful to formulate a set of shared assumptions and goals with the school and not assume a rigid "expert" stance regarding the best ways to facilitate the children's development. The process of defining goals should result from a mutual examination that draws on the expertise of both teachers and clinical staff. Consultants must also recognize and appreciate the opportunities available in this environment to have an impact on a wide number of children, parents, and educators. Although clinicians of diverse backgrounds and experience can function in this role, the effective consultant must be flexible and team oriented, enjoy community-based settings, and be comfortable working apart from other clinicians. The consultant must also be adept at handling multiple roles and responsibilities, including crisis intervention, parent workshops, child observations and assessments, teacher training, and systems work (see Figure 1 for a list of possible roles for mental health consultants). Perhaps most important, consultants should acknowledge their own limitations as sole agents of change, and they must seek to share their knowledge and training with teachers and parents who will have the greatest impact on the young children in their community.

The preschool staff entering a collaborative relationship should likewise utilize the opportunity it presents. The work of Goldman, Botkin, Tokunaga, and Kuklinski (1997) suggested that the receptivity and readiness of teachers to participate with consultants greatly influences the success of the collaboration. The partnership is enhanced when staff are willing to consider their educational role in broad terms that encompass the social and emotional development of children and to share their expertise and insight regarding children's academic strengths, creative abilities, and learning readiness. The mental health collaboration will also be strengthened if both partners are open to new ideas and disciplines and are willing to integrate these in the class-

I.   ASSESSMENT AND TREATMENT OF CHILDREN
          —Classroom observation/assessment
          —Developmental screenings/psychological evaluations
          —Socialization groups
          —Circle time/classroom interventions
          —Individual or group therapy

II.   WORKING WITH PARENTS AND FAMILIES
          —Parent workshops
          —Drop-in service
          —Crisis intervention
          —Dyadic or family therapy
          —Mothers (grandmothers, alternative caregivers) groups

III.   COLLABORATION WITH TEACHERS
          —Consultation on individual children
          —Classroom management/structure
          —Building an emotion-centered curriculum
          —Planning for troubled children: team meetings
          —Managing teacher stress/personal problems

IV.   STAFF DEVELOPMENT
          —Child development training
          —Communication workshops
          —Support groups/stress management
          —Team-building exercises

V.   ADMINISTRATION
          —Consultation with directors, educational coordinators, social workers
          —Defining structure/management training: staff roles
          —Managing contact with oversight agencies, boards

VI.   COMMUNITY OUTREACH
          —Preparing for kindergarten, school readiness training
          —Assisting in special education process
          —Working with Child Protective Services
          —Recommending mental health and medical evaluations/referrals

Figure 1.   Possible roles for mental health consultants.

room. Ideally, the teachers and the consultant can together confront the often painful realities of children's lives and reflect on and discuss their own feelings and reactions elicited in their work with the children.

The preschool–mental health collaboration will flourish in an atmosphere of mutual respect and encouragement, in which consultants and the preschool staff work to build bridges, allay fears, and address conflicts that might arise from differences in professional status, compensation, ethnicity, or community identity. This can only happen over time and with a long-term investment from both ends. Too often such partnerships have failed because of a lack of funding, short-lived program initiatives, or an inadequate understanding of a community's needs. Yet when successful, a strong preschool–mental health partner-ship can lead to decisive change and can leave programs with more effective tools to meet their children's needs (Donahue, 1996; Goldman et al., 1997). The shared vision of professionals can give staff renewed hope and strengthened resources for confronting difficult behaviors and emotionally charged situations in the classroom. It can also build a program's resilience and reduce the stress of staff as they join to-gether to face the day-to-day challenges of meeting the educational and emotional needs of young children.

section 1

The Collaborative Process

chapter two

Across the Threshold

Establishing the Relationship in Early Childhood Programs

The nature of the collaboration between the mental health consultant and early childhood staff is greatly affected by a broad range of well-established personal, professional, cultural, historical, and social forces that are in place well before their first face-to-face meeting. As a result, it is no surprise that the process of building bridges between early childhood educators and mental health consultants is as varied as the histories, the programs, and the individuals themselves. Although some collaborations seem to flow almost effortlessly, with consultant and staff ready and eager to work together to serve the mental health needs of children, others are fraught with resistance, requiring much time, effort, and commitment before a working partnership is forged. Just as the structure, needs, and "personalities" of the centers vary, so too does the context of the consultation. In some settings, the directors initiate and implement the arrangement; in others, oversight agencies or previous administrations arrange the consultation. These differences can significantly affect a center's readiness to engage in the collaborative process, leading to considerable variability in the early course of the preschool–mental health partnership. The following three examples highlight the variability of the entry experience from the perspective of the consultant.

> When the consulting psychologist, Dr. Jennings, had been at the Head Start center for about a month, she held her first parent support group. The meeting was scheduled for 9:30 A.M., and Dr. Jennings arrived early to set up the space in preparation for the meeting. As she entered the building, she noticed that someone had posted copies of the flier she had sent home to parents to announce the group. Dr. Jennings then went downstairs and saw more fliers posted by the classrooms and in the hallway. In the room where the meeting was to be held, a circle of chairs was already neatly set up. On the side of the room was a table, draped with a brightly colored paper tablecloth, and on the table were pitchers of water and orange juice and plates of small muffins. Dr. Jennings went back upstairs to the office to find the "magic genie" who had so thoughtfully prepared everything. After learning that it was the program's family worker, Ms. Ramirez, Dr. Jennings thanked her and expressed surprise and happiness at all Ms. Ramirez had done. "Hey, no problem," Ms. Ramirez casually responded, as if such assistance was routinely provided.

In this example, the consultant found herself entering a system that was open to her presence. The program was well established and had many administrative and teaching strengths. The staff as a whole seemed to have only minimal issues and conflicts within the "family system" and were thus free to welcome the consultant on board, eager to take advantage of the services she had to offer. In this instance, the program was unencumbered by internal barriers to entry so that the staff had no need to resist the process and, in fact, were able to provide support to the consultant as they welcomed her to their program.

This seamless entry is, however, not always the case. For some new consultants, the entry process is a difficult and slow-going experience. Depending on past history and current stresses within the setting, as well as potential clashes in personality, style, and philosophy between consultant and staff, the entry process can be more problematic.

It was Dr. Lee's first day as a consultant at a large child care program serving homeless families in an urban setting. Although Dr. Lee had been an early childhood consultant in the past, she had never worked with homeless families and was new to this mental health agency as well. The 20-year-old child care program, however, had many senior staff members with extensive experience with this population and a long history of ambivalent associations with various mental health agencies. In general, the staff appeared to be overwhelmed by the growing neediness of the children and families they served. They seemed to welcome the consultant as a "savior" but were also prepared to see her as a scapegoat in their highly stressed system.

Dr. Lee spent much of her first morning as consultant becoming acquainted with the administrative and teaching staff. Suddenly, at the end of the day, the program social worker, Mr. Akeem, caught her in the hall and expressed great alarm at a troubled youngster's provocative comments, which raised concerns of potential abuse at home. Mr. Akeem accompanied Dr. Lee to the classroom and initiated a discussion with the teacher and the child, Jessica. The consultant agreed that Jessica's comments were indeed worrisome and warranted close examination. She then decided to contact Jessica's mother and arrange a meeting. As Dr. Lee proceeded to make the call, she was astounded to find that the only telephones on site were located in a large, undivided office housing the director, assistant director, social worker, receptionist, and nurse. The room was an open passageway for parents, children, and teachers as well. As Dr. Lee picked up the telephone, she became aware of the wide range of individuals attending to her call without affording her even the pretense of privacy. Dr. Lee felt scrutinized, at once compelled to address a potentially abusive situation while aware of the evaluative monitoring of the observing staff.

When Dr. Lee did reach the child's mother, she introduced herself and requested a meeting to discuss some concerns that had arisen, relaying Jessica's comments in a general way. Jessica's mother became immediately enraged, challenging the consultant with abusive and hostile language while expressing extreme anger toward her "lying" child. Dr. Lee was overwhelmed by this outburst; not only did she fear for this child's welfare, but she also felt personally

*vulnerable and upset and was unsure how to proceed with
the parent before the watchful eyes of the observing staff.
Despite this inner turmoil, Dr. Lee attempted to be strong
with the parent, setting limits around the amount of abusive
speech she would tolerate. She also invited Jessica's mother
to attend a meeting to explore the situation and to determine
what subsequent actions, including the potential
involvement of child protective services, were warranted.
Dr. Lee told Jessica's irate mother that she hoped the parent
would attend but remarked that the meeting would take
place regardless of whether Jessica's mother agreed to
participate. Dr. Lee hung up the telephone near tears; she
felt judged if not betrayed by the staff members, who were
likely familiar with this explosive parent, and wondered
whether she was "set up" to be confronted in such a public
forum. Fortunately, Dr. Lee was able to remove herself from
the scene and contact her supervisor, who helped the
consultant take a breath, slow down the process, and make
the best possible clinical decision.*

*Later, when her distress subsided, Dr. Lee was able to
review this harrowing entry and understood herself to be the
victim of bad luck—how could such a loaded, painful, and
difficult issue of potential abuse arise on her very first day?
In addition, she was able to see the behavior of staff not as a
vindictive act of public humiliation but as a kind of
hazing—how will this young, professional woman handle
the challenges the program staff face every day? Will she
care enough? Will she be tough enough? Beyond that, Dr.
Lee began to recognize the events as a call for help from the
staff: "These are the overwhelming challenges encountered
every day; can you help us?" With the luxury of hindsight
and the support of her supervisor, Dr. Lee was able to
review the events of the day, to consider alternate courses of
action that included taking time to process the material, and
to find a way of contacting the parent privately with greater
preparation for her potential response. In addition, Dr. Lee
examined her role in similar crises that might arise in the
future, questioning whether it was her place to make the
initial contact and reflecting on how she could best support
the program, the child, and the family when such difficult
issues of potential abuse emerged.*

This consultant's first day was indeed a most unusual and painful entry into a difficult and overwhelmed system. Though baptized by fire, the consultant did eventually become an integrated member of this community, sharing with staff the overwhelming struggles as well as the equally intense rewards of working with young children from this highly stressed neighborhood.

Most entries do not fall into the extremes of either example. It is more likely that the consultant will not be immediately met with overt challenge or resistance; neither will he necessarily feel particularly welcomed, supported, and put at ease. Most consultants initially report feeling somewhat uncomfortable in the new, unfamiliar terrain. Typically, the consultant is unsure of the staff's feelings about him and may be unclear about his role in the program.

It was Dr. Holt's first visit to the small nursery school to which she had been assigned as a consultant. After being greeted warmly by the director, Ms. Watts, Dr. Holt expected to learn more about the center and to talk with the director about her consulting role. Instead, Ms. Watts immediately launched into a story about the illness of a friend. Throughout the lengthy exposition, the director described her friend's ordeal in great detail and included a complex description of the multiple interconnections of the people in her life and in the community. At first, Dr. Holt felt confused. What was going on? As she listened, she wondered why the director was telling her, a stranger, all of this. Was Ms. Watts temporarily using the consultant as her own therapist because she desperately needed to talk? It didn't appear so. She was telling a good story, her pain contained and secondary.

It gradually became clear, as the story unfolded and the consultant relaxed, that the purpose of the story was to introduce Dr. Holt to the life of the community of which the director was an intimate part. Behind the neighborhood's difficulties combating drugs and poverty was a richly alive, connected, and caring group of people to which the center was inextricably linked. Ms. Watts was introducing all this to Dr. Holt and also closely observing her response: Will this outsider be able to appreciate the many facets of the community—its strengths as well as its weaknesses? Will she enter and become a part of it? Or will she remain outside,

seeing it as dangerous and foreign, something to be kept at a
distance and judged?

These examples illustrate the complexity of entering an early childhood program, particularly when both consultant and program staff are new to the work. For the program, it is opening a door to the outside, showing strengths and vulnerabilities, hopes and fears. It can be a threatening experience as well as a hopeful one. For the consultant, who is often trained in very different ways of intervening, it means entering a complex system as an outsider whose role is not clearly defined. This ambiguity can create many opportunities but can also cause the consultant to feel ungrounded as she struggles to define her role. This chapter provides ways of thinking about the initial stage of the collaboration as the foundation for more intensive interventions.

ESTABLISHING COLLABORATIVE RELATIONSHIPS

Forming a collaborative relationship is an exciting and challenging endeavor. In the model this book describes, it is also, by definition, a two-way process. Just as the consultants enter a new system, attempting to form relationships and to assess the situation, so too are the child care staff observing the consultant: Will this person understand the difficulties faced by the staff? Will he be compassionate? Harsh? Undermining? How can he help? How much should we tell him? Whose side is he on? It is extremely important for the consultant to be sensitive and responsive to the feelings and perceptions of the staff as they evaluate each other in the early stages of their work together. This involves spending time together, listening to staff, and establishing a dialogue with them. Openness, flexibility, a desire to listen, and the ability to empathize with various staff members are all important tools that the consultant can use to begin this dialogue.

Not only should the consultant address any preconceptions the staff has about his role, but he should also step back from his own ideas about the way the entry process should proceed. Although the consultant may indeed have an agenda for this early phase of entry, he should avoid developing fixed notions regarding the sequence and pacing of this process. For example, in the previous vignette involving Dr. Holt, the consultant had to relinquish her expectations about the purpose of the first meeting with the director. In particular, she had to let go of her initial impulse to learn more concrete information about the center up front and instead allow the process to unfold in a less controlled manner. She could then respond to the director's indirectly expressed desire to introduce the consultant to the life of the community.

In terms of the staff's preconceptions, the consultant should become apprised as soon as possible about the center's previous experience with consultation in general and mental health consultation in particular. The consultant is advised to listen closely to the various representations of past experiences in this area. It is important to develop an awareness of both the positive and negative aspects of these relationships. In this way, the consultant can begin to understand the hopes and fears of the staff in relation to the new consulting experience. In some cases, he will want to emphasize his plans to maintain a role that has continuity with that of the previous consultant and only gradually begin to assert himself in new ways. In other cases, it is necessary for the new consultant to differentiate himself and his role from past disappointments. One way to do this is to address any lingering negative feelings with respect to the past experience. The staff may be mourning the loss of the previous consultant, or they may feel abandoned and angry. There could be feelings of distrust. As the new consultant listens and responds to these concerns, he can begin to establish a sense of assurance in the new relationship.

The experience of one consultant-in-training, who entered an early childhood program where the previous consultant was out on sick leave, illustrates some of these dilemmas:

> *Upon entering this new system, Mr. Block, the consulting social worker, began to explore the feelings the staff had for Ms. Donatello, the previous consultant. As a result of this process, he came to understand the sense of deep loss the staff was experiencing as well as the unspoken fears and group denial of the seriousness of Ms. Donatello's illness. The staff believed that she would be back very soon and that Mr. Block was only a temporary substitute. In fact, they seemed to feel as if any acceptance of him signified giving up hope for their friend's recovery. As a result, Mr. Block was kept at arm's length as the staff resisted accepting him as a potentially permanent replacement. As he was able to recognize their loss, empathize with their painful experience, and help them maintain the presence of their previous consultant, Mr. Block was gradually accepted in his role. The staff no longer felt at risk of losing their ill friend if they accepted her replacement.*

Very often consultants face the difficult challenge of addressing historical concerns that, although greatly affecting their entry into the system, predate their arrival and are not based on their personality, style, or professional ability. Nevertheless, the sooner consultants understand and address these concerns, the greater the opportunities will be to gain acceptance within the community.

Although the need for flexibility should be emphasized, there are some general guidelines that are helpful to consider when entering into an early childhood program. First and foremost is the need to work closely with the director of the program, particularly in the beginning. This is the first relationship, the "port of entry." As soon as possible, preferably before meeting with other staff, it is important to begin a discussion about the director's plans for the preschool–mental health consultant partnership. This is key not only in beginning the assessment process but also in exploring the possibilities for the collaboration as a mutual and interactive relationship. The collaboration formally begins as the consultant and the director discuss a plan of entry and a means of introducing the clinician to the staff.

The introduction to the staff can be a sensitive process. Clearly, the consultant needs to present herself as useful to the program. She should acknowledge her expertise in relevant areas, such as child development, the effect of stress and trauma on young children, classroom management of acting-out behaviors, and how and when to intervene when children show signs of emotional distress or developmental delays. However, the consultant wants to avoid being narrowly defined as the expert, the "fixer of problems," which connotes a far different role from that of collaborator and professional colleague. The consultant can work toward this goal by communicating a genuine collaborative mind-set— welcoming the professional expertise of the center's staff and openly sharing the evaluation process, not merely presenting its end product.

As the consultant introduces herself to the director and staff and discusses possible roles she may have in the program, she must be careful to build in time for the entry process. She should present the need to develop relationships with the staff, children, and parents—by observing, helping out in class, and meeting with parents informally—before being asked to commit to specific interventions or goals. Often this entails holding back on responding actively to calls for help, which can be very difficult for the consultant looking to prove herself to staff or welcoming the chance to engage the children directly. Similarly, the consultant may feel pressured to respond quickly when the center's needs appear intense. Issues of safety always require immediate action, but the consultant must nonetheless strive to act thoughtfully and appropriately, avoiding hasty interventions. Although it may be difficult to tolerate this seemingly slow and unstructured entry, the consultant must recognize that a thoughtful and gradual beginning helps establish appropriate and effective relationships and lays the foundation for the success of future interventions. This initial period of observation and assessment is needed to discover how the consultant's skills and abilities fit into the needs of the program. Gradually the consultant's role will become more clearly defined, and goals can be set and plans made for the use of the consultant's time. These goals will, of course, be constantly reevaluated, and the consultant's role will shift as a result.

Working with the Program Director

One exception to this early unstructured stage is the need for regular and frequent contact with the director. In most settings, the consultant and director find that regularly scheduled meetings facilitate the establishment of a healthy collaborative relationship. These meetings afford the director the opportunity to observe and develop comfort with the consultant as a clinician, a confidant, and a member of the community. Similarly, by emphasizing the importance of these meetings with the director, the consultant acknowledges the director's role in the functioning of the organization and his centrality to the collaborative process. If the staff is led by a director who is well connected to his employees and eager to establish the collaboration, they will more easily welcome someone who is proceeding under his auspices. The consultant then will also have access to the director's wealth of day-to-day information about what is happening at the center, and together they will be able to determine how to make the best use of the consultant's time on any given day. If, however, the director is ineffectual or insecure, if there is a division between him and the staff, or if he is resistant to the collaborative process, then the consultant needs to use the time to address the difficulties the director is experiencing. The relationship between the consultant and administrative staff is explored more fully in Chapter 3.

The director's style has a profound impact on the overall qualities of the center, including the feelings of staff and the attitude toward children. This is particularly evident when a change of leadership results in a significant shift in program style.

> Ms. Hannon was preparing to retire after 20 years as the director of a large suburban preschool and child care program. She was intimately involved in the life of her center and was known to have an unwavering memory for the names and family histories of all the program's students. In addition, she was genuinely concerned about the lives of her staff, handing out personal advice and financial assistance when needed. The door to her office was always open

wide. The consultant, on a chance visit, found a member of the kitchen staff taking a coffee break in the director's office. There were two teachers in casual conversation at the desk and an unhappy toddler on the lap of the director, who stroked the little girl's hair while engaged in an animated telephone conversation. When Ms. Hannon retired, her replacement decided to implement a number of changes. Coffee was no longer allowed in the office, children were not permitted to enter, and when a teacher walked in the room, she was publicly challenged: "Why are you here? I don't think we have an appointment."

Needless to say, the sharp contrast in styles had a great effect on the staff and eventually led to a shift in the program's approach to children, which became more structured, formal, and behaviorally focused.

During the time the consultant is getting acquainted with the director and assessing his needs, the director is becoming familiar with the consultant, evaluating her competence and deciding how the consultant can best support the program. Again, the presence of mutual trust and respect greatly enhances the collaborative process. Nevertheless, such a relationship does not exist *de facto;* it must evolve over time as both consultant and staff observe and become comfortable with the other's behavior and abilities. Some directors may feel intimidated by the consultant, assuming her actions and decisions are somehow legitimized by virtue of her status as a mental health "expert." But, unfortunately, not all clinicians, even those with solid professional credentials, are well suited to the demands of early childhood consultation. In some cases, the consultant's professional competence is not an issue, but her personal style may not mesh with the personality of the center. The director should not hesitate to observe the consultant's behavior with staff, children, and parents to ascertain whether the consultant indeed deserves their confidence. Just as the consultant is comfortable observing and evaluating others, so too should she expect and accept the same process for herself.

The director should feel free to evaluate both the style and content of the consultant's communications. Although the director is not a trained mental health professional, he should nonetheless feel a certain degree of comfort with the consultant's clinical judgment, finding it compatible with his expertise in early childhood as well as the dictates of simple common sense. It should be understood that the mental health professional operates within certain confidentiality guidelines that place some limits on the specificity of shared clinical material.

Nonetheless, the director should feel that relevant information is communicated to him and the staff in a timely manner. If planning to engage in direct clinical work with children on site, the consultant should explain how aspects of the treatment remain private, but she should not present therapy as a mysterious and secretive process that yields results concealed from teachers and staff. Rather, the director should feel that the consultant shares observations, assessments, and interventions in an appropriate and useful manner and is able to invite the participation of involved teachers, social workers, and specialists throughout the various stages of this process.

During this entry period, the director should feel comfortable voicing needs and feelings to a responsive consultant who respects the director's position and maintains confidentiality. The director should be able to express program matters that range from more formal planning and decision making to less structured explorations of her concerns about specific children, teachers, or families. In addition, the director should agree with the level of formality devised for ongoing contact—whether arranged as a standing appointment or on an "as needed" basis. The director should also feel free to evaluate the consulting agency. The director may examine the availability of related services, the potential for direct communication with administrative authorities, and the structure or demands that this agency places on the consulting professional, particularly as they affect the consultant's availability to the program.

Connecting with Staff

Once a positive and ongoing dialogue with the director is in effect, the consultant can begin to form connections with the rest of the staff. The consultant can do this in a formal manner, structuring time to spend in each classroom and making appointments for contact with staff outside the room. Typically, however, the process unfolds in a more natural and informal way. The consultant may be asked to observe a child and, in turn, spends time with all the teachers and children in the classroom. As a result, she begins to get to know the teachers and to establish herself, ideally, as an interested, nonjudgmental, and supportive professional.

This process evolves over time and occurs in many contexts. Spending time in the staff room, drinking coffee, and chatting with staff are means of creating a more relaxed tone. Providing needed help is another way, such as by covering the classroom when a teacher steps out, helping on the playground or with a special project, or joining mealtime preparations and cleanup. The goal is to let staff get to know the consultant at the same time as she is getting to know the center. Many consultants find themselves in settings that are more like a large family than a rigidly hierarchical agency or company. As a result, exchanges with staff may be more casual and intimate; a consultant may find herself sharing more personal information than she typically does in other professional settings. Depending on the style of the consultant, this may be an enjoyable experience or a disconcerting one that shifts her usual professional stance. Many clinicians choose to disclose little personal information in therapy for theoretical reasons: Psychodynamic therapists do not want to predetermine the way in which an individual conceives and thus uses the therapist. It is hoped that part of the work of therapy occurs around this relationship that is, at least in part, determined by the qualities that the patient transfers to the therapist. If coming from that type of background, the clinician new to the setting might be taken aback by the free sharing of personal material.

> Dr. Chin had recently announced her increasingly obvious pregnancy. She recognized that the undeniable reality of this very personal event was an issue for all the patients in her clinical practice, but Dr. Chin generally communicated only the most basic information about her pregnancy to them. As a consultant, however, she found that teachers asked with much warmth and openness about her pregnancy, her health, her children at home, her husband, and her plans for work. For Dr. Chin, it was a relief to open up, to complain about her persistent morning sickness and other associated discomforts and concerns. She did not expect, however, for so many details to be shared with the children, who now knew her due date and the baby's gender and name as well as the ages, names, and genders of the other children in her family.

Although the consultant would not have chosen to share these specifics with all the children, particularly not with those she saw for individual therapy, she found that the information did not impede the therapeutic process but did, in fact, speed her entry into this preschool family system.

How long does the entry process last? There is, of course, no fixed time frame because the length of the process is unique to each consultant and program. It only gradually recedes in importance as the nature of the consultant's role becomes established. Many factors—including issues associated with the consultant, the program, and the nature of the fit between them, in addition to practical considerations such as how many hours per week the consultant is on site—will determine the time needed to establish the collaboration. Usually, however, it takes most of an academic year to become a completely integrated part of the program's operation, and not until the second year does the consultant begin to feel fully utilized as an active member of the community.

POTENTIAL PITFALLS IN THE ENTRY PROCESS

There are several common pitfalls that beginning consultants might confront. The consultant often faces the risk of becoming embroiled in preexisting power struggles at the child care center. This may occur if the consultant identifies with one group within the staff—for instance, the teachers or the administration—and becomes seen as an advocate for that particular group. Although it may eventually become part of the consultant's role to address these conflicts, it is very important in the beginning of the collaboration that the consultant stresses the neutrality of his position and his lack of affiliation with any one group.

Another common problem occurs around setting up goals. Some consultants may envision "rescuing" the center, hoping that their interventions will solve even the most insurmountable challenges—a wish that can be particularly damaging when shared by the center's staff. Such ambitious designs can be a clear setup for failure. The consultant should be careful to establish modest, attainable goals, particularly in the beginning of the relationship. This point is illustrated by the vignette about Dr. Lee, the new consultant who was confronted on her first day with a possible abuse scenario. She inadvertently gave the impression she would "take on" all abuse issues, implicitly accepting the unspoken mandate that abuse was her terrain, and when such concerns arose, they could be handed over to her. She began to devise plans for assessment and reporting before she realized, with her supervisor's help, that she would be ill-advised to imply to the center that she alone would henceforth handle these matters. Instead, she returned to the center with the recommendation that the key players within the program formulate a reasonable approach to such issues; she did offer to participate in the process, although she was careful to avoid accepting ownership of its outcome.

A related pitfall for the consultant entering a new program is falling into the role of the professional who enters a center to "fix" its problems. Instead of becoming a collaborator, the consultant is seen as an outside expert who dispenses wisdom and advice. This kind of relationship can feel reassuring to the beginning consultant who is struggling to establish his expertise and to create a useful and well-defined role for himself in the center. Again, this desire may fit with the wishes of the program that searches for a quick and easy solution to many deep-rooted problems. Yet such a stance places great limitations on the consultant's effectiveness, as he is then seen as aloof from the life of the center, creating expectations that will ultimately lead to disappointment and failure when he is unable to satisfy such impossible demands. Instead, the consultant should work toward being seen not as a unilateral solution, but as part of a well-rounded team approach, as a genuine collaborator contributing his knowledge.

Furthermore, the effective consultant recognizes that part of his role is to place himself behind the staff in their quest for growth, supporting their ability to contribute substantially to the challenges they face. This stance does not, however, imply that the consultant should withhold useful advice. Rather, it means using the consultant's area of expertise to empower the members of the staff to develop their own voices. This may take the form of helping a teacher articulate *her* perception of the child about whom she is concerned. Then teacher and consultant will work together to construct a way of understanding the child and a plan for an intervention. With an administrator, the goal may be to explore feelings about making difficult referrals to social service agencies, with the intent of building confidence in her own abilities. The consultant works with the idea of facilitating the growth of individual staff members as well as that of children and families.

Finally, and perhaps most important, a consultant is often tempted to begin interventions too quickly, without completing a full assessment of the program. Without understanding the dynamics of the system, the consultant may plunge into an intervention with a child or parent only to find that, in doing so, the family worker has become alienated or the teachers feel bypassed. In another scenario, the consultant begins engaging in direct services and then becomes too busy, unable to provide for the needs of the setting. The consultant should try to withstand the pressure to act hastily in the first couple of months; he should instead strive to engage the system and establish key structures and relationships that will provide the foundation for the success of future interventions. During this early stage, the consultant seeks to foster optimism about the possibilities that he is exploring, working to help the various staff members feel that he is responsive to their needs and feelings and is willing to incorporate their recommendations. Simultaneously, the consultant begins a careful and systematic assessment of the context and structure as well as the strengths and weaknesses of the program.

ASSESSING THE EARLY CHILDHOOD PROGRAM
The consultant typically becomes acquainted with the program by observing key features of the environment that range from small, structural details of the physical setting to the overall atmosphere and emo-

tional tone of the center. The consultant observes the general working order of the system, including the strengths and weaknesses of the staff, the pervasive mood and philosophy of the program, the resources available to the center, and the program's relationship to the community. Even before such an assessment can begin, however, the consultant must determine the extent to which the program is willing and able to make use of the mental health collaboration.

Readiness to Collaborate

A certain level of functioning is required of the center in order for the partnership to be successful. Some systems may seem ill-equipped to meet the basic academic, nutritional, and even safety needs of the children. If the level of disorganization is too great or if the primary needs of the center lie in areas other than mental health, the consultant will then be obliged to address these immediate concerns prior to focusing on the emotional needs of children and families.

> *Mr. Bell was assigned the job of consulting with Monroe Child Care. Almost immediately, he discovered a disturbing level of dysfunction in the center. The director was overwhelmed and lacked proper qualifications and experience. There were no staff meetings and no curriculum guidelines. There were also grave concerns about safety and supervision of the children, culminating in a child exiting the school building without the knowledge of her teacher. Mr. Bell offered to assist the director in devising a plan to address these concerns but was met with anger and resistance. He then decided to have a joint meeting with his supervisor and the executive director of the child care center. The consultant expressed his concerns and what he felt needed to be done to satisfy basic licensing requirements for the center and to allow him to continue the collaboration. As a result of this meeting, the senior administration decided to conduct a careful assessment of the program and made the difficult decision to replace some unqualified teachers and, eventually, to reassign the director as well. During this process, the consultant temporarily shelved his concerns regarding individual children and focused on more fundamental needs of the program until some degree of stability was achieved.*

This example, while extreme, shows how important it is to assess whether any given center is ready for collaboration with a mental health professional. In other cases, there may be less profound but nonetheless significant hurdles for the consultant. The center may be focused on areas other than mental health and may not be receptive to broadening its vision. For instance, a highly structured, cognitively oriented program may not welcome the presence of a mental health professional who attends primarily to social and emotional development. The collaborative stance outlined in this book may overcome some hurdles and initial skepticism, but it is important for the consultant to recognize and respect the program that does not want his services.

Both the consultant and the program director need to examine the nature of the fit between them. How does the style, training, and background of the consultant interface with the center's needs and orientation? In the previous example, the collaboration was made possible by the consultant's expertise, not only in the area of children's mental health but also in early childhood education: He had extensive experience working as a teacher and educational director in child care. The needs of the center could be well addressed by this particular consultant, but without this background, he would most likely have felt overwhelmed by the extent of the basic shortcomings of the center.

An Assessment Tool

The initial assessment of a preschool setting is, in some ways, like assessing a complicated family system. Relationships, lines of power and communication, early childhood philosophy, and attitudes toward the "outsider" all need to be looked at and understood. There are the "parent figures" whose wisdom, strength, and support are sought out or whose authority is unquestioned and absolute. There are the perceived strengths of the system: a multicultural emphasis, perhaps, or a strong outreach program. Often there is an "identified patient": a child, parent, or staff member who becomes the scapegoat. In this constellation, the presence of the particular individual is seen as threatening the system's ability to function effectively. Symptoms become evident: acting out, high turnover of staff, low enrollment, and apathy. Finally, the system will have developed coping strategies for dealing with the symptoms and the stresses of working with groups of young children. It is extremely important for the consultant to take the time to assess the situation carefully and accurately. The initial assessment is much like the intake in therapy: It gives the consultant an opportunity to appreciate assets and to develop a sense of what is causing the difficulties so they can best be addressed.

By conceptualizing the early childhood program as a large and complex family system, the consultant can understand the center's strengths and weaknesses in the context of the program as a whole. Although the metaphor of the family system is valuable, there are none-theless significant differences between assessment in family therapy and in preschool consultation. The consultant is not an outside observer who independently conducts the evaluation and creates the treatment plan for the center. Rather, the work of the consultant is to forge a col-laboration with other professionals in the child care system to evaluate jointly and then intervene within that system. Consultants are encour-aged to think about the following assessment process outline as a way to help structure their impressions and observations. Nevertheless, it is equally important to maintain an attitude of collaboration, mutuality, and respect, all of which are central to the development of a healthy consulting relationship.

To facilitate the assessment process, the authors have developed a tool for consultants (see the Appendix) that is based on standard evaluation procedures for individual and family psychotherapy but is adapted for use with a child care center. To give the reader an idea of how this tool could be used, each category is discussed, using as an ex-ample a fictitious combined Head Start/child care center called Small World Head Start.

Physical Setting   Just as in therapy, where the therapist's office can convey to the client a sense of safety, warmth, and welcome, so too does the physical space of the early childhood center create a mood and reflect an attitude. What is the physical state of the building and neigh-borhood? Is it welcoming to children? Does the site have a staff lounge or cafeteria where the staff feel welcomed? What about parents—is there a parent room or other open space? Are the classrooms well lit with age-appropriate material in good condition? Are toys within reach? Is there a wide variety of gross and fine motor activities, books, and creative art supplies? How well organized are the rooms? Are they too messy or too neat? Is there a good balance of organization, safety, and open exploration of materials? All these indicators tell much about the center—its place in the community, its availability of resources, and its attitude toward the children, their parents, and staff.

The Small World Head Start was located in an old community cen-ter, adapted for the program's use. The classrooms were bright, cheer-ful, well organized, and large. It was a pleasant and child-centered en-vironment. The administrative offices, while small and cramped, were also inviting and warm. As one spent more time there, however, one was struck by the lack of privacy in the space. The classrooms were di-vided by thin, temporary partitions. As a result, the teachers and chil-dren could hear everything going on in the two classrooms. This was extremely important for the consultant, Dr. O'Rourke, to remain aware of, especially when dealing with tense staff relations. Finding creative ways of using the space, as well as addressing how this layout affected teachers and the staff in general, became an important piece of this consultant's work.

Community   The consultant should be aware of the economic, ethnic, cultural, educational, and geographic variables of the larger community in which the center is located. In addition to noting the type of community in which the families live, it is also important to assess the quality of the relationship between the center and the community. How has it been viewed historically? Are there many recent immigrants? What is the economic status of the community? What about the ethnic mix? Is it an urban community? Is the staff drawn from the community, and do most live there presently? Are there differences in language and culture between staff and the community, and, if so, how are these handled? The consultant can begin to collect this information by talking with long-time staff members about the nature of the center's relationship to the community and by asking the director if there is anything written about the history of the center. The depth of a center's roots can have great impact on the degree of community acceptance and involvement. The strength of centers that have long histories, including intergenerational legacies for both parents and staff, is striking. When a teacher has known a new student's father since childhood, her potential impact within the family is indeed magnified. If the center is seen as being separate from, outside of, or new to the area, the quality of the interactions between staff and families will differ from those in a center that is perceived to be a mainstay of the neighborhood.

In addition to understanding the links within the immediate area, the consultant is advised to evaluate the relationship between the center and the larger community. How does it interact with other agencies, such as child protective services, the department of social services, foster care, mental health clinics, preschool special education services, and other early child care providers? The center's intake and referral process offers a glimpse into its connections in the community. For instance, does the center have clearly established ways of making and following through on referrals to parents? Is there a system in place for contacting involved agencies when conducting intakes? Is there knowledge about local services that offer support to parents, children, and teachers?

Small World Head Start was nestled in a city full of the problems troubling urban areas in the late 20th century. On the positive side, there was a strong feeling of connection among people and agencies in the community, many of which had been there for generations. It was an ethnically mixed neighborhood. The children in the program were African American, Caucasian, Hispanic, Middle Eastern, and Asian.

The program was well established and had strong links to the neighborhood. Most of the staff had lived in this neighborhood at some point in their lives and felt a deep connection to the community—they knew many of the families they served and shared the stresses and pleasures of life in this area.

Approach to the Consultant   The center's approach to mental health consultation and other community partnerships is important in determining how the consultant's entry into the system will be perceived and further reflects a general attitude toward outside agencies. If there is a history of unsatisfactory contact, there will almost certainly be resistance to the consultant's presence. Similarly, if there is a history of strong collaborations, there may well be associated positive, and perhaps unrealistic, hopes and assumptions. Regardless of the content of prior contacts, the consultant will need to understand this history and address the staff's thoughts and expectations about the meaning of the consultant's presence in light of past experience.

In the case of Small World, this was the first contact with ongoing mental health consultation. These circumstances enabled Dr. O'Rourke to have greater freedom in determining how to proceed and where to focus her attentions. The director, Ms. Sanchez, was very welcoming and eager to have Dr. O'Rourke's services. Rapport was established quite easily in the classrooms. The difficulty here was the pressure Dr. O'Rourke felt to address some of the issues immediately. She noted, for instance, that a child was acting out in class. Rather than talking about this with Ms. Desmond, the teacher, she actively intervened with the child without getting a complete sense of the dynamics of the situation. Later she realized that Ms. Desmond, who was quite passive, needed encouragement to act on her own initiative. Dr. O'Rourke's hasty intervention may have inadvertently contributed to Ms. Desmond's passive stance rather than supporting the teacher to make her own assessment of the situation and act accordingly.

In general, however, the staff was quite receptive to Dr. O'Rourke. In particular, they were eager for increased support and assistance with the challenges they faced in their classrooms. In addition, the considerable seniority of most staff members, as well as the well-developed sense of community among them, did not prove to insulate them from this outsider. Rather, their tight-knit, multicultural community seemed to function as a secure base, supporting the staff as they accepted others into their system. There was, however, one exception to this general rule involving a new teacher who was having difficulties gaining acceptance within this preschool family.

Staff   The staff form the heart of the child care center. For the consultant, establishing a collaborative relationship with staff is crucial to the work. It is also often the most difficult part of entry. When evaluating the staff as a whole, the consultant strives to understand its composition, including its history and level of experience, amount of education and training, as well as the salient issues of race and culture. The consultant also assesses the key interpersonal relationships and seeks to understand the lines of power within the system. In particular, the consultant evaluates how the director functions in her role and how the staff responds to her. A careful examination of the team structure of the program is an important aspect of the assessment process. Is there a well-developed team approach, or do individuals tend to function more independently?

The staff of the Small World Head Start consisted of the director, an administrative assistant, six teachers, a family worker, a cook, and a maintenance worker. Except for one male assistant teacher, the staff was all female. In addition to the core staff, there were a number of part-time aides and volunteers in the classroom. The staff were composed primarily of members of the African American and Latino populations from the community—the sole exceptions were the cook and one teacher, who were both Caucasian. One teacher resided in a distant and more affluent community whereas the rest of the staff lived within the center's neighborhood and thus confronted the same economic, educational, and social challenges that the Head Start families faced. In general, there was a feeling of racial harmony that pervaded the center, with the celebration of many cultures evident in the pictures displayed, the curriculum devised, the wide range of cultural events and holidays celebrated, and the types of food enjoyed. There was little evidence of racial or cultural tension within this long-standing staff.

Most of the staff had been there for years, and there was a very low turnover rate. There was a clear sense of a communal bond between these members with a relatively strong team-oriented structure. There was one critical exception to this rule: A new head teacher named Ms. Alonzo was experiencing considerable difficulties relating to the other staff members. She had a great deal of experience and was hired a year earlier to supervise the other teachers. In general, the staff had the minimum qualifications required for their positions. They had little formal education and training, areas in which they seemed eager to receive more support. This desire had increased in recent years, particularly as the staff experienced greater challenges in the classroom for which they felt unprepared.

Ms. Sanchez had been the director at Small World for 10 years. Very affable and engaging, she favored a strong, managerial style. With her forceful ideas and dynamic personality, Ms. Sanchez would dominate any meeting or classroom she entered. Yet this strength was tempered by an inconsistent availability. When present, she would actively engage the staff with her plans and ideas but would then be suddenly gone, leaving the building for days at a time. As a result, the staff was anxious for contact with Ms. Sanchez but found her unavailable. In part, her lack of accessibility was the result of increasing demands on her time. The administrative and executive pressures involving the network of child care providers in the community kept her busy. However, Ms. Sanchez also lacked an understanding of the impact this had on the staff and failed to recognize the strain it placed on them. When something went wrong in her absence, she tended to blame staff for not following through on her suggestions.

The supervisory structure was complicated. Most problematic was the relationship between Ms. Alonzo and the rest of the staff. Hired as both a head teacher and the educational coordinator, she moved in and out of these roles. This was coupled with a somewhat rigid, if not abrasive, personality style that permeated both her skills as a teacher and as a supervisor. The "old" teachers were upset, the director frustrated, and the children affected as the emotional atmosphere of the school reflected these conflicts. However, Dr. O'Rourke quickly learned that there were many interconnected problems that were both masked by and played out in this problematic area. Various circumstances contributed to the situation: the passivity and helplessness of the "old" teachers, the director's inconsistency, and the lack of recognition of the teachers for their dedication and hard work in a very demanding job.

The preceding assessment exemplifies the process of looking more systemically at presenting problems among staff. New consultants need to keep an open mind as they begin to look at these complicated, often long-standing relationships. Dr. O'Rourke used a variety of techniques to gather information and develop positive relationships during this early stage of entry into the system. She was careful to ask relevant questions, to speak with and observe as many staff as possible, and to remain empathic to all the "players" while maintaining a more neutral stance vis-à-vis the particular conflicts that emerged.

Approach to Children   Assessing the center's approach to children is a central element of the consultant's work. When evaluating the program's overall attitude toward young children, examine the school's general theoretical framework, including the beliefs about and goals for emotional and academic development. Consider how these are carried out on a day-to-day basis. What is the general approach to structure in the classroom? Are creativity and unstructured play encouraged? Is the attainment of early academic skills considered paramount? Are children encouraged to be independent thinkers? Is the program oriented more toward individual or group experience? To what extent are the children expected to conform to strict behavioral codes? How are acting-out behaviors handled? What is the usual approach to withdrawn and fearful behavior? How are separation difficulties handled?

At Small World, two things were immediately apparent. One was the difference between the classrooms. The classroom run by the new teacher was well organized, highly structured, and cognitively enriching. It was also teacher centered, with little attention paid to the individual needs, interests, or emotional concerns of the children. A second classroom seemed chaotic and overwhelming, but the warmth and caring of the teachers for each of the children was quite apparent. Although all teachers at Small World Head Start showed a strong desire to help the children, they generally placed little emphasis on understanding or attending to the emotional concerns of the children. This was clearly evident in the difficulty handling separation issues: Children and parents were left to manage this matter on their own. Also problematic was the teachers' approach to discipline. When a child hit another child, for instance, he was told not to, that it "wasn't nice." There were no consequences and no follow-up. Basic issues around safety of the children were also quite obvious.

Evaluating an early childhood center's approach to children can be done in many ways. Indirect means—such as reading teacher notes, the parent handbook, or other promotional literature—can provide useful information. These methods can indicate much about how a program wishes to present itself, yet the value of such literature pales in comparison to firsthand experience. Similarly, conversations with children, parents, teachers, and other staff can indicate some general qualities about the center. Nonetheless, the obvious, and arguably the best, method of obtaining such information is through direct observations. Sitting in, absorbing the atmosphere in a classroom without actually having the responsibility of teaching or managing the children, provides the consultant with a rich source of information. In the same manner, the chance observation of a director's contact with a parent or a social worker's interaction with a child can reflect much about the center's general attitudes.

A consultant also learns about the program's general approach to children by participating in the life of the center. Helping out at the beginning or end of the day can give the consultant a chance to see how transitions are handled. Joining in classroom activities gives the consultant a direct sense of what it feels like to be a teacher or a child in the classroom and may be more comfortable for teachers, as they have an additional helping hand and are less likely to feel judged by a distant observer.

At Small World, Dr. O'Rourke had difficulty entering one class-room and was given subtle cues that the teacher, Ms. Jeffers, resented any infringement on her authority. One day, Dr. O'Rourke heard the teacher discussing plans to begin a topic entitled "All About Me." Dr. O'Rourke was intrigued by this idea and openly expressed her genuine interest. She inquired into Ms. Jeffers' plans and found that the teacher was going to introduce the topic by having the children trace their bod-ies on paper and create life-size replicas of themselves. Dr. O'Rourke was impressed by the plan and found Ms. Jeffers to be responsive to this interest, sharing future plans and asking for the consultant's input. By putting emphasis on the teacher's role, Dr. O'Rourke was confirm-ing Ms. Jeffers' ultimate authority in the classroom, which lessened Ms. Jeffers' defensiveness and allowed her to welcome the consultant into the teacher's domain.

Approach to Children with Special Needs   Observing the center's attitude toward children with special needs is an important part of the evaluation process. Some programs are quick to provide multiple services for their children with the slightest indication of a delay or impairment in functioning. Others, however, tend to deny the severity of problems or disability, thereby reducing the opportunity for potentially useful interventions. Part of the consultant's role is to evalu-ate the program's overall approach to children with special needs, encouraging early detection of problems in those programs that may underrepresent these needs and helping others slow down the decision-making process to be certain children are correctly identified and re-ferred. The consultant will observe a number of salient features in the center's approach to special services: Are children with special needs identified in a timely manner? What is the referral process? Is the cen-ter comfortable recommending evaluation for alternative placements, or do they tend to see this as a reflection of the school's failure? What is the school's general attitude toward the specialist who may pull chil-dren out for services? Is there resentment about the interruption or a cooperative spirit? What resources are available to staff for addressing the special needs of children in the classroom?

In recent years, there has been an increasing demand to integrate children with special needs into the general classroom. This mandate can generally be met with considerable success, particularly with young children who need not be isolated as a result of their emotional or physical challenges. Nonetheless, the inclusion model has shifted many educational, emotional, and behavioral demands onto the class-room teacher. It is therefore incumbent upon the preschool program to provide teachers with the educational and psychological tools that best support the development of these children as well as the class as a whole. Unfortunately, many programs do not provide such supports, thus limiting the effectiveness of both special services and classroom activities. After examining a school's attitude toward children with special needs, the consultant can then help the program develop reasonable expectations and approaches toward these children while providing their teachers with the appropriate level of assistance and training.

At Small World, the staff had grown accustomed to reviewing the educational, medical, and behavioral needs of all children early in the academic year, and they usually referred a small number of children for extra services. They had grown accustomed to working with outside providers who would come to the center to offer cognitive enrichment, speech-language therapy, or other services to individual children, but they did not always welcome the presence of these other professionals in the classroom. The teachers were more vocal in wanting to refer children with moderate to severe behavior problems to self-contained programs, and at times they were at odds with the director, the family worker, and the new educational coordinator over when to make this decision. During the consultant's first year, a 4-year-old girl with limited hearing entered the child care program. The teachers were struggling to accommodate her needs and had begun to question to what extent they could manage children with physical challenges.

Approach to Families   The center's approach to parents is frequently more difficult to assess directly in the beginning of a consultation and, consequently, can be easily overlooked. In many programs, particularly in those whose children arrive by bus, the staff has little face-to-face contact with families on a daily basis. Parental involvement may be sporadic, limited to workshops and planned meetings or random contacts. It is important to establish from the start that this is an area in which the consultant has the potential to become active, especially in programs that lack family workers or other social work staff. The consultant should assess the history of parental involvement at the center and evaluate the availability of opportunities for increased participation through volunteering in the classroom, sitting on committees, and coming to workshops.

At Small World, Dr. O'Rourke's initial assessment was incomplete in this area. Families were not fully integrated into the daily activities at the center, and there was limited attendance at workshops and formal meetings. Faced with some very complex issues in other areas, Dr. O'Rourke allowed this part of the evaluation to remain incomplete. Later, she had the opportunity to learn how families were invited into the center and how information was gathered about the children. Had Dr. O'Rourke fully assessed these variables at the outset, she might have been able to address parent issues earlier, helping the parents feel more fully welcomed at the center. In addition, Dr. O'Rourke would have discovered concerns about the family worker, Ms. Booker, that became apparent later in the collaboration. Ms. Booker was inexperienced and had difficulty gathering sensitive information from the parents. The resulting lack of important family data for both teachers and the consultant had a negative effect on their capacity to intervene with children in a rapid and appropriate manner. In addition, Dr. O'Rourke failed to observe the conflicts between Ms. Booker and teaching staff that emerged as a result of this situation, which might have become apparent sooner had Dr. O'Rourke attended more closely to Ms. Booker's role in the center. However, it should be recognized that although the lack of a formal intake procedure tends to produce some gaps in the assessment process, the information generally emerges as the collaboration unfolds over time.

Overall Formulation   The formulation is a general understanding of the strengths and weaknesses of the program. How well is the program functioning as a place for young children to develop and grow and for families to be fortified? What is the overall feeling? Is it a happy place? Depressed? Anxious? What stresses do the families, teachers, and administrators face, and how are they interrelated? Is it a well-established program, or is it a fledgling operation, just beginning to form ties within the community? In general, the overall formulation is an attempt to make sense of the whole program in terms of its stage of development, its internal strengths and weaknesses, and its niche in the community.

It is of primary importance to note the strengths of the early childhood setting. In the process of assessing and acknowledging these assets, the consultant begins to form an alliance with the staff and to work toward change by first building on what the program does well. The weaknesses, however, are much like a list of symptoms or problems. They may form the basis for an initial plan of intervention or may be kept in the background to be addressed at a later date, when the consultant feels she has developed a comfortable working alliance.

In the case of Small World Head Start, the strengths were in the overall sense of connectedness and commitment to the children. The school felt like a family—involved with each other, warm, caring, and having an interconnectedness and lack of privacy that almost felt natural in this context. The weaknesses were, nevertheless, also apparent. In particular, Dr. O'Rourke saw the lack of understanding about the emotional needs of the children and some issues around safety. The advent of a new teacher/supervisor had upset the equilibrium of the "family," and the resulting strife was making everyone tense. Perhaps most important, Ms. Sanchez's frequent unavailability was a cause for concern and seemed inextricably linked to the other shortcomings of the center.

In formulating a conceptual overview of her impressions of Small World, Dr. O'Rourke identified four central themes:

1. The center served children and families with increased emotional vulnerability because of the multiple community stresses they faced. These included pervasive economic hardship, decaying community infrastructure, and limited social and educational resources and assistance.
2. The staff felt ill-prepared to address these heightened emotional concerns as they lacked adequate training, supervision, and support. In addition, as most of the staff lived within the same community as the families they served, they shared many of the same stresses and vulnerabilities.
3. The director had a powerful yet inconsistent presence in the center and did not fully appreciate the impact of her absences.
4. The well-established program was ambivalent about admitting a new teacher into the closely knit staff "family."

In trying to understand how these factors related to each other, Dr. O'Rourke believed that Ms. Sanchez's personality and role were key. Her authoritative personality and dedication were evident in the numerous strengths of the program and its positive reputation in the community. However, her inability to recognize the staff's need for her consistent presence left them feeling overwhelmed and, at times, unsupported. As a result, they were emotionally less available for the children in their care. Ms. Alonzo was hired to provide them with educational guidance and greater availability but was hampered by her own interpersonal issues and lack of fit with the center.

INITIAL PLAN OF INTERVENTION

After having formulated a concept of the overall functioning of the setting, it becomes easier to develop priorities for intervening within this system. In the Small World example, Dr. O'Rourke met with Ms. Sanchez first and later with other staff to begin articulating her sense of the child care center and its needs. The consultant should be open to feedback, asking how it feels to have her there and what about her style is helpful and what might be experienced as disruptive or missing the mark. Together, staff and consultant should work at reviewing, revising, and fine-tuning the formulation and plan of intervention.

At Small World, Dr. O'Rourke believed that forming a supportive relationship with the director was the first major objective. The goal was to help Ms. Sanchez feel strengthened in her role by exploring the personal, systemic, and administrative obstacles that impeded her capacity to be adequately available to her staff. This goal would be achieved through regular, preferably weekly, meetings with the director. She hoped that by offering her assistance, Ms. Sanchez would, in turn, be better able to provide consistent support to the staff, who were struggling with the considerable vulnerability of the children and families they served.

A second area for intervention was working to foster more cohesion among the teachers. A primary goal was to establish relationships with the teachers and the new educational coordinator and to begin to explore with them their concerns and needs. The consultant also wanted to work with them to devise ways to increase a sense of support for staff and to expand the opportunities for staff development. In addition, she hoped to find a regular mechanism for teachers and other staff to discuss their feelings, to address their frustrations and stresses, and to develop effective ways of working together.

There were a number of other key issues that needed to be addressed and would likely require further observation and intervention planning on the part of the consultant. She would assess the rooms for physical safety, emotional warmth, and academic appropriateness. In addition, Dr. O'Rourke planned to become actively engaged in classroom activities. She believed that by interacting with children in the classroom, she could model an emotionally responsive approach to children, provide practical assistance, and demonstrate her willingness to "get her hands dirty." Over time, Dr. O'Rourke would also address the numerous community stresses by devising workshops to help parents and families. In addition, she planned to support Ms. Booker's role and to determine other ways the consultant might assist in outreach work to meet the growing needs of the families and the community they served.

In discussing the plan with the director, Dr. O'Rourke found Ms. Sanchez to be attuned to the goals around staff development, in particular around creating better working relationships among the teachers. Although she agreed in principal to regular meetings with Dr. O'Rourke, Ms. Sanchez had difficulty maintaining this commitment on a regular basis—an occurrence that mirrored the teachers' experience. Over time, however, Ms. Sanchez began to find these meetings useful and, as she examined the factors that interfered with her ability to remain engaged on site, she was better able to attend on a regular basis. The teachers were eager for help and readily agreed with Dr. O'Rourke's setting up regular times to spend in the classroom and to meet with them as a group.

Once a plan is set up and agreed upon, the consultant is ready to begin the work. However, she will periodically need to check in, ask for feedback (informal or otherwise), and revise her goals and her allocation of time. It is a constantly evolving process, based on changing needs, perceptions, and foci. Ideally, this process of mutual evaluation has begun in the critical point of entry and continues to be nurtured throughout the duration of the mental health–early childhood collaboration. In this way, the mental health agenda is both responsive and flexible, emerging from a dynamic collaborative process that reflects the assessment of the consultant, the needs of children and families, and the concerns of teaching staff and administration. The mental health agenda that emerges from the entry process most typically addresses a wide array of systemic and individual concerns but generally begins with a focus on the needs of the administrative staff, who function as a gateway to the program, its teaching and support staff, as well as the children and families they serve.

chapter three

Bridging the Divide
Working with Administrative Staff

A strong relationship between the consultant and the preschool administrators is central to the development of an effective collaboration. The director and senior staff members not only set the school policies but also do much to establish the tone and tenor of the school and its connection to the surrounding community. The administrative staff members charged with ensuring the overall quality of the preschool and planning for the future can benefit from sharing these tasks with another professional with expertise in child development and organizational skills. Administrators may also seek counsel and collaborative input regarding other issues, including supervision of staff, curriculum development, staff training, crisis management, parent workshops, community outreach, board management, and fund-raising. These endeavors can be time-consuming and lengthy, and in the initial phase of the collaboration, the consultant needs to establish priorities with the senior staff. The aim of these meetings is to create a working agenda for the consultant as well as to brainstorm with the administrators about their goals for the children, teachers, and the program as a whole. The consultant who instead enters with a standard blueprint for mental health services that lacks any serious input from the program staff is destined to fall short of her goals and will be unlikely to meet the center's needs.

STAFF ALLIANCES AND CONFLICTS

The effective consultant comes to appreciate the system of interconnected relationships in the preschool and how his presence alters that system. This is particularly critical regarding the consultant's role in supporting and advising the administrative staff. Although most child care settings do not have a formal management design or a rigid hierarchical structure, they nonetheless must wrestle with their own power struggles and communication problems. Child care centers are often grassroots, community-based organizations, and the preschool staff can come to resemble an extended family whose members embrace an egalitarian philosophy of shared ideas and resources. However, if applied too rigidly, these same ideals can be used to resist an open and honest dialogue about control issues and organizational structure. If the staff are all committed and "in it together," how can they become divided?

Yet some splits are inevitable, even among the most harmonious child care staff. The consultant must anticipate this from the outset and avoid becoming too closely identified with one group. If the mental health consultant was a former teacher or a "frontline" worker of another sort, he may lean toward the classroom staff in disputes. He may see parallels to his own struggles with administrators who did not always have a clear sense of the burdens of clinicians in the field. Likewise, if he has had more administrative experience or past difficulties with others he supervised, the consultant may take his cues from the program director and her immediate staff and be quicker to hold the teachers in judgment.

The following situation illustrates the potential dilemmas the consultant might face in this regard.

> *Ms. Andrews, the consultant at a large child care center, was concerned about the structured academic work that Ms. Lazlow introduced to her class of 4-year-olds; most of the material seemed to be lost on the children. The consultant spoke briefly with Ms. Lazlow after the lesson but did not believe she was making any progress. Ms. Andrews felt compelled at that point to go to the director of the program, Mr. Morgan, to report what she had witnessed—much as she would have done when she worked as a staff social*

*worker in a local preschool program years before. Ms.
Andrews had always felt a solid connection to Mr. Morgan
and admired his candor and his commitment to the
children. However, Ms. Andrews had not adequately
assessed how Mr. Morgan's additional administrative duties
outside the school had affected the staff. The teachers
continued to praise and support Mr. Morgan while
demeaning and resisting the efforts of the educational
coordinator to whom he had delegated the classroom
supervision duties. Mr. Morgan was sympathetic to Ms.
Andrews' concerns, but he also made it clear that the day-
to-day workings of the preschool classrooms were no longer
his main focus. Ms. Andrews needed to report her
observations to the educational coordinator instead. In a
later peer group discussion with other consultants, Ms.
Andrews recognized that she had acted too hastily and had
not given Ms. Lazlow adequate time to explain her
philosophy or a chance to digest the new ideas with which
she was presented.*

In this example, the consultant was faced with a delicate issue and
turned first to the person with whom she identified. Because it was not
a dangerous situation or one that required the director's immediate
input, Ms. Andrews was rebuffed by Mr. Morgan and instructed to report her concerns to the teacher's supervisor. Ms. Andrews was not
necessarily comfortable with that option: She recognized this approach
as a potential breach of trust with Ms. Lazlow and not a logical first
step for maintaining an alliance and effecting more long-term change.
Once Ms. Andrews was disentangled from her personal allegiance to
the director and reviewed her biases from her history as an administrator, she was able to see more clearly the structural issues and pick a
better point of intervention.

Staff alliances and conflicts can also be played out in other more
subtle ways. When presented with clinical information in a school environment, a consultant must listen with two ears, much like the therapist who carefully notes the current events in patients' lives while
paying close attention to hints of repetitions from their pasts. Every
school has its own history, and staff members in early childhood programs have often been entwined for years. Relatively straightforward
descriptions of children acting out or parents who are hard to reach almost always include pieces of these preexisting entanglements. There
are times when difficulties in the classroom are far less important than

the systemic divisions that they come to represent. Sometimes the consultant needs to veer away from the presenting problem, and his intervention must first address his role in the relationship matrix of the school. This point is addressed in the following example.

> *Four-year-old Janice was wreaking havoc at her nursery school. She was disruptive in class, disrespectful of her teachers, and aggressive with peers. Her teachers had given her the first few weeks of the school year to settle down, but by mid-October they were at a loss, and they began to fear for other children's safety after Janice began angrily throwing blocks and other objects about the room. Unsuccessful in their in-class attempts to set limits, they resorted to taking Janice to other staff in the program, including administrative workers. Due to safety concerns for Janice's classmates and themselves, the teachers pleaded for others to take Janice for a short while. Though uncomfortable with this arrangement, some staff would oblige and keep her for brief periods. Janice seemed to welcome this one-to-one attention.*
>
> *After a few weeks, during which the situation remained largely unchanged, the teachers were summoned to discuss Janice's case with the director, the new educational coordinator, the special needs teacher, and the mental health consultant, Dr. Simmons. The teachers approached this meeting warily, having felt unsupported in the past by their director, Ms. Daniels, and believing that the staff in the "back offices" had little appreciation for the stresses of teachers' day-to-day classroom tasks. Despite this, the meeting initially proceeded well. Ms. Griffin, the head teacher, noted some recent improvements in Janice's conduct and acknowledged that removing Janice from class might reinforce negative behavior. The group also brainstormed on how to help Janice's mother, who was struggling with her at home.*
>
> *Sensing an openness to further suggestion, Dr. Simmons made recommendations for how to respond to Janice's behavior in the classroom. At that point, Mr. Taylor, the assistant teacher, grew exasperated and again complained that the teachers had not been heard. He angrily and pointedly suggested that the administrative staff replace the teachers for 1 day to see if they could adopt any new strategies. The director and the educational coordinator*

replied that this idea was inappropriate: The children, who were unfamiliar with the administrators, would be confused and have their routine disrupted. They were also clearly angry at being put on the spot by the teachers.

Dr. Simmons felt the urge to support the administrators' points of view as more sensible but paused to consider the structural implications of this discussion and assess the risk of aligning against the teachers at that moment. He instead decided to take up the teachers' challenge and offered to spend time with Janice in their classroom the following week if acceptable to all present. Dr. Simmons told the teachers it would be helpful for him to have firsthand experience with their problem and agreed it would be the best way to test any proposed solutions. This diffused the tension in the meeting somewhat. Dr. Simmons made a few summary remarks about the progress the teachers had made, which, at that point, they appeared more willing to hear.

In the preceding example, the consultant's decision-making process was informed less by the teachers' literal request for hands-on help and more by their sense of urgency, despair, and isolation from the administrative staff. As a person within the system but with a less fixed role or natural alignment, the consultant had the opportunity to bolster this team of teachers without taking sides or further alienating the administration. Within 3 weeks, the situation with Janice had calmed considerably, though this change appeared to have little to do with any of Dr. Simmons' suggestions or help. The teachers decided that they would no longer stand for this girl's behavior or allow her to leave the room, and they were clear and direct with Janice, leaving her visibly relieved and more content in class. Rather than give advice, the consultant reinforced the teachers' strategies and newfound resolve and accepted the premise that only the teachers could handle their student. Ms. Griffin proudly reported her results to Dr. Simmons one morning and related a recent conversation with Janice's grandmother. The grandmother wanted to know how they worked such magic with Janice, who was now much more responsive at home as well.

Although Janice had definite difficulties with aggression and impulsivity, the center's systemic weaknesses had been exacerbating her problems. Feeling stressed by the new demands Janice presented, the teachers sought support from the administrative staff but did so in a way that undermined their chance of getting adequate help. The teachers' inability to manage this difficult child frustrated Ms. Daniels, raised further questions in her mind about the teachers' overall competence, and made her slow to respond to the immediate call for assistance. Not surprisingly, Janice began to act out even more frequently and intensively because she sensed that the system could not contain her. As the teachers increasingly focused on Janice, the class in general became more chaotic and less structured.

Here the consultant functioned much like a family therapist, looking to reinforce the structural integrity of the system and to right the power alignments. The teachers wanted to feel that they were back in control and that Janice was responsive to them. Although they could learn more effective ways of drawing support from the administration (and later did obtain an additional classroom staff person), they needed to know that they could prevail and that this child did not have the power to disrupt their room. The consultant supported their efforts, not to side with them against the senior staff, but to meet Janice's needs at that point. By maintaining this clinical perspective, he was able to lessen the tension between the teachers and the administrators and to help them pursue a common goal for the child.

This example demonstrates the importance of the consultant retaining his independence within the system. He must actively avoid the tangled web of alignments and splits among the child care staff. Otherwise, he will be inevitably drawn to one side or the other or, worse, become engaged in a triangular arrangement in which he tips the balance in favor of one or more staff members. This note of caution is not meant to imply that the consultant must refrain from having warm relationships with staff members. The consultant's independence should in no way preclude his ability to become an active member of the community and to be a real person with teachers and administrators alike.

This dilemma can be addressed in another way. If the consultant is clear that he will address each clinical situation on a case-by-case basis and will want to gain information from all parties in equal measure, he can allay some of the fears regarding his allegiance. More important, if the consultant follows through on this pledge and makes every effort to treat each staff person as an individual and a professional, he will be far less likely to take sides or be seen as a pawn of one group. This respect and concern for staff begins with addressing each member by name, saying hello in the morning, and offering to help in even the most basic classroom tasks. Small oversights in respect are quickly picked up by staff and, thankfully, are often commented on by them. Larger failures in this regard, such as addressing only head teachers and not assistants or reporting on classroom observations without reviewing them with staff, will likely derail future attempts at inquiry or intervention with those teachers.

Again, this independence should not be misconstrued as equivalent to remaining aloof from the child care staff or maintaining a "therapeutically neutral" stance toward the children and their families. Unlike most consultants in private industry who tend to strive for objectivity and distance, the mental health consultant can become intimately involved in the life of the preschool. The task for the consultant is not just to observe, to comment, or to instruct, but to live with staff and become part of their community. Taking part in daily rituals, eating meals with staff, learning about their families and interests, getting to know the neighborhood, sharing recipes and customs—all are opportunities for the consultant to become a more integrated member of the child care center. Approaching the work with warmth, enthusiasm, and a sense of shared purpose does not have to compromise the consultant's objectivity; instead, it increases the likelihood that his suggestions and supportive comments will warrant consideration by a greater proportion of teachers and administrators alike.

MAINTAINING AN ONGOING DIALOGUE BETWEEN THE CONSULTANT AND THE PROGRAM DIRECTOR

Running a preschool is a challenge for even the best prepared early childhood professional. Caring for, educating, and preserving the well-being of young children is a noble endeavor but still brings relatively little acclaim in American society, paling in comparison, for example, to how European countries treat their nursery school principals (Simons, 1997). In addition to the limited recognition and salary, preschool directors often are not adequately trained for the tasks they must confront. Many do not have formal training in administration or management and may have relatively little experience supervising teachers and other staff members. Typically, they have risen from the ranks of experienced educators and are chosen because of the respect they have earned for their performance in the classroom.

In getting to know the director, the consultant must bear in mind the myriad tasks he oversees. The director is frequently the educational supervisor, the building manager, the controller, the director of development, the head of safety and security, the transportation coordinator, the nutritional planner, the community advocate, and the point person for all crises and emergencies. He may be ill-prepared to take on some of these roles and others are doubtless ones he does not relish. The first task for the consultant is to survey the scene, to try to step into the director's shoes, and to appreciate the delicate balancing act that the director faces every day. One critical mistake that some consultants make is to criticize directors glibly for not focusing on the children, for losing sight of the ultimate goal, or abandoning the educational hat for more managerial tasks. Few directors welcome these administrative roles, which they too view as distractions. But like their peers in other human services agencies, directors recognize that they must take care of business if their centers are to survive. In many child care settings, particularly in communities with limited child care subsidies and other fiscal constraints, survival is not taken for granted.

In this regard, the consultant has a unique advantage. Free from the fiscal demands of the setting and without its administrative concerns, she can spend time with the children at a more leisurely pace, at least in the director's eyes. Rather than holding on to these experiences or sharing them only with the classroom staff, the consultant has a chance to bring the director into the heart of the program in ways that other observers cannot. Directors often cherish the consultants' stories of the children, from a boy sharing a dream about scary monsters, or another asking if he could marry his mother when he grew up, to a shy girl who had been crying for her mother joining her peers at the water table for the first time. These moments can help reinject a sense of purpose and a feeling of "it's all worthwhile" in directors and perhaps momentarily relieve some of the stress of the job's other demands. The consultant may also wish to point out the developmental advances implicit in these examples, but experience suggests that it is the affective tone that is nearly always the most critical element conveyed in these stories.

For the director, there is often the temptation to extend this role and to have the consultant report on a much larger range of experiences that she witnesses. This request can be innocuous enough, but it should give the consultant pause, and it is a chance to discuss with the director the consultant's role and the importance of maintaining independence. Other situations are more vexing. In one instance, a new Head Start director asked the consultant-in-training to check up on one teacher who appeared sluggish and less involved with the children than she had been in previous years. Although uncomfortable with this request, this inexperienced consultant thought she should comply to further her alliance with the director. Fortunately, in this case, the consultant's supervisor was also on site. The supervisor was able to explain to the director the importance of the teachers' trust and sense of safety with the new consultant, especially as they were first getting to know each other. The director reluctantly agreed to withdraw this idea and decided to address the issue more directly in a team meeting and through her own observation.

Although he must carefully avoid taking on a monitoring role, the consultant should feel free to emphasize the positive points he observes in the classroom. Often the director hears more about a teacher's shortcomings or missteps and less about the ongoing relationships with the children or subtle developments taking place in the classroom. The consultant's experience may run contrary to these negative perceptions, giving him the opportunity to present a more balanced view to the director.

> *Ms. Harris had a reputation for being overbearing and harsh with the children in her nursery school class. At first, the consultant could only concur with this view, after seeing her bark orders and carry herself in a somewhat threatening way. But over time, he saw beneath Ms. Harris's gruff exterior and was able to experience and observe her warmth and generosity. The consultant related one instance in which he watched Ms. Harris comfort and console a child from another classroom on the playground. She had taken a strong interest in this boy who had been having extreme separation problems. Ms. Harris patiently held the child's hand and walked him around the playground, assuring him that things would get better. Pleasantly surprised by this account, the administrative team and director in particular began to soften toward Ms. Harris and to consider her strengths both in limit-setting and in comforting children in distress.*

In this instance, the consultant had the opportunity to point out the strengths of a teacher whose weaknesses tended to be more apparent. This approach is not meant to obscure this teacher's need for growth but rather to balance a negative perception and to give hope that further progress could be made. In this case, the teacher responded to continued positive support from the director and also seemed to be somewhat more willing to hear constructive criticism.

Early childhood program directors face the difficult task of managing staff and defining a workable team structure while nurturing staff members who may be inexperienced, underpaid, or experiencing job-related or personal stress. Directors tend to be strong in one of these areas and may find that providing support comes more naturally to them. Yet without a solid team approach, well-defined lines of authority, and clear job descriptions for both administrative and teaching staff members, a preschool program will not run effectively. In some instances, complaints will come from teachers who long for more structure and clearer expectations and wish to be treated and respected as professionals.

As discussed in Chapter 2, the consultant's initial assessment of the center will usually include a review of team structure. Some pre-

schools have solid, long-standing teams that take an active role in running the program. In these centers, the mental health consultant generally has an easier time finding a role in the system and can join together
with administrative and classroom staff in a more seamless manner. In
other programs, the consultant may have to play a more active role in
helping to build or reinforce the team structure. He may start by asking the director to describe the organization of the program, to outline
the extent of authority of the administrative staff, and to explain the responsibilities of head and assistant teachers. Often in this process, it
will become obvious where job descriptions are murky and responsibilities unclear. It is also essential to ascertain how these groups communicate with each other. Though an aversion to staff or team meetings is somewhat common in early child care programs, there is often
a need for more group contact, albeit with a clear and well-defined
agenda. Some of the resistance might be attributed to traditional models of education, where individual classrooms have their own rules and
arrangements and, to a large extent, function independently. However,
at no other point does the educational process intersect with so many
aspects of a child's cognitive, social, and emotional needs than in the
preschool years. Programs that are open and inclusive and have input
from a diverse group of professionals can best address these areas of
development.

The consultant can help the director by making requests to meet
with groups of staff members on a regular basis. In Head Start and
other preschools with more administrative staff positions, this might
initially include briefings with the director, the educational coordinator, and the social worker to review the week's events and any pressing matters with children and families. The consultant might also help
this group develop action plans and report back at the following meeting on the progress in the interim period. For instance, the consultant
might suggest that she observe a child who is acting out and meet with
the child's teacher, while the social worker speaks to the parents and
the educational coordinator observes the classroom and offers alternative management techniques. At the next meeting they can compare
notes and involve the classroom team in this process, who in subsequent weeks may take responsibility for designing and implementing
new strategies and bring in other staff and the consultant as necessary.

Through this process, the director may come to see the value of the
team structure and begin to delegate authority to other staff members.
Ideally, the educational coordinator can manage classroom team meetings, the social worker can oversee family interventions, and the nurse
or health coordinator can handle specific health-related issues. Each of
these administrative staff members should then report back to the director on a regular basis so that she remains informed as to the day-to-

day goings-on in the program. If this system is functioning well, the director may be better freed up to spend time with the children, to visit classrooms, and to get to know parents. Obviously in programs without the staffing described here, the director will initially be called on to take a more active supervisory role but might then shift more of the responsibility to the individual classroom teams.

An efficient team structure not only provides for built-in support from colleagues, but it also allows the director to focus more actively on providing support and assurance to staff. If less constrained and stressed by daily issues with children, the director can focus on staff training and development and may seek out the consultant's advice on arranging relevant discussions or training sessions. More important, the director will likely be increasingly available to support staff under stress or needing assistance with their responsibilities. This task is psychologically easier to undertake if the director feels that the school is in generally good working order and that the teams will provide staff with additional aid. The director might plan training in child development for less experienced staff, provide education for staff regarding appropriate expectations for academic progress and behavior, or offer more individualized help to staff experiencing personal struggles or a life crisis.

Although not typically trained as a therapist, the preschool director will often have to assume a supportive role with staff, balancing their needs with those of the children and the program as a whole. This can include concrete backing, as in one Head Start program where the director organized a clothing and fund-raising drive for a teacher and her family who were forced out of their apartment by a fire. More often it will involve helping staff who are stressed by the demands of the children or circumstances in their own lives. The consultant can sometimes help the director frame a discussion with staff and can offer to be a resource for the staff member in question. Occasionally, this will entail brief consultation or problem solving with staff or referring an individual with personal or family problems for further treatment.

If a healthy rapport has been established, the mental health consultant and the director can sometimes provide a brief intervention that helps reduce a teacher's stress, both by offering her concrete advice and by sharing and empathizing with her concern.

Mr. Flynn, the head teacher at a nursery school, was becoming increasingly exasperated by one parent who seemed to question his judgement constantly, particularly concerning her child's safety. Mr. Flynn had come to dread interactions with Timothy's mother in the afternoon, always

*feeling he had to be on the defensive. This strained
relationship was dampening Mr. Flynn's spirits during his
first year as a head teacher, in what had otherwise been a
promising start to a new school year. For the consultant, the
first task of the meeting was to reassure Mr. Flynn that he
was indeed doing a good job and that he had the full
support of the director, who quickly seconded this opinion.
The discussion then shifted to reexamining this mother's
behavior in light of her own separation issues with Timothy
and her anxiety over working full time, both of which had
emerged in her first meeting with Mr. Flynn and the
director. The group discussed ways of involving Timothy's
mother more in the classroom, such as inviting her in
during her lunch break once a week, and they also talked
of having another meeting with both parents to discuss
safety concerns and their son's considerable progress. The
director was clear in her support of Mr. Flynn; she
acknowledged how upset Mr. Flynn felt about the situation
and did not suggest any changes in his classroom setup
or routine.*

Mr. Flynn welcomed the advice regarding Timothy's mother and
was a bit more hopeful afterward; but more important, the teacher was
relieved to know that he could voice his concerns without any fear of
retribution. The consultant in this case mainly echoed suggestions the
director had already considered and helped the director explicitly express her full support for Mr. Flynn.

Other more daunting challenges for the director can sometimes be
met more easily with support from a mental health consultant. Perhaps
chief among these duties is deciding when an employee's ongoing concerns significantly interfere with her ability to function in her position.
Directors take this responsibility quite seriously and rarely relish the
task of confronting a staff member with a negative evaluation or,
worse, terminating her employment. Although not easy in any human
services organization, these issues are particularly thorny in early childhood programs, which are often tightly knit communities that come
to be extended families for many teachers and other staff members.
In these cases, directors can benefit from consultants' objective assessments of situations and their recognition of the struggles involved in
making difficult decisions.

In times of crisis in the community or the school, the director often
finds himself in the position of supporting all others in the community
and may need someone to help him shoulder the burden. The death of

a teacher or other member of the community can weigh heavily on a preschool director, who may be unsure how to respond to the grief and other emotions staff and families present. Incidences of abuse and neglect can be particularly distressing for directors, and they can benefit from having an outside professional review the events, explore their feelings about them, and support the directors as they decide on a course of action. Fires, hurricanes, and other devastating occurrences can have a lasting impact on young children, and preschools often have an opportunity to provide both concrete assistance and reassurance to the children and families. Again, directors can almost always use a partner in these endeavors. These subjects and other examples are addressed more specifically in Chapter 8.

Such moments may also serve to remind the consultant that the director needs backing and encouragement at other times as well. A director may be overwhelmed by the volume of tasks that come his way and can feel bogged down by the minutiae of his job. It is essential that the consultant makes a point of assessing the director's needs and reaching out to him. The support may take tangible forms: helping a director plan for board meetings or visits from oversight agencies, reviewing curriculum materials, or making presentations together at community or professional meetings. No one person can fill all these roles, but it is often the availability of the consultant that is most comforting to the director, especially when he is stressed or needs to "blow off steam." Having another professional on board who shares similar goals and values yet remains outside the system can sometimes help the director weather the program's turbulent times without feeling as isolated.

Preschool directors also frequently want to be included in staff training or support groups. Ongoing meetings with all staff members and the consultant can sometimes diffuse tensions regarding status and role in the school and can reaffirm a sense of being a part of one community. Teachers can come to feel that senior staff members have more of an appreciation for their work when the entire group hears about the challenges teachers face and their efforts to meet the needs of all their children. (This concept is discussed in greater detail in Chapter 4.) Likewise, as the following example demonstrates, directors and other administrators have reported feeling more accepted and part of the team when they have been able to embrace teachers' concerns and share their own stresses in these large forums.

At the Open Door Child Care Program, the new director, Mr. Bennet, was determined to put his stamp on the

*program. He had a solid early childhood background and
clear ideas about curriculum development and classroom
structure, and he was particularly invested in seeing
creative, child-driven group projects in each classroom.
Although the teachers recognized his energy and
knowledge, they felt he had unrealistic expectations and did
not fully appreciate the background of their students. Many
of the families in the programs were severely impoverished
and a large number of children had experienced multiple
traumas.*

*Open Door had a long-standing collaboration with a local
mental health clinic, and a consulting social worker had
facilitated a staff support group for teachers for 3 years. After
Mr. Bennet's arrival, much of the group was focused on the
teachers' complaints regarding his assertiveness and lack of
appreciation for their needs and their job-related stress.
Although invited in for two meetings to discuss these
concerns, Mr. Bennet was skeptical of the group and
wondered if it had outlived its usefulness. He did, however,
make some concessions to the teachers, and over the course
of the year he came to more fully appreciate the intense
needs of the individuals they served.*

*Over the summer, Mr. Bennett asked the consultant, Ms.
Driscoll, if the group could be expanded to include all
teachers, administrators, and support staff. Although hesitant
at first, Ms. Driscoll agreed to test this format, and, to her
surprise, the group began to flourish during the next
academic year. The teachers were more open about their
needs and concerns, and Mr. Bennet was able to address
these issues more directly in the group. He was a much
stronger advocate for the staff than anyone suspected and
welcomed the chance to prove to them that he heard their
pleas. Mr. Bennet was still somewhat authoritative and at
times assumed too active a role in the group, but he could
hear complaints about this from the teachers. He also
confided to Ms. Driscoll outside the group that he was trying
not to act as the director in that forum.*

*During his second year, Mr. Bennet grew more
comfortable referring children and families for therapeutic
services, and he became a strong advocate in the local
community for mental health resources for children and
preschools. He also sought Ms. Driscoll's advice on a wide
range of staff and personal issues, unlike the first year of his*

tenure, when he rarely took advantage of this opportunity. The teachers still sometimes questioned his personal style and methods, but by the end of the year few doubted that Mr. Bennett had their interests at heart and that he was firmly committed to the children and families of Open Door.

In this example, the director initially believed that the group challenged his authority, and he was left feeling alone and isolated. However, as he became a full-fledged member of the group, he began to appreciate the role it played for teachers and used it to share his own stresses and frustrations. In the process, Mr. Bennet became more humanized in the eyes of the staff. At the same time, he grew to see their struggles in a different light and began to praise their work more openly.

CONSULTATION AND EDUCATIONAL PLANNING

Some Head Start and other early childhood programs are fortunate enough to have an educational coordinator to oversee curriculum development and teacher training. In other programs, the director and senior teachers usually fill this role. In either case, those in charge of educational supervision may welcome the consultant as a potential partner in 1) expanding curriculum planning to include a focus on social and emotional development; 2) designing educational and treatment plans for children identified with learning, developmental, or emotional needs; and 3) providing support to teachers. The relative emphasis of the joint efforts of the consultant and educational supervisor will, of course, depend on their areas of expertise and the requirements of the program.

Educational supervisors and senior teachers often need assistance in overseeing other staff, especially if they have limited administrative experience. It is helpful for the consultant to point out the positives in classroom observations of teachers and to help supervisors do the same. This is critical both in helping supervisors establish a more collaborative relationship with teachers and in giving the supervisors confidence that they can advise teachers and improve their classroom skills. In some early childhood programs, the educational supervisors have more training and experience than the other teachers, so they may be challenged by the extent of the teachers' knowledge of developmental principles or preschool curriculum training. If they can first see the positive interactions in the classroom and view them as building blocks or a foundation for their work, the educational supervisors will be far more likely to remain connected to teachers and to feel that their efforts are worthwhile.

Teachers are more inclined to adopt new strategies in working on either an emotional or cognitive level with children if they can see someone else do it first. Didactic programs and seminars are useful reviews for teachers but pale in comparison to on-site demonstrations of new techniques. The consultant has a chance to model for the educational supervisor by inviting her to observe his efforts, for instance, to introduce family story time or to talk about scary monsters at lunch. He might do the same in return, sitting in on the educational supervisor's demonstration of group premath exercises or participant storytelling. Ideally, the mental health consultant and the educational supervisor would then share their observations of the children's responses and the teachers' level of enthusiasm and interest.

Without overstating the case, the consultant can point out advances teachers have made in trying new ideas and methods, such as allowing more emotional expression in the classroom. Often this will start with an acceptance of the consultant's own attempt to try something different, such as a group sharing of the children's weekend or vacation experiences. Sometimes it is manifested by changes in the affective tone of the class or in the teachers' acceptance of varied mood states in the children, gains that are easily overlooked or that may seem elementary to a supervisor with extensive training and experience. The educational supervisor may need help acknowledging these steps and encouraging the teachers to continue using new techniques. It is also useful to review baseline observations from previous years with the same teachers or from the start of the current academic year.

Along with recognizing and complimenting the teachers on gains in learning new skills and enhancing curriculum planning, the educational supervisor can sometimes benefit from taking a long-term approach to supervision. Administrators and consultants frequently hold disparate expectations regarding appropriate rates of change for accepting and implementing new ideas, either personally or professionally. Mental health professionals are accustomed to taking a long view during which change can be expected to occur in small increments. Discussing these differing approaches may help the educational supervisor set more realistic and attainable goals for classroom teachers and may help her recognize modest advances toward her ultimate objective. This is not to imply that the educational supervisor should set her sights low and accept an inadequate level of performance from teachers. Even staff with only a limited background in early childhood education have much to offer the children and families they serve. Their energy, enthusiasm, and ability to relate to children often compensate for a lack of more formal training. It is just these teachers who need support and guidance from a supervisor, who in the best settings can help turn their raw talents into well-honed educational skills.

In addition to modeling for teachers, the educational supervisor often helps them establish goals with particular children and chart their development over time. Although the consultant does not usually have a direct role in designing these interventions and goals, he may work with the educational supervisor to keep them incremental, attainable, and time-limited. For a 3-year-old boy who knows few words in September, this might mean having a month-to-month chart in which the teachers track the new words he learns. Together, the mental health consultant and educational supervisor may brainstorm about ways of extending this charting to the entire class and expanding it to include the children's knowledge of colors and numbers or their capacity for attending to a story. In these instances, the consultant is clearly an invited guest and must, of course, recognize the educational supervisor's training, expertise, and prime responsibility in the areas of curriculum development and classroom planning.

The educational supervisor may also call on the consultant to help cultivate teamwork in the classroom. Together, they may discuss ways of helping teachers learn to share tasks in their class, with team members developing their own specialties and interests. One might focus on storytelling and songs whereas another focuses on art projects, having each display her wares in parts of the classroom. The goal is to foster a mutual support network among the teachers in which they encourage each other or offer aid to one another when necessary. The mental health consultant may be charged with seeing to the teachers' responsiveness to this arrangement. In group meetings, he might ask if the team believes that the supervisor has reviewed and appreciated each member's work. In a less collaborative room, teachers may feel they have to compete for their supervisor's attention, or one teacher's disenchantment and lack of enthusiasm may hold sway, limiting the initiatives of the other staff members. The educational supervisor will likely want to know soon if something is amiss and may want help from the consultant in promoting teamwork and developing pragmatic ways to give teachers feedback on their efforts.

Besides building teams, the educational supervisor has a real chance to bolster staff morale by providing concrete support to teachers. The consultant might highlight this function as the supervisor decides on requests for classroom materials and supplies, especially for new projects, or plans for enjoyable off-site visits to local libraries and cultural institutions. He may suggest that the educational supervisor arrange staff recognition luncheons or other social events that serve the same purpose. In perhaps her most important role, the educational su-

pervisor can encourage teachers to further their education and training
by taking college or graduate classes or attending workshops and seminars. In one Head Start program, a new educational coordinator had
the opportunity to counsel and assist two teachers who were taking
college-level classes as part of a scholarship program during her first
months in this position. She went out of her way to aid the teachers by
tutoring and encouraging them and helping them with their papers.
Clearly above and beyond a typical mentoring role, her efforts did not
go unnoticed by staff, and the consultant frequently pointed to this
support as one of the cornerstones of the educational coordinator's success. The other teachers in the school not only began to develop interest in taking classes, but they also quickly grew to respect this supervisor and to appreciate her tangible efforts, leaving them more receptive
to their supervisor's work-related comments and suggestions.

CONSULTATION AND SOCIAL WORK
Social work duties are common and numerous in preschools and are
often shared by several staff members. Early childhood programs
make referrals for special education services; provide family outreach;
help families gain access to medical care and other services for families
in the community; and offer linkages to schools, recreational facilities,
and cultural centers. Some preschools have an assigned social worker
who handles many of these duties while on site for 1 or more days per
week. In Head Start, the family worker completes intakes and family
needs assessments, organizes parent workshops and social events, and
visits families in their homes. In other programs, the director, support
staff, and, in some cases, classroom teams handle these responsibilities.

Many Head Start family workers and others handling social work
duties in preschools do not have formal training in the field. The director may ask the consultant to spend extra time with them developing their skills and sense of professionalism. Reviewing key questions
for parents and other family members is often a good starting place,
and these discussions might help define and systematize the school's
intake forms and procedures. Joint meetings with parents for family intakes are often helpful because the consultant and the social worker
can later review the issues raised and the interview procedure. These
collaborative efforts are even more critical in programs where the family worker is struggling to delineate boundaries and elucidate her role
in the school and in the neighborhood.

In many preschools, the social worker is knowledgeable, experienced, and well established in the community as well as the person
most aware of family issues or concerns that need to be addressed in
school. She is often the person to whom parents or teachers first turn

for support. When concerns arise about a child in the classroom, the mental health consultant will naturally rely on the social worker to obtain relevant background information and to gain a sense of the child's previous experience in school. In establishing this relationship, the consultant needs to be aware of potential overlaps in duties and tasks with the social worker, and early on they should sit together to clarify roles and responsibilities. This process is critical when there are overt or covert issues of professional status and recognition or if the consultant is a social worker with similar training and experience. In a preschool with a well-functioning parent program, the consultant might spend little time on planning outreach activities and instead design workshops on topics within her specific area of expertise. It is important that both the consultant and the on-site family worker feel that they have their own definable niches, can work together to reach out to families in need, and support each other as peers. This may involve the social worker making initial contact with families and recommending a meeting with the consultant. Often joint meetings are most successful, as shown in the next scenario.

> *Ms. Thomas was hesitant to come to her daughter Lisa's preschool program as she feared that Lisa would be asked to leave due to aggressiveness and hyperactivity in the classroom. Ms. Thomas agreed to meet with the consultant, Dr. Wagner, and the school social worker, Ms. Baker, to discuss ways to help Lisa. Ms. Thomas was overwhelmed by Lisa at home and by her own responsibilities as a single mother who had just returned to school. Dr. Wagner reviewed his observations of Lisa in class, focusing mostly on her playfulness and her attention-seeking behavior. He suggested that Lisa might benefit from some one-to-one counseling sessions with him and that she would also make progress if a rewards system was used in the classroom and at home. Ms. Baker spoke next, mainly of her own experience as a single mother with two daughters and of her respect for Ms. Thomas' attempt to get her life back on track. Ms. Baker advocated counseling and the consultant's other suggestions as ways of supporting and strengthening Ms. Thomas's resolve in caring for her daughter.*

In this case, the consultant believed that brief interventions would significantly help Lisa, but it was the on-site social worker who, by sharing her own experiences, convinced Ms. Thomas that the consultant's suggestions were worthwhile and that there was reason to be hopeful. The social worker herself served as a model for Lisa's mother, and her acceptance and support of on-site mental health interventions made them a more reasonable course of action. By sharing their terrain in this way, neither the consultant nor the social worker was left alone with the needs of the family, and both could call on each other for support, advice, and direct planning of services.

It is not unusual for preschool social workers and teachers to find themselves focusing on different members of the same family. To a certain extent, this division of labor is expected, with teachers concentrating on their work with children in the classroom and social workers attending to other family needs such as helping parents with school registration, medical appointments, and entitlements. Yet at times each group can come to feel that the other does not appreciate their work or that theirs is the "real" work that will have the most impact on the family. Again, despite an overall shared sense of purpose among staff members, such splits are not uncommon in preschools.

The mental health consultant can play a key role here. As previously mentioned, he can encourage team meetings in which members have an opportunity to share their work and their goals with the children and families. He can model some of this by describing his own work and by respecting and responding to the plans of other team members. The consultant may also help define appropriate boundaries between staff in terms of intake and assessment of children, classroom placement, ongoing family outreach, and ways of presenting concerns about children to parents. The consultant may also encourage joint projects, having the social worker joining the class for a specific lesson each week, or suggest parent conferences with all team members. The goal is to avoid splitting the children or families into discrete units, with each staff member attempting piecemeal solutions rather than contributing to an overall treatment and educational plan. Once more, there is no substitute for regular staff meetings to make and follow up on plans and to give staff continuous opportunities to share ideas and draw support from each other.

LIAISONS WITH COMMUNITY AGENCIES

The social worker and mental health consultant can work closely together when advocating for children outside of the early childhood program or when seeking other services for families in the community. Often they share their observations regarding specific children and work together to seek early intervention or special education services. At times, especially in school districts with fewer resources, obtaining adequate services for children is not an easy task. In these cases, consultants may be called on for both their professional opinions and for the potential force of their arguments. They may have to adopt a more combative and activist role that might otherwise be unfamiliar but can often bolster the case made by teachers, social workers, and evaluating professionals. Here the consultant may lend the weight of professional expertise in support of the school's recommendations for services and the child's right to receive them. The consultant may intentionally step out of a collaborative, backing role into an advocacy position that requires a more explicit use of professional status and privileges. In these instances, he must prepare and debrief staff and parents, reminding them that this shift is indeed a temporary one to help them achieve their goals.

The objective of the consultant in these specific instances, and in outreach in general, is to enhance the professional standing of the early childhood program in the larger community. Too often health, mental health, or educational concerns are taken lightly when they come from preschool staff, and social service and medical providers tend to downplay the relevance or seriousness of symptoms in young children. Although this trend largely reversed in the 1990s, there are still some agencies and professionals that dismiss preschool staff and, perhaps even more so, child care providers. If referrals are made in collaboration with an on-site mental health professional, there is a greater likelihood that they will be addressed in a timely fashion. Sometimes the referral or recommendation might have to originate from the consultant who can then transfer future contacts to the family worker or teacher and, in the process, work to revise the bias against preschool staff.

In addition to helping obtain services and negotiate external systems, the consultant can also assist staff contending with the frustration and stress engendered in the process. Referrals and evaluations frequently involve a slow process that takes from several weeks to months to become implemented treatment plans. Securing social services and entitlements for families is similarly taxing and can weigh especially heavy if the families have urgent needs for food, shelter, or medical assistance. Perhaps most distressing to child care workers is the occasional lack of investment in families that are clearly in need of preventive services. Each of these situations can contribute to feelings of helplessness and despair among staff and reduce future efforts to obtain needed services for families.

The consultant's role in this process is to encourage the social service staff to continue in their efforts while maintaining realistic expectations regarding the time and energy they might expend on any one case. Again, the consultant can help point to the positive outcomes—the child whose speech is progressing thanks to teacher-recommended early intervention services or the family that, with the social worker's help, has secured Medicaid and now can receive coverage for a child's chronic condition. The social work staff and consultant might also discuss which services families can negotiate themselves and where else in the community they may receive support for housing, medical, and other questions not under the purview of the child care center. Developing a systematic tracking system for referrals and evaluations can also ease the burden of this often frustrating process and give staff a definite sense of ongoing progress.

The consultant may also be called on to help programs make difficult decisions, particularly those related to suspicions of child abuse and neglect. Although in a healthy collaboration the consultant becomes a part of the system, she still has a fluid role that usually allows for more objectivity and professional distance in these sensitive situations. The consultant can help the director, the teachers, and the social worker review their mandates and also assess the current situation in a thorough, team-oriented manner. This does not necessarily mean a preschool will be more likely to report abuse. Taking a little more time and speaking frankly with parents or caregivers may alleviate the need to report concerns to other agencies.

The director of Alliance Nursery School, Ms. Berry, told the consultant that on two occasions she smelled alcohol on the breath of Jimmy's grandfather, Mr. Dunn, though Mr. Dunn did not seem impaired either time. Dr. Ash, the consultant, had been working with Jimmy for 3 months. Dr. Ash had also been working with Mr. Dunn for the past 3 weeks because he had just assumed full-time caregiving responsibilities from his daughter who was receiving residential substance abuse treatment. Dr. Ash suggested that Ms. Berry broach her concerns directly with Mr. Dunn, considering the director's role as the person ultimately charged with maintaining the children's safety and well-being. Ms. Berry was hesitant to step on the consultant's "clinical turf" but did bring it up at the next opportunity with Jimmy's grandfather, which Dr. Ash followed up in his next meeting with Mr. Dunn. The grandfather denied the use of alcohol on the days mentioned and reiterated his concern for Jimmy's emotional and physical health. No further steps were taken at that point except to tell Mr. Dunn that any concerns of staff would be raised with him directly. He continued both his weekly meetings with Dr. Ash, which

included exploration of alcohol and drug use in his family,
and his regular visits to Jimmy's classroom to check in with
the child's teachers.

Although no great revelations occurred in the preceding example, the director spoke honestly with the caregiver, shifted some of the burden to the consultant, and thus greatly relieved her stress. Ms. Berry knew that the situation was now in the open and could be monitored on an ongoing basis by the teachers and the consultant and understood that if Mr. Dunn had a serious issue with alcohol, signs would reappear in his own or Jimmy's behavior. No outside interventions were deemed necessary at that point, especially as Jimmy clearly was enjoying a warm relationship with his grandfather and was in a much more secure and stable situation than he had been previously.

This case illustrates the importance of the consultant's modeling and encouraging frank dialogues between both administrative and teaching staff. Whether the issue is alcohol or substance abuse in families, chronic illness, death, divorce, or child maltreatment, the adults in early childhood programs need to establish a comfortable way of discussing these topics. Chapter 7 explores ways of raising important issues with children, an area that staff are frequently resistant to address. Questions of privacy and confidentiality do emerge, but there often is also an implicit message that talking will only make things worse for all involved. Understandably, fears of being engulfed or overwhelmed by these problems abound, and the administrative staff do have to set a standard of appropriate limits and expectations for staff in these cases. However, preschool staff who share these stories and learn to cope as a group with the sometimes difficult realities they face are far more able to maintain their good humor and commitment to the work.

chapter four

Joining Hands

Collaborating with
Early Childhood Educators

Effective collaboration begins with a strong relationship between the mental health consultant and the person who is most directly involved in establishing an emotionally responsive classroom environment, the teacher. Any high-quality preschool or child care program strives to create an environment where children feel safe, well regarded, and understood. The consultant and teacher collaborate on establishing such an atmosphere. Although the mental health professional focuses on the emotional adjustment of children, he must recognize that these needs are not partitioned from other areas of children's lives. Rather, the consultant works with the teacher in addressing the emotional life of a child, not as a separate entity, but as a central aspect of the whole child, inextricably intertwined with all other aspects of growth and development.

The successful consultant strives to develop a working partnership with the teacher that is respectful, open, and transactional. Such a relationship takes time to establish and varies with the interpersonal dynamics of the individuals involved, as illustrated in the following example.

> Dr. Green began working with two excellent and
> experienced teachers in a large, inner-city Head Start
> program. One head teacher, Ms. Stone, was reluctant to
> accept mental health services in her classroom and
> maintained a guarded stance toward the consultant.
> Although always polite and respectful, she merely tolerated
> the presence of the consultant and avoided sharing
> information directly. When relevant issues did arise, she
> would discuss them with the director who would in turn
> discuss these concerns with Dr. Green. The consultation was
> slow to develop and tended to be limited to work with
> individual children needing special services, thereby having
> minimal effect on the classroom as a whole.
>   In contrast, Ms. Ortiz immediately told the consultant that
> she was thrilled to have this new program, invited Dr. Green
> to join in classroom activities, and shared her concerns and
> ideas openly with the clinician. Consequently, the
> consultation developed at a swifter pace and with a higher
> level of warmth, trust, and mutual exchange; this was, in
> turn, reflected in the gains of individual children as well as
> in the entire classroom. In Ms. Ortiz's class, the children and
> teachers freely engaged the consultant not only when issues
> emerged but also during the daily classroom routines.

In those relationships that are not as well developed, the teacher and consultant may co-act or engage in parallel activities with the children. In higher-functioning collaborations, the consultant and teacher are able to create a more integrated and shared agenda that can have a broader therapeutic effect in the classroom. Of course, one cannot expect to achieve the same degree of success in all classrooms. Whereas the collaboration between Ms. Stone and Dr. Green did eventually become a good working alliance, it never achieved the high degree of reciprocity, trust, and effectiveness that evolved in Ms. Ortiz's classroom. As a result, the mental health needs of the children were never as fully served.

When there is trust, respect, and affection between the consultant and teachers, there is a greater opportunity to infuse the classroom with warmth, understanding, and openness. The consultant and the teacher who are perceived to be a team, to hold each other in positive regard, and to be united in their primary concern and caring for the children are more likely to establish a "holding environment": an atmosphere of warmth, safety, and emotional nurturance. When such an environment is successfully created, the children as a group can reap the psychological benefits of a classroom with "good mental health." In addition, individual children can begin to engage the consultant in the role of a mental health professional with the consent of their teachers. This support takes many forms, ranging from basic instrumental assistance to more subtly communicated psychological approval. Just as the degree of parental acceptance and involvement shapes the form and effectiveness of individual child therapy, so too is teacher approval a critical component of the consultation and treatment process.

The teacher allows the consultant to engage with her class on both a concrete and a psychological level and also determines the extent to which she accepts and trusts the consultant, which, in turn, informs the teacher's willingness to become an active part of the consultation process. The teacher who has gained confidence in the consultant will begin to seek the mental health professional's advice and support and will use the clinician's presence in the room to build the emotional well-being of the class. If a consultant attempts to bypass this important step, she could find that her impact is limited to a few select children who may be reluctant to trust her and slower to develop a therapeutic alliance. Not only would the consultant miss an occasion to support work with individual children, but she would also lose the critical opportunity to contribute to the emotional atmosphere of the entire classroom and, thus, the program. Although a consultant hopes her work has important, direct effects on children, the indirect effects mediated through the teacher are likely to have the most far-reaching results. This chapter focuses on the nature of the successful collaboration between mental health consultants and teachers, including the key factors involved in creating and maintaining a good working relationship.

DEVELOPING AND MAINTAINING RAPPORT

Effective collaboration does not instantly emerge. It is contingent on the personal qualities, expectations, and beliefs that the consultant brings to his relationship with the teacher; that the teacher brings to the consultant; and those embedded within their cultural, educational, economic, and social systems. The quality of the alliance between the mental health professional and the teacher is colored by forces in place even before the very first contact between these two individuals. The mental health professional frequently has a greater degree of training and, consequently, receives greater monetary compensation, more professional autonomy, and more social respect. At times, this imbalance is compounded by cultural and socioeconomic differences that affect the relationship. Of course, the complex balance of power between the mental health professional and the teacher does not sway solely in the favor of the consultant. Very often, it is the teacher who is more firmly embedded within the community, who speaks the same language—both literally and figuratively—as the families served. The consultant should maintain an awareness of the numerous preexisting factors that shape the nature of the collaborative relationship and recognize that the delicate power balance is continually shifting, because it is formed as much by genuine differences as by stereotypic expectations and social context. Finally, and perhaps most important, consultants must respect teachers and their critically important work with children and, whenever possible, find ways of communicating this sentiment.

Although so many factors beyond the control of the key players do indeed affect the quality of the relationship, the ultimate success of the collaboration is primarily determined by the personal attributes that the individuals bring to the work and the degree to which this relationship is nurtured over time. Just as the consultant observes and evaluates the teacher's qualities, so too does the teacher assess the consultant. The teacher is likely to note the consultant's sensitivity to classroom routines, her degree of activity, her willingness to pitch in and help in the class, and her comfort level with young children in the environment. Many personality traits are fixed, yet both consultant and teacher can develop an awareness of their expectations and styles that can be modified when needed to cultivate a functional and mutually satisfying collaboration.

Race, Class, Culture, and Profession

The success of the collaboration ultimately relies on the personal relationship forged between the consultant and teacher, a partnership that is influenced by a number of preexisting factors. These variables include broad cultural and social matters, systemic issues within the program, and professional discrepancies as well as the personal experiences and dispositions of the individuals involved. A consultant may wish to avoid acknowledging these factors, particularly when attempting to gain acceptance in a place where he feels like an outsider entering a close-knit community. Yet denial of these professional, social, cultural, and belief differences can promote an artificial relationship that may be cordial but ultimately limited in depth and scope. A willingness to examine these factors often helps promote a more genuine acknowledgment of both difference and common ground that can eventually lead to a warm and effective collaboration.

In an ideal world, there would be great cultural and ethnic diversity among the teachers as well as the consultants, but, unfortunately, this is often not the case. Most commonly in urban programs, the teachers share the predominant ethnicity of the students but the mental health professionals do not. In most Head Start environments, for example, both the children and the staff tend to live in the local community and are typically an economically disadvantaged group. How then do these cultural factors shape the development of a good rapport between clinician and staff? The following vignette illustrates some pertinent issues.

> *Dr. Rowen, a Caucasian therapist beginning work as a*
> *consultant at a Head Start program, met for the first time*
> *with a seasoned African American teacher to discuss*
> *selection of children for treatment. Historically reticent to*
> *share "her children" with outsiders, the teacher joined*
> *Dr. Rowen for a review of potential referrals from a wide*
> *range of children facing multiple and severe psychosocial*
> *stressors. The first issue the new therapist wished to address*
> *was his concern that one particularly well-liked African*
> *American child might develop gender identification prob-*
> *lems because he wore his hair in shoulder-length braids.*
> *Regardless of whether gender confusion was a relevant issue*
> *in this instance, Dr. Rowen clearly selected a matter of low-*
> *level, if any, concern and also tagged himself as an "out-*
> *sider" unfamiliar with the traditions and styles of the center's*
> *dominant culture. He created a difficult entry for himself*
> *and had persistent difficulties working effectively with*
> *this teacher.*

Of course, one cannot be faulted for unfamiliarity with a behavior or style associated with a particular ethnic group. Nonetheless, when mental health professionals consult with organizations where a culture divergent from their own predominates, they must be sensitive to differences and remember a key maxim: "When in doubt, ask." It is critical that consultants avoid making assumptions or value judgments about practices with which they are unfamiliar.

Individuals have a wide range of reactions to cultural difference. Some, like Dr. Rowen, may have a rigid and culturally specific lens through which they view the world. Others may assume the dress, style, and mannerisms of the culture in an attempt to belong. However, such external adjustments tend to have limited success, particularly when unaccompanied by a deeper appreciation of ethnic customs and traditions in the local community. Still others may be uncomfortable and routinely choose to avoid the subjects of race and culture, stating

"We are all the same." Not only can this approach negatively influence the consulting relationship, it can ultimately have a stifling effect in the classroom, where young children may seek to address issues of race and culture that are often stimulated by the presence of ethnic diversity among staff and students. This atmosphere can indeed provide an important arena for such explorations that are often not tolerated in society at large.

> *A social worker was consulting in a small child care center that served the children of hospital employees. During free play, a 4-year-old African American girl was gently stroking the consultant's arm and commented that she liked the consultant's "nice white skin." The social worker responded that she also liked the little girl's "pretty, smooth brown skin." Another child joined the conversation, asking the consultant whether she was born "a white baby or a black baby." These comments evolved into a full-group discussion about skin color as well as racial difference and continuity. It was not self-evident to these children that race was a fixed attribute; they were able to struggle as a group to understand this concept, which was a cognitive challenge for them.*

In many settings, such discussions would be discouraged, given the many layers of emotional response that can be evoked by such examinations of race. These conversations could be stimulated by the presence of any member of a divergent racial group. However, it is not unusual that the consultant is one of the first adults of a contrasting ethnicity with whom the children develop a closeness that allows them to freely examine such themes.

There are many styles of addressing cultural difference, but the best approach is an acceptance of one's own culture paired with an interested, respectful, and nonjudgmental willingness to learn about the community one hopes to enter. This can be accomplished in many ways but often begins in the classroom. Most early childhood programs address culture through the curriculum and when planning for holidays and special events. These classroom-based activities often give consultants the chance to ask about unfamiliar holidays, customs, and history in an open and interested manner. Consultants may offer to enrich these themes with books, experiences, and information with which they are familiar, thereby setting the stage for a mutual exchange of cultural experience.

A clinician working in a community that differs from her own has the opportunity to reexamine her individual as well as professional biases, and the consultant is also reminded that current diagnostic frameworks are embedded within a social and historical reality that can never be entirely culture-free. Those who enter a culturally distinct community with a willingness to learn about its culture-specific features and to reexamine their own notions of health, disorder, and cultural difference often find themselves best able to develop a good working relationship with the individuals from that community. This does, however, take time. It also demands an ability to tolerate feelings of social isolation, as illustrated in the following vignette.

> *Dr. Long began working as a consulting psychologist in a large Head Start program located in an urban setting. She was the only Caucasian individual among a staff of African American and Latino teachers and administrators. Dr. Long, unfamiliar with the neighborhood and uncomfortable venturing out without direction, would bring her lunch and eat alone during the lunch hour while the staff, in various combinations, would dine together. Although many factors probably contributed to this isolation—the long history of preexisting friendships among the teachers, different professions, the role of past consultants as well as the assumptions of the staff regarding the wishes of the clinician—the cultural differences no doubt added to her experience of isolation. Gradually, Dr. Long was welcomed into the more personal social activities of the group, occasionally joining others for meals, breaks, and after-school chats. Dr. Long eventually left the program and was particularly gratified when the staff threw her a potluck Spanish lunch as a good-bye party. At the end of the day, the teacher who was initially the most distant asked, "How can you leave? You're one of us now."*

In addition to issues of culture, there are often many professional differences between consultants and teachers. As mentioned previously, the consultant has typically attained a more advanced educational level, receives greater financial compensation, and is afforded more respect and authority from society at large. Although the consultant should not deny or apologize for these differences, he is likely to help rapport develop when he truly respects the teachers and recognizes that early childhood teachers are, as a group, undervalued, underpaid, and inadequately respected as professionals. The consultant may further gain the esteem of the teaching staff if he explicitly acknowledges their critical role: Teachers spend the most time with children, addressing the broadest aspects of their academic, physical, nutritional, and emotional well-being.

Although some staff may come to resent consultants for enjoying more professional privileges, others can bestow an exaggerated sense of importance on their ideas and comments along with some unrealistic expectations of their capabilities. This admiration can be gratifying, but most consultants recognize that they are not likely to live up to these lofty expectations and that being seen as the fix-it person with the Midas touch does little to enhance the teacher's own sense of competence or to foster a collaborative relationship. Yet the consultant might not want to dismiss out of hand this position of authority, as it gives him the chance to bolster staff who feel underappreciated or unheard. He can offer the ear of a supportive professional who is willing to listen and to give honest feedback without being compromised by his alliances or position in the hierarchical structure. More important, words of encouragement and support, which should be omnipresent in the consultant's work, can have significant meaning to staff members who may not usually have that kind of forum. While maintaining his professional identity, the consultant can talk to teachers and other staff implicitly as peers and equals and, at times, explicitly recognize their wisdom and experience, which may not be reflected in an advanced degree.

Past Experience with Mental Health and Related Services

As discussed in Chapter 2, there can be many site-specific historic issues that influence the relationship between consultant and staff. Many centers have had previous experience with consultants who provide specialized services, such as speech-language, assessment, and ongoing psychological services. The consultant is advised to evaluate the history of outside services at the program and determine how it affects the current collaboration. How do teachers feel about these other practitioners? What is the tenor of the individual teacher's professional experiences and personal impressions vis-à-vis psychology and intervention for special needs?

> Dr. Brown found that one particular teacher, Ms. Ahmed,
> seemed reluctant to allow her children to leave the
> classroom for individual therapy sessions, claiming problems
> with scheduling or suggesting that services were not
> indicated for that child. Finally, Dr. Brown arranged a
> meeting with Ms. Ahmed, who discussed with great concern
> and insight the children's psychological difficulties. After

*some discussion, Ms. Ahmed stated, "I know these kids need
extra help, but I have to tell you I have a problem with how
special needs services have worked around here. Very often,
a professional whom I have never met stops in without
addressing me or the children, selects a child without ever
having told me why, pulls the student out of the room, and
does something mysterious behind closed doors. He then
drops off the child without ever letting me know what is
being worked on or how the child is progressing."*

Ms. Ahmed's criticism had a great impact on the consultant, who
examined his own practices and renewed his effort to share relevant information with the teachers. Dr. Brown worked to communicate more
fully with them throughout the entire diagnostic and treatment process
in the hope of developing a true team approach. Ms. Ahmed ultimately
became one of the most responsive, informed, and engaged teachers in
the collaborative process.

In addition to outside consultants, many programs have their own
family workers or special needs staff. The consultant typically considers
the relationships between teachers and staff social work professionals.
As the next example illustrates, any preexisting conflicts are likely to
have a negative effect on the relationships among these central players.

*At an early childhood program for homeless families, the
school had formed a partition between direct work with
children and services for the family. The staff social workers
conducted all intakes at the shelters and continued to work
with families throughout the year, developing special trips
and workshops for mothers. The teachers, who were
uninvolved with this component, focused directly on the
needs of the children in the classroom. As a result, the
teachers identified closely with the children and felt angry
toward parents, whom they often perceived as uninvolved, if
not negligent. The teachers therefore resented the social
workers' special programs and bowling trips, feeling that the
parents were being indulged while their children were
neglected. Similarly, the social workers believed the
teachers were failing to appreciate the needs of the family
that must be addressed in order to best meet those of the
children.*

*When Dr. Rhodes, the outside consultant, entered the
system, both teachers and social workers had expectations
regarding her place in this split—the teachers feared she too*

would "indulge" the parents while the social workers were
concerned Dr. Rhodes would vilify the parents. Of course,
the task of the consultant was instead to help broaden the
perceptions of the teachers and the social workers and to
encourage a shared vision that included empathy for family
and child. Once Dr. Rhodes recognized this dynamic, she
attempted to bridge the gap, reminding both sides that their
perceptions were understandable, and to extend the scope
of their understanding to include the group they dealt with
less directly. Dr. Rhodes worked to accomplish this goal
through individual contact with teachers and social workers
as well as discussions in team meetings and informal
contacts. Furthermore, the consultant helped develop joint
activities for teachers and social workers through outreach
meetings in the community as well as events in the
classroom, thereby affording the two groups the opportunity
to work together as a team and expand the breadth of their
daily focus.

As discussed in Chapter 3, there are other systemic matters, which exist within the history and administrative structure of the program, that can affect the rapport between the teacher and the mental health professional. This range of dynamic issues within the system has the potential to influence the teacher's feelings of efficacy and self-worth. There may also be conflicts that emerge from concerns of power and control among the teachers and between teaching and the administrative staff. It is important to recognize that the relationship between the consultant and the teacher is greatly influenced by many broad, and often unarticulated, systemic issues. The consultant may or may not be able to address these subjects directly. Nonetheless, she will be affected by them and often find that an understanding of these "family dynamics" within the school and the classroom can help guide her in creating successful collaborative relationships. By carefully establishing her allegiance to administration and teaching staff while determining the boundaries of confidentiality, the consultant seeks a place in the system that allows her to be a supportive and trusted advisor as well as a facilitator between these groups as problems arise.

Personality and Individual Style
In addition to being influenced by preexisting global factors, the relationship between consultant and teacher is considerably affected by a number of personal and stylistic qualities of the individuals involved. Particularly in the early stages of the collaboration, the consultant will

engage in an evaluation process. To what extent is the teacher psychologically minded? What is his experience with and attitude toward mental health professionals? How dedicated is he as a teacher? Is he overly stressed? What is his teaching style? Does he tend to be cognitively and task oriented, or is he more emotionally focused? Is he affectionate? How does he handle structure and discipline? Unavoidably, the consultant will be evaluating these dimensions within the teacher and will develop an internal response to her assessment of these qualities. Yet the effective consultant will continually reevaluate her inherent standards and perceptions so that her definition of "the good teacher" is not too narrow. Very often, the conception of an ideal teacher is a smiling, soft-spoken, highly verbal, and sensitive person. Many of these qualities are indeed important, but the experienced consultant learns not to confuse substance with style.

> *Dr. Allen, the consultant, walked into Ms. Rosa's classroom and was somewhat startled to hear a voice booming across the room, shouting rather forceful directions at José, who was in the process of climbing on the table. The child was also quite startled and quickly complied with the teacher's request. Ms. Rosa continued her activities and gathered the children on the rug for an animated and joyous storytelling session while José, found his way onto her lap.*
>
> *Although Dr. Allen was initially taken back by the loud and strong personality of the teacher, she soon recognized that Ms. Rosa was a sensitive and caring teacher who expressed warmth and affection with an intensity that surpassed her expressions of dissatisfaction and anger. Dr. Allen did work with Ms. Rosa on strategies for effective discipline and, over time, helped Ms. Rosa modulate her style in this area. Nonetheless, Dr. Allen learned that she had underestimated this teacher's ability because of preconceived expectations of style and personality that likely included some cultural bias.*

Of course, the teacher will simultaneously evaluate the characteristics of the mental health professional as well. How does it feel to have the consultant in the classroom? Is she willing to get her hands dirty? How comfortable is she with young children? Is she familiar with the community? It is the interaction between the consultant and the teacher that will greatly determine the success of the collaboration. What is the personality mix between the two? All of these personal dimensions will substantially influence the development of rapport over time. Whereas some may be fixed aspects of personality and experience, others are more amenable to change and can be approached directly.

Professional Differences

Ideally, there develops a sharing of information and experience that allows both teacher and consultant to work together to best meet the needs of the children as a group and to address the particular needs and abilities of individual children. The consultant can help foster this relationship when she genuinely respects the teacher's important and difficult occupation, a job that appears to be multiplying in its degree of difficulty as classroom size grows and psychosocial and financial challenges to children and families intensify. The inclusion of children with special needs has also increased the everyday challenges within the classroom. Even teachers who work in more affluent settings, where some of the experiences faced by more impoverished families are not present, will nonetheless confront considerable stress in their children who are affected by changes in family structure, financial shifts, family conflict, and other events. Furthermore, teachers typically feel undervalued by society—a response common to most early childhood teachers, irrespective of the community in which they work. Consultants who recognize these realities are better able to empathize with and admire teachers as well as communicate these feelings to them.

The relationship benefits when the consultant acknowledges that the teacher's particular training or background in education differs from her own and makes a unique professional contribution to the collaboration. Although the level of formal training varies widely within the field, all teachers have some experience or perspective that is potentially new and enriching for the consultant. Many consultants have learned a number of stimulating curricular activities from teachers; these include creative arts and crafts projects, books and storytelling, music, and dance. It is not unusual for a clinician to integrate these discoveries into her clinical work outside the consultation site. Teachers also frequently broaden the mental health professional's understanding of the academic, social, and physical skills that can be expected of and imparted to young children. In this way, teachers enhance the knowledge base of consultants and can increase clinicians' practical understanding of the scope of behaviors that comprise the normal range. This is especially important for therapists who have found that their formal training in these areas, particularly regarding young children, may have been incomplete—a finding that is all too often the case in psychology, psychiatry, and social work training programs. Many individuals with excellent training also have not had the extensive, hands-on experience with young children that serves to solidify academic knowledge, elevating it to a more meaningful and internalized level. The early childhood teacher who has achieved this level of understanding can be instrumental in facilitating this learning process in the consultant.

Similarly, the consultant brings her expertise to the table. The consultant has professional training in the psychological, emotional, and social development of children, including those with special needs. In addition, the mental health professional is typically well versed in the process of assessment, treatment, and service coordination; the consultant can help the teacher by intervening directly with children and families as well as by assisting staff as they navigate the vast array of services and agencies with which they may be involved. The consultant is usually trained and experienced in working with larger systems and is thus qualified to lead groups and run workshops. Although the consultant hopes to be respected for these professional skills, she also wants to be recognized as someone who cares deeply for children and who is able to listen and learn from others. Most consultants want to be seen as team players who are able to share information and impressions so that conclusions are the result of an ongoing collaborative process. This mutual respect tends to evolve gradually and may be expressed directly or nonverbally.

How then does the consultant communicate his respect for the teacher? As discussed in Chapter 2, the effective mental health professional is sensitive to the manner in which he begins to establish a rapport with the teacher. He attends to even the most subtle nuances of communication—carefully balancing the relative weight of observation and comment, passivity and activity—while maintaining an awareness of classroom routine and atmosphere. A consultant communicates respect most powerfully through his manner in the classroom. His primary focus is the developmental gains and emotional well-being of the children, but the consultant is in no way precluded from wiping noses, tying shoes, taking a sick child to the nurse, or even covering the room for a few moments while the teacher steps out. In fact, it is often these simple acts that help a consultant to be welcomed into the classroom and avoid being pigeonholed within the narrowly defined limits of a detached "expert."

In sum, the effective collaboration develops over time when the key players respect each other as individuals and as professionals; are flexible; are open to learn from the unique perspective of the other; and are willing to communicate openly, even when differences arise. The early stages in building these relationships are critical to the establishment of a good rapport, but both consultant and teacher must be willing to continue nurturing their relationship over time—to monitor,

communicate, and process issues as they occur—if they hope to cultivate an increasingly constructive collaboration. How then does this
collaboration function in the classroom? What are the activities of the
consultant, and how does he work with the teacher to have a positive
impact on the children?

COLLABORATING IN THE CLASSROOM

The effective teacher–consultant team learns to balance a multitud2 of
goals when in the classroom. The consultant must address the psychological needs of the children as a group; the individual needs of
children who have been identified for special services; the curriculum
goals of the teacher; the feelings among the adults in the room; and the
concrete, everyday caregiving and supervision inherent in working
with a large group of young children. The consultant may find that
managing these multiple tasks proves to be the greatest challenge
of the consulting process but also the most rewarding. The consultant
has the unique opportunity to collaborate with teachers, conduct therapy, and play with children. Whereas the numerous roles of the consultant as therapist are more fully discussed in Chapter 7, the current
section examines these issues as they relate to the teacher–consultant
collaboration.

Developing Shared Goals

There are a number of logistical issues that can affect the consultant's
ability to develop an effective collaboration with teachers in the classroom. The successful consultant is flexible, open to learning about
classroom activities, and willing to embrace an expansive job description that includes assessment and therapeutic intervention as well as
serving lunch, pushing swings, and helping out on trips. The consultant needs to learn classroom routines and find ways to conduct therapeutic endeavors in the least disruptive manner possible. This includes
sensitivity to classroom activities when entering and leaving the room.
In general, when visiting a class or removing a child from the room, the
consultant should check in with the teacher to be sure that her plan
does not hinder the teacher's agenda. The consultant needs to demonstrate sufficient flexibility to shift her plans if they do not fit with the
classroom routine. Similarly, the consultant should greet all children
with warmth and interest but should be careful to avoid creating a
major classroom disruption. The clinician should exit the classroom at
an appropriate moment that does not sidetrack the activity or leave any
child at loose ends. If, for example, the consultant is returning with a
child who had joined her for an individual session, she may facilitate
this child's transition to the classroom by remaining a little longer. Ide-

ally, the teacher will feel comfortable educating the consultant about his classroom rules and routines and will offer feedback about the activities of the consultant as they affect the children in his class. In addition to teaching the consultant about the structure of his classroom, he will introduce the clinician to the individual children as well.

Just as the teacher educates the consultant about his students, classroom routines, and educational techniques, so too does the consultant educate the staff about the mental health needs of young children. In the context of such a mutual exchange, the teacher is less likely to be resistant to the consultant's psychological approach. Furthermore, the consultant strives not only to gain the teacher's acceptance of interventions but also enlists the teacher as participant in the therapeutic process. In general, the task of interpreting behavior and linking the child's feelings and actions to family issues and past history is best left to the mental health professional. Teachers can, however, best serve this process by being open to a wide range of children's emotional expression while offering a warm and supportive classroom environment. The overt functions of consultant and teacher may be defined as distinct but, in reality, these roles overlap considerably: The effective therapist participates in the educational process and the effective teacher supports emotional development. Yet there are instances when the goals of the teacher and those of the therapist may seem to conflict. At times a consultant may unknowingly disrupt the routine or break a classroom rule, as shown in the following case.

Laura was a little girl with considerable emotional issues who attended a therapeutic class in the morning and then joined a general Head Start class in the afternoon. She was having great difficulty handling this transition, becoming oppositional and defiant as naptime began. The consultant, Ms. Collins, happened to be present during one time when the teachers were struggling with Laura's disruptive behavior as the class prepared to nap. Ms. Collins turned her attention to Laura, encouraging her to join the other children while acknowledging how difficult and confusing this transition was for her. Laura was able to remain on her mat only when assisted by the consultant, who held Laura close. Ms. Collins then read a story to Laura, which seemed to calm the child during this rest period.

The next day, Ms. Collins initiated a discussion with Mr. Osborn, the head teacher, about Laura's difficulties. It gradually became evident that Mr. Osborn was displeased with the consultant's decision to read a book to Laura, as this was against the "naptime rules" and created difficulties for the children not receiving this special attention. The consultant apologized for inadvertently breaking this rule. Ms. Collins then explained the reason for her activities, yet she assured Mr. Osborn that these goals could have been achieved in another manner. She also encouraged the teacher to express his views at the time such an incident occurs. The consultant proceeded to model for Mr. Osborn that he might say, "Ms. Collins, in our classroom, we read stories after snack but put them away at naptime." The consultant stated that such comments would be welcomed and even useful to the children, who would have the chance to observe adults effectively negotiate conflicts.

By verbalizing and exploring their differences, the teacher and consultant in the previous vignette developed a greater degree of trust in their collaborative relationship. Mr. Osborn was able to communicate his concerns as a teacher to the consultant. In turn, Ms. Collins was able to emphasize the importance of supporting Laura's individual needs while maintaining a respect for classroom rules and routine.

The next vignette shows, however, that at other times the objectives of the therapist and those of the teacher seem to conflict.

During a visit to Ms. Simpson's class, Dr. Johns joined the group at circle time. Justin, a depressed child who was being seen by Dr. Johns for individual play therapy, came and sat on his lap. The teacher and her aide simultaneously chided Justin for failing to sit in the proper "crisscross-applesauce" manner, causing the child to withdraw silently. Given the consultant's position as therapist to this youngster who was acutely sensitive to rejection, Dr. Johns felt quite conflicted. He recognized this important therapeutic moment and wanted to respond to Justin's newly expressed desire for contact, yet he wished to maintain respect for the established classroom routine. The consultant decided to assist Justin in sitting next to him, carefully maintaining physical contact by unobtrusively placing an arm around Justin's shoulder. At a later date, when reviewing Justin's progress in a team meeting, Dr. Johns chose not to discuss this incident directly; he instead took the opportunity to highlight Justin's experience of rejection, heightened

*sensitivity to perceived rebuffs, and need for reassurance
and warmth.*

In this example, the teacher's demand for order and group confor-
mity conflicted with the consultant's perception of Justin's therapeutic
needs. The therapist was able to modify his approach to fulfill Ms.
Simpson's expectations, but he also tried to expand the teacher's awareness of Justin's psychological issues. Subsequently, broader matters regarding the place of affection and physical contact in the classroom
were examined, as were the more dynamic issues of Ms. Simpson's ambivalent feelings toward this particular child and her perception that
others inappropriately indulged him.

*In another instance, Ms. Simpson reported that Justin had
been acting out on the bus by spitting at another child and
was subsequently placed in time-out as punishment for this
behavior. Dr. Johns began to inquire into this event and the
possible sources of Justin's behavior when Ms. Simpson
responded rather curtly, "I knew you'd just take his side."
Rather than attempting to disabuse the teacher of this
perception or, conversely, explaining the reasons why Justin
truly did need someone "on his side," Dr. Johns suggested
that Justin was indeed behaving as if he were a "bad" boy
because he felt like one. In fact, Justin so believed in his
badness that he found ways to fulfill his own prophesy and
make people angry with him. The consultant and teacher
then examined how they might work to reverse this self-
perception before Justin became even more adept at
fulfilling this role that seemed to have been so unfairly
assigned to him.*

The therapist tried to communicate his understanding of this child's
needs without denigrating the teacher for feeling angry toward Justin
or questioning her decision to set limits. As a result, the consultant
sidestepped the issue of "taking sides" in this child's life. Dr. Johns also
worked to help the teachers gain insight into Justin's behavior and to
develop increased empathy, two central goals of the mental health collaboration. The teacher was eventually able to assume a therapeutic
stance with Justin by affirming his "goodness," as she identified the
child's successes and reflected them back to him. The consultant was
able to support the teacher's efforts with this child many months later.

After Justin had graduated from preschool, Dr. Johns con-
tinued to work with the child and his family within the clinic.
Justin had a summer of major life upheavals: His parents re-
lapsed into drug use and became violent, and Justin's mother
was sent to prison. Justin became more withdrawn and de-
pressed but was making small gains in his ability to explore
his inner emotional life verbally. At the end of one session, in
which Dr. Johns attributed the child's sadness to the numer-
ous difficulties experienced at home, Justin informed him,
"I'm so sad because I miss my teachers from school."

The consultant relayed the preceding story to staff during a
teacher workshop. He used it as an example of the effect on children
when teachers provide a stable and empathic environment in the midst
of chaos at children's homes. At times, this impact is greater than staff
realize; it can occur despite or even because of behavior challenges in
the classroom when teachers successfully set limits and maintain consistency while communicating a positive regard for the children.

Classroom Interventions

A consultant facilitates a teacher's participation in the mental health
collaboration directly, through an educational process, and indirectly,
by modeling and working conjointly with the teacher to enhance the
emotional quality of the classroom. Direct teaching occurs primarily
outside the classroom in individual conferences, team meetings, and
didactic seminars, all of which are discussed later in this chapter. In the
classroom, the consultant both demonstrates for and co-acts with the
teacher to enhance the therapeutic quality of the environment. The
therapist strives to achieve these goals in four general ways: 1) intervening in a therapeutic manner as issues arise, either alone or in concert with the teacher; 2) modeling approaches to communicating with
and listening to children; 3) supporting the teacher as she addresses
emotional or psychological needs of children; and 4) observing, assessing, diagnosing, and creating hypotheses that are then offered as feedback and recommendations to the staff. These elements are further examined in the discussion of therapeutic interventions with children,
found in Chapter 7.

Typically, the consultant begins the collaborative relationship in a
role that is primarily one of observer. A clinician often spends the first
few weeks becoming acquainted with the children and teachers as they
simultaneously get to know him. At this stage, the consultant usually
remains in the background, observing the class in general and focusing
on the specific children who may have been identified by teachers and
staff as having particular needs or concerns. The consultant will join in

activities when invited to do so, following the lead of teachers and children as he gauges his level of involvement. During this early phase, the consultant generally shares observations with teachers outside the classroom, and together they develop plans for assessment of individual children.

Gradually, as mutual trust develops, the therapist becomes more active, intervening when psychological issues arise. The next scenario demonstrates this role.

> When Dr. Chen, the consulting psychologist, joined a circle time discussion, Billy raised his hand for show and tell. He proceeded to relate a tale about Freddy Krueger, the infamous villain of a violent adult horror movie. Billy told his story replete with blood and gore, adding that this all "really happened" as Freddy was "a real person." The group virtually erupted with tales of violence they had either witnessed in reality or viewed on television. Dr. Chen was internally debating whether she should actively intervene in this discussion, which she thought would likely be handled in a skillful and sensitive manner by the head teacher, Mrs. McGrath. Would her intervention be infringing on the teacher's classroom territory? At that moment, Mrs. McGrath turned to Dr. Chen and said, "I have no idea what to do with this."
>
> After receiving her permission to take control of the discussion, the psychologist sought to affirm the children's affective experience and engage in some group reality testing, helping them to define the boundary between fantasy and reality. She stated that "Freddy Krueger is a scary guy in the movies; he's not real, but sometimes it's hard to tell the difference." Dr. Chen then helped to draw the discussion to a close by turning to questions of mastery and self-soothing. She elicited from the children some coping mechanisms by asking, "What do kids do to feel better when they're scared?" The children responded with a number of strategies, ranging from snuggling with teddy bears to getting their parents. The group seemed visibly comforted as they addressed this difficult topic, achieved some degree of mastery, and then moved on to more typical preschool themes.

In this vignette, with the teacher's consent but without her participation, the consultant intervened directly at the group level while modeling an approach to handling such disturbing material. The child who stimulated this discussion was referred for individual sessions with the consultant but continued to evoke themes of violence during group conversations. Over time, the teacher observed the therapist's interventions and became increasingly adept at handling these difficult themes, both in concert with the consultant as well as on her own.

At times, however, it is difficult to draw the line between material that is appropriate for group discussion and that which is best addressed in individual sessions. Consultants and teachers must develop a shared comfort level and mutually define what is acceptable in class. This line is not always easy to establish, as it must take into account the professional views of each collaborator and the demands of the classroom. Whereas a therapist would rarely, if ever, set limits on the content in an individual therapy session behind closed doors, she may feel the need to set some boundaries on the material explored in a normal preschool group setting.

> Tasha was a precocious, vivacious, and highly verbal 4-year-old with a history of sexual abuse. One day during circle time, Tasha declared that she wanted to "do sex" and proceeded to discuss an elaborate fantasy involving a boy in her class and their visit to "a sex house." The distress and confusion experienced by the children was matched only by that of their teachers. The staff turned to the consultant, Dr. Lynn, who helped them draw this discussion to a close without rejecting the child for simply verbalizing her thoughts. The consultant stated, "Tasha has a lot on her mind, and maybe it would be helpful for her to speak about these things with me in my office when circle time is over." Dr. Lynn sought to redirect Tasha by encouraging the child to express herself in a private context. The consultant was careful not to reject Tasha or disavow the topic by labeling it as bad and unacceptable for discussion. Tasha was then referred for individual play therapy and eventually developed the ability to raise her hand in circle time to request an appointment with Dr. Lynn when she felt the need.

The substance of the child's fantasy in this instance was clearly outside the comfort zone of a typical circle time conversation, and the staff and consultant agreed that individual sessions would be a more appropriate arena for such explorations. It was nonetheless important that the consultant help the staff maintain an open and accepting stance if the children became curious, raising age-appropriate questions about their own bodies.

Sometimes the consultant and teacher have more difficulty establishing boundaries that are mutually acceptable. This can occur during those unsettling moments when a child has blurred the distinction between reality and fantasy, as shown in the following case.

During one circle-time discussion, Alisha, a child with serious emotional concerns, told the group about her friend who was "sitting next to her on the rug." It soon became apparent that she was referring to an imaginary friend who frequently engaged in highly aggressive behaviors. The overwhelmed children became upset; the boundaries of reality were momentarily shaken for the group. The consulting psychologist, Dr. Diaz, took the initiative and tried to articulate for them that Alisha's friend was a pretend one who was not in fact in the room, despite Alisha's insistence to the contrary. The consultant then led a discussion about what was pretend, what was real, and how it was very frightening to hear Alisha talk about such violent things. When the group appeared to regain some stability, Dr. Diaz left the room for a scheduled meeting.

In a subsequent discussion with teachers, the head teacher informed Dr. Diaz that the class continued to "fall out," becoming increasingly agitated. She further suggested that the group discussion was simply too much for the children and the staff, who felt unprepared to handle the disruptive behaviors. It became evident that the teachers attributed these difficulties to Dr. Diaz for "opening up" painful feelings and leaving the staff to contend with the consequences. The psychologist expressed his willingness to rethink various approaches to handling such occurrences in the classroom and considered whether a more rapid "sealing over" of such painful content might better suit the demands of the classroom. He acknowledged how difficult it was for the teachers, who felt ill-equipped to cope with the defiant behavior and painful content with which they were left. However, Dr. Diaz asserted the importance of helping the group process the confusing material and recognize that it was, in fact, fantasy. He also emphasized the importance of acknowledging the violent material that had been voiced by the child and was heard by all. The child's comments had

*the power to stimulate such strong responses only because
she touched on a theme that was already all too present for
many of the children. If the adults denied the content of
Alisha's comments, they would run the risk of adding insult
to injury by leaving the children alone to contend with what
they heard quietly and internally. The subsequent acting-out
may have been an unavoidable consequence of the child's
comments. Dr. Diaz did nevertheless agree that it would
have been better handled if he had remained in the room for
a longer period of time. He then could have supported the
teachers as they sought to respond to the challenging
behaviors that had been stimulated by the group discussion.*

The teacher and the consultant differed in their perspective on handling such evocative comments in class. Whether they ever achieve consensus, each one can develop an appreciation for the other's viewpoint; they can incorporate some managerial needs of the teacher and therapeutic goals of the consultant, even when these items seem to conflict.

COLLABORATING OUTSIDE THE CLASSROOM

Teachers and mental health professionals work together outside the classroom in a multitude of roles and contexts. The consultant often encounters teachers in scheduled classroom team and staff meetings, workshops or seminars, and support groups. In addition, consultants and teachers may meet individually. The purposes of such contacts vary broadly and may include staff development, administrative activities, examination of classroom issues and individual child needs, staff support, and, in some cases, teachers' personal concerns that affect professional roles.

Establishing Boundaries

The various scheduled meetings that take place in most center-based early childhood environments are the core mechanism for staff communication, administration, and development. In most Head Start and mandated preschool programs, there are formal meetings organized by classroom or job description. These group settings afford important opportunities for consultants to offer and obtain information as well as to facilitate the examination of group and individual issues in the classroom or the center at large. In home-based and small center settings, the staff may not be large enough to build in such formal group meetings. However, even in a staff of two, time should be set aside for discussing practices and policies, examining the particular needs of individual children and families, and exploring concerns that emerge among the various caregivers.

When a consultant participates in broader staff meetings, she often finds herself involved in discussions regarding managerial issues, staff complaints, or interpersonal problems. The mental health professional is typically trained in group process and, by virtue of her position as a consultant, has a unique vantage point that is both inside of and outside of the system. In this way, she can maintain a more neutral stance and aid the processing and solving of broader systemic issues. However, the clinician must take care to establish comfortable and varied allegiances so that all staff members feel trust and support that is not poised against any other staff alliance. See Chapter 2 for an elaboration of these important concerns.

A typical preschool team meeting includes the classroom teachers and some combination of other staff members, such as the director, the educational supervisor, special needs providers, and the family worker. During team meetings, the teachers typically report on the classroom behavior of individual children, the family or social workers share family history and other relevant background material, and the consultant may offer observations from classroom visits or therapy sessions. This sharing of information is designed to strengthen the center's team approach so that children are not viewed through the narrow lens of one person's direct experience and training. Each player can have access to multiple information sources and can then work in a group to process the material and develop a more complete understanding of a child and his environment.

Nevertheless, sharing sensitive material can raise difficult issues of confidentiality—something that is less likely to emerge in clinic-based interventions. The following example highlights this situation.

Christina's behavior was becoming increasingly alarming to the staff. During a team meeting, the group members shared their concerns about this 4-year-old girl. One teacher observed how Christina seemed to throw herself at a policeman who came to visit the classroom. Christina's behavior seemed both indiscriminate and sexualized as she clung to this unfamiliar man. The group agreed that the consultant, Ms. Hahn, should discuss this matter with Christina's mother and propose therapeutic intervention for the family. In the initial parent–therapist meeting, Christina's mother was quite upset by the rumor that her daughter was flirting with the policeman and asked why the family was not first contacted with this information. Ms. Hahn affirmed the understandable concern that this issue may have been inappropriately discussed and agreed to share this confidentiality issue with the staff. Ms. Hahn further reassured Christina's mother that the current meeting was set up to share this information and to consider how to address Christina's behavior. Fortunately, the parent was able to overcome this difficult entry into treatment, and she and her daughter successfully engaged in therapy with the consultant.

Very often, the teachers live within the early childhood program's community and may be in contact with families outside of the school setting. This proximity can pose challenges regarding the appropriate flow of information, particularly for staff members who have not been fully trained in the importance of maintaining confidentiality and who may, in fact, have a lesser burden regarding the privacy of information than does the on-site therapist.The mental health consultant has the opportunity, therefore, to work with the director and staff in establishing reasonable limits regarding family confidentiality. It is often the job of the consultant to question whether every bit of background information obtained at intake is necessary to share in a team meeting. He may suggest that only information that is clearly relevant to a child's development and behavior be discussed; even then, this material should be carefully selected and generalized. It might, for example, be pertinent for the teachers to know that Johnny's father is incarcerated, but it is not necessary that the entire staff be made aware of the specific nature of the man's offense. In addition, it is often very useful for the consultant to remind the staff that although it may be in the child's best interest to disclose some sensitive information, it is always critical that this material is shared only with those involved in the child's care. When information is inappropriately divulged outside such circles, the professionalism of the program is undermined and can result in potentially damaging gossiping. In fact, the welfare of the child may be compromised if parents, concerned that their privacy is not respected, avoid disclosing personal details or even refuse the help that might be available to them.

The consultant must further remind himself that team meetings are not equivalent to supervision or other formats for group process in a clinic where all participants generally observe the same confidentiality guidelines. As a result, the consultant must exercise a greater level of restrictiveness when sharing information with the team. He typically shares classroom observations and offers general impressions and understandings that will assist teachers as they work with children while avoiding the specific clinical material on which these impressions were built. In this respect, the clinician acts no differently than when meeting with any teacher as collateral to his therapeutic work. Of course, it remains critical that the consultant obtain informed consent from parents regarding his intent to communicate with teachers and other staff.

Confidentiality matters often extend beyond the concerns of the family and emerge for teachers and other staff members as well. It is not unusual for a consultant to make himself available for individual meetings with teachers to address a broad range of issues impinging on the teacher's ability to function most effectively in the classroom. When a teacher discusses personal concerns that may affect her job performance, can she expect that the content will be kept confidential? If she wishes to disclose relevant systemic or programmatic concerns, can she be assured that her privacy will be guarded? The consultant is most effective when he is available to "lend an ear" to teachers and other staff when personal or systemic matters might influence their professional positions, yet he must clarify the limits of his therapeutic duty.

> *Assistant teacher Ms. King was struggling with a number of personal issues stemming from her pregnancy and relationship difficulties with her partner. The other teachers in the classroom believed that Ms. King's problems were affecting her physical and emotional availability. In particular, they expressed concern that her depressed mood was having a negative effect on the children. They confided in the consultant, Ms. Lewis, who agreed to talk individually with Ms. King and later facilitate a conversation among the team if everyone agreed. During this individual meeting, Ms. King acknowledged her personal difficulties to Ms. Lewis, who sought to be empathic and to express support. Ms. King then asked the consultant to be her personal therapist. Ms. Lewis informed the teacher that such a role would not be appropriate given the nature of her work as a consultant for the center. She did, however, agree to help Ms. King find a therapist and redirect the conversation toward issues in the classroom and within the team. Unfortunately, the other teachers did not feel comfortable exploring these issues in a group meeting, and they never directly addressed their concerns with Ms. King. Nonetheless, the independent discussion of these classroom*

*topics with each teacher seemed to improve the team's
functioning. When asked by the director about the
interrelationships among teachers in this class, Ms. Lewis
responded in general terms about the conflicts of which the
director was already aware, using care not to disclose the
specific nature of the issues divulged by the teachers.*

It is often a great challenge for the consultant to define the boundaries of her position as therapist and confidant within the preschool—
an environment that often mirrors both the strengths and stresses of a
close-knit family. When sharing information, the consultant is advised
to use caution in maintaining alliances with all staff members. She
should be careful that her systemic interventions are not enacted in the
service of more dynamic "family" issues such as gaining the favor of
the director ("parent") at the expense of a teacher ("sibling"). When
such situations occur, the therapist is most effective when she has a supervisor with whom she can comfortably examine these issues. Then
the consultant can make decisions based on the needs of the center
rather than on her own personal reactions. She may find that the
preschool "family" setting stimulates responses within her that may
not arise in other clinical contexts but, nonetheless, demand careful attention. With this supervisory support, the consultant can examine the
influence of her own emotional responses and make choices that best
meet the needs of the individual teachers as well as the entire program.

Another common function of the individual meeting with teachers
is to address issues about children who are being seen in therapy.
These sessions are essentially the same as those occurring in clinic-
based interventions: The consultant and teacher share observations
and work together to set up appropriate emotional, behavioral, and educational goals that can be addressed in the classroom. In this format,
teachers and consultants work as a team, ensuring that appropriate information is shared, that goals for individual therapy, family contact,
and classroom activities are compatible and appropriately addressed.
These collateral meetings have a number of advantages compared to
traditional teacher–therapist contacts. When addressing individual
child issues with teachers, the consultant has credibility as a well-
known and trusted team player, possessing direct knowledge of the
teacher, the center, and—most important—the child. The traditional
clinician usually is an unfamiliar outsider who never observes children
in their natural environments: at the center, in the community, or at
home. As a result, the clinician's recommendations can seem to originate from a contextual vacuum. An ongoing and well-functioning

collaboration forms an ideal context in which teachers and consultants work together to address the requirements of individual children.

Staff Meetings and Workshops

The consultant typically participates in the staff meetings by focusing on the mental health needs of children and families, but she may also work as a team facilitator, helping the group members cope with issues that affect the cohesion of the classroom team. This frequently includes helping teachers confront issues about each other or the consultant as well as those that emerge between the teachers and administrators, social workers, and other specialists. Team meetings are a key arena for processing a wide range of concerns directly related to the classroom, so the consultant can address critical programmatic and systemic issues. Furthermore, these gatherings provide a central opportunity to promote the growth and development of numerous collaborations involving teaching, administrative, special needs, and consulting staff members.

In addition to team and individual meetings with teachers, the consultant often joins full staff or administrative meetings. In these group contexts, the consultant has the unusual occasion to work with staff on larger policy and procedural decisions, adding a mental health perspective to structural changes and plans for special events, holidays, and other activities at the school. Although choices regarding graduation and Christmas celebrations may initially appear outside of the consultant's domain, a closer look reveals that the planning, preparation, and enactment of such events have a great psychological impact on children, families, and staff.

In these meetings, the consultant often has the chance to address general themes that affect the entire early childhood program. At the start of the year, the consultant helps staff prepare for issues that accompany the children's arrival: separation difficulties for children and parents, adjustment to classroom routine, and appropriate developmental expectations. Holidays afford wonderful opportunities for celebration and joy but can also heighten feelings of loss and sadness; the consultant may assist the staff in addressing these more painful feelings. As the year draws to a close, the consultant can help children and staff anticipate another separation by facilitating early preparation. The clinician also should encourage the designation of ample time to review the year and to say good-bye—a difficult process that often requires specific attention. The broader administrative and full staff meetings are excellent mediums for examining these important psychological concerns as they relate to the specific needs of each center.

Whereas ongoing staff meetings are the core mechanism for addressing site-specific concerns, teacher workshops are excellent settings for general didactic and process-oriented group explorations. Rather than turning to external sources, many directors are pleased to discover that in-house consultants are equipped to educate staff on a variety of relevant psychological topics. In turn, the consultant has the unique opportunity to instruct a broad audience that works directly with young children in many capacities and encompasses a wide range of previous training. Although it is not unusual for clinicians to train other students in the field, most do not have the chance to engage teachers and other staff, who typically have had little or no mental health training yet address children's emotional concerns daily. As the next vignette shows, such training can be an exciting experience for both staff and consultant.

> Ms. Benton was a young assistant teacher who was feeling somewhat frustrated as she struggled to meet the demands of teaching and school. She found it difficult to arrange her schedule and did not feel that her course work was relevant to her job as a nursery school teacher. As a result, she seemed to be withdrawing at work, resenting all administrative demands that placed an added burden on her crowded schedule. When the director announced the upcoming child development workshop to be conducted by the consultant, Dr. Lawrence, Ms. Benton did not hesitate to voice her disinterest.
>
> Dr. Lawrence's workshop included a didactic presentation, useful examples from current classroom experience, and staff participation. At some point during the workshop, Dr. Lawrence noted that Ms. Benton's entire demeanor had changed. She eagerly raised her hand and actively participated in all discussions. After the seminar, Ms. Benton told the consultant how exciting it was to see that her school studies did relate to her work at the center and that she knew more than she realized. Ms. Benton also noted that she felt like a "real professional," and she returned to both school and teaching with more enthusiasm.

Such an experience is as gratifying to the student as it is to the teacher. Carefully devised teacher workshops can elevate the teachers' professional level and stimulate an interest in additional training (see the Appendix for a listing of some potential topics for staff development workshops). Moreover, staff training can boost morale by communicating respect for teachers as valuable professionals.

Dr. Moore planned a workshop entitled "The Psychological Problems of Young Children and Their Families: How to Identify and Manage Behavioral and Emotional Concerns." This workshop was conducted for teachers and staff at a large Head Start program. At the request of the director, the seminar focused on how to determine which children are coping with typical developmental issues and which might have concerns requiring therapeutic intervention. The workshop also educated teachers about the work of mental health professionals and their goals with children and families. The group then explored the teacher's role in a child's psychological development and her significance in the life of a child with special needs. The lecture was highlighted by real-life examples from the teachers' current experiences. At the end of the presentation, an older woman who had been teaching at the center for 20 years tearfully told Dr. Moore, "All my friends ask me why, at my age, I continue to put up with all the hardships of working here—its nice to be reminded why I do it."

The previous scenario emphasizes that formal workshops not only help educate staff, but they also offer a much-needed view of the larger picture and remind people of the valuable work they are doing. In addition, it is not unusual for workshops to begin as vehicles for didactic instruction and become a means to examine personal experiences that affect individual teaching styles and philosophies. For example, a workshop on discipline may evoke childhood memories that can be shared and processed within the group setting, leading to important personal and professional insights.

Groups for Exploration and Support

Some large, center-based programs also use full staff meetings as opportunities for group and personal growth. These workshops typically focus on professional issues (e.g., communication skills, staff conflicts, other school-related issues) as well as more personal concerns (e.g., relaxation and meditation, recreational and fitness activities). Again, the consultant with experience in group process can serve as facilitator or lead the support group. Although early childhood programs vary by degree of interest in pursuing these arenas, those that elect to participate find that when staff openness is paired with qualified leadership, such experiences can improve staff morale and communication skills. However, in the process, some painful feelings can emerge.

Mr. Jones was a new director at a center-based preschool. Prior to his arrival, the staff had operated for some months without any director and without certainty that the program would continue. Upon his arrival, Mr. Jones decided to discontinue a number of ongoing staff meetings, including a teacher support group that had been in place for 2 years. The teachers were dismayed to see this format dismantled, discussed their feelings with the consultant, and requested that she convey their feelings to the director. Mr. Jones agreed to reserve a portion of staff day to discuss the teacher support group, asking the consultant to facilitate the conversation. What began as a discussion of that particular group expanded into an exploration of the overall supportiveness of the center in general and the new director in particular. The consultant sought to help the teachers voice their grievances while avoiding counterproductive confrontation of Mr. Jones, who was clearly uncomfortable in this group context. However, by expressing his sadness about the staff's general discontent, Mr. Jones revealed his concern for the teachers; in turn, the teachers saw for the first time a more compassionate side of their new director. Mr. Jones did reconsider the usefulness of a support group, expressing the desire to meet teachers' needs, but he also requested that it not be utilized as a forum for divisiveness. The staff then set guidelines for the appropriate use of the support group; everyone agreed that it should not be an aimless complaint session, but a platform to examine issues relating directly to a teacher's classroom work.

Although the undefined nature of group process can be a frightening prospect for some, it can ultimately lead to greater staff participation and cohesion. A staff support group can be an ongoing opportunity for such experience.

Many teachers and administrators, particularly those working in smaller and more affluent settings, may not feel the need to structure ongoing support groups. In contrast, educators who serve children from multiproblem or impoverished families may choose to build forums for staff support. At one preschool program, a teacher support group was formed following a period of crisis. It grew and changed over a period of 3 years, with shifts in focus mirroring the changes in staff and in the key issues they faced. The history of this support group is presented to illustrate its myriad functions as it evolved over a substantial period of time.

At the close of one school year at South Street, a large
center-based program, one teacher died suddenly in an
automobile accident. As would be expected, the children
and staff were overwhelmed by this teacher's death and
struggled to cope with their feelings. As the death occurred
at the end of the school year, the intervening summer meant
that the staff and children were not able to process this
tragic event as a group. When school reconvened in the fall,
the pain and complexity of emotions, the time·spent apart,
and the arrival of new individuals unacquainted with the
event all conspired to leave this loss unaddressed in any
overt way. Nonetheless, the teachers and children continued
to face this tragedy alone and often unconsciously, as its
effects reverberated throughout the center.

The returning consultant was well aware of the event and,
as an integral part of the community, she also grappled with
her own reaction to the teacher's death. She began to
observe how painful emotions were rampant yet
unexpressed and suggested forming a support group to
address these powerful and undiscussed feelings. The staff
was very responsive to the idea, and the group was
established, meeting weekly to process their sadness and
loss, fears about safety and death, as well as some
ambivalence toward the deceased teacher that later
emerged. This support group operated in a process-oriented,
self-help manner, allowing the staff to avoid the negative
ramifications of unexamined loss and, instead, to complete
the mourning process as a functional, cohesive group.

Although the event at South Street may be an atypical stimulus for
the organization of a support group, it nonetheless demonstrates how
a group formed around a crisis and can have a positive effect on the
center's collective psyche. The mourning process continues for some
time after a tragedy, and leaving it unaddressed can have a detrimental effect on the program. Staff can use support groups to examine
these issues in a supportive context, working toward resolution rather
than merely sealing over painful losses.

Generally, such groups offer support to staff facing not an extreme
tragedy but the day-to-day concerns that arise in their work with
young children who are disadvantaged or highly stressed. These
groups can be open-ended, with no fixed agenda, so that teachers are
free to determine the direction of discussions; this encourages important themes to emerge in an organic, unplanned manner. Alternatively,

support groups can be topic driven, allowing the group to select relevant subjects that will determine the content of each session. Depending on the needs of the center, either model can be used, or they can be
combined, to address the teachers' concerns. Whereas the topic-driven
groups tend to be more educational and leader directed, the open-
ended groups usually are more introspective, allowing themes to emerge
from the teachers.

   After enough time had passed and the mourning process waned,
the support group at South Street assumed the more typical purpose of
examining day-to-day issues in an open-ended forum.

> *The support group continued to meet on a weekly basis
> during its second year, with one consultant staying on and a
> new consultant joining as co-leader. As discussions about
> the tragic death declined, the teachers turned to concerns
> regarding their work with children from impoverished and
> sometimes dysfunctional families. Themes included feelings
> about parents, particularly anger toward perceived
> mistreatment of children; struggles with discipline in the
> classroom; and frustration with "the system" that offers too
> little help, too late. Teacher burnout was another prominent
> subject, as staff examined the stresses and frustrations
> associated with their work with young children.*

   This function became the core service of the support group and
was probably the most effective use of the meeting. However, there
were instances when the group focused more on institutional or systemic issues relating to their particular center.

> *At the start of the third year, there was a sudden absence of
> leadership at South Street. The director resigned her position
> and was replaced by her assistant, who soon followed suit,
> leaving the center rudderless and in fear of being shut down.
> During that time, the staff continued to meet and found that
> this time was useful: The group members addressed feelings
> about the program's uncertain future and also made
> practical administrative decisions as they worked to keep
> South Street afloat. The teachers planned for parent
> conferences and special events while discussing fears that
> they would soon be unemployed and their children
> abandoned.*

At that point, the support group had the unusual but important task of continuing the center's daily operations and providing an opportunity to address feelings provoked by uncertainty. Each child care center must establish fundamental guidelines as to the nature and scope of its support group, but the most useful group is sufficiently flexible to evolve and meet the changing needs of a program.

CONCLUSION

The collaborative relationship between teachers and consultants forms the foundation of the mental health consultation. Consultants can offer formal staff training and provide teachers with support for personal, professional, and programmatic issues that impinge on their abilities to fulfill their roles as early childhood teachers. Given the breadth of their role as educators, as well as the scope of the challenges they face, early childhood teachers often experience considerable stress with few opportunities to voice their concerns or to develop the skills that can minimize their own distress and that of their students. Ideally, the mental health collaboration provides structured as well as informal avenues to meet these needs.

Most important, teachers and consultants work together in a wide range of contexts—formal and informal, individual and group—to address the mental health concerns of children. This end is achieved when the teacher facilitates the consultant's work with children, endorses the therapeutic process, and joins in interventions. In addition, the consultant offers support of the classroom's mental health by providing guidance and recommendations to the teachers as they attend to the emotional needs of young children. Teachers play a similar role in a consultant's work with families. Typically, the teacher makes the first contact with families and begins to build relationships that help parents feel comfortable meeting, accepting, and working with the consultant.

section II

Center-Based
Interventions with
Young Children and Families

chapter five

Engaging Families

Chapter 4 details how the consultant becomes acquainted with the preschool teachers through an ongoing process of meetings, observations, and informal conversations. As this chapter details, when working with families, the consultant implements these same methods and strives to develop both an appreciation of the personal histories of families and an understanding of their relationships with the early childhood program. In this way, the consultant can define and address the mental health needs of families while supporting the children's emotional development. Consultants pursue this goal indirectly through work with teachers and staff and by strengthening the parent component of the school program. Clinicians also provide direct services through their formal and informal contacts with families.

The first step in this process involves talking with staff about the backgrounds, interests, stresses, and strengths of the families they serve. Although it should begin in the early stages of the consultation, this inquiry process is not meant to be a one-time demographic survey or needs assessment. The consultant must be careful to view the information gleaned from initial discussions with staff members as a valuable resource, not as data to be used to develop universal assumptions or generalizations about the families at the center. These early discussions will also give the consultant an understanding of the center's approach toward and methods of relating to families. Of course, this information is enriched by the consultant's direct observations and experiences with the families themselves.

Despite the diversity among the families in most child care centers, the general information provided by staff reports and the consultant's observations can help in planning family activities. For example, first-time mothers or newcomers to the community may need concrete support and advice on child-rearing practices and obtaining services for children. More experienced parents with extended family nearby may not need as much practical advice on how to handle tantrums, sleep problems, or poor eating habits. However, these families may be interested in issues pertinent to them, such as sibling rivalry or intergenerational conflict. Experienced parents may also be an extremely rich resource for younger or more isolated parents.

A consideration of the economic constraints on families will also help the consultant to frame relevant discussions with staff. Working parents may welcome help in balancing their responsibilities and roles, especially if both parents work, and will need to make the most of the limited time they have available for meetings. Centers serving a large proportion of impoverished families will often face additional issues, from helping the families cope with a lack of resources—including, perhaps, funds for child care—to assisting the pursuit of employment.

An understanding and appreciation of the families' cultural backgrounds is also essential if the consultant is to forge meaningful relationships with parents (Lynch & Hanson, 1998). This requires that consultants be aware of their own histories and traditions and examine their preexisting assumptions about other groups (Harry, 1992). Consultants must be willing to learn from families and staff about the program's predominant culture and to openly address differences in child-rearing practices as they become apparent. If clinicians maintain rigid notions of "developmentally appropriate" ways to facilitate separation, toilet training, impulse control, language acquisition, social competence, and other early childhood milestones, they will be limited in their attempts to have real dialogues with families.

RELATIONSHIPS AMONG
FAMILIES AND EARLY CHILDHOOD STAFF

Early childhood programs have a wide variation in their approaches and connections to families based on the needs and interests of both parties. Some child care centers have active family involvement, ranging from in-class volunteering and parent workshops to fundraising, transportation, and administrative assistance. There are even separate lounge areas in some programs, with books, resources, and a quiet place for parents to gather informally. Other centers have little contact with families other than at drop-off and pick-up times or even less if transportation is provided by the program. As in many elementary schools, much of this variability lies in the time families are available. Working parents often have harried schedules that permit little free time for teacher conferences, workshops, or fundraising activities. Preschools are often stymied in their best attempts to involve families, and staff may resent offering enticements to pique interest. As a result, some programs decrease their family activities rather than address the concerns that cause low turnout and minimal enthusiasm.

In addition to time constraints, families may be less involved because of their beliefs regarding early childhood education. Many parents still associate early childhood programs with babysitting, especially if the center is formally identified as a "child care" setting. When this message is transmitted to staff, whether through direct comments or by casual disregard of in-class work and outreach efforts, teachers may feel unappreciated. Unresolved issues around respect, competence, and professionalism can prevent the development of a more collaborative relationship between teachers and families.

The preschool staff may also consciously or unknowingly place limits on family involvement. Many early childhood educators are much less comfortable with parents than they are with children and can feel ill-equipped to discuss the developmental changes and advancements they observe in the classroom or to raise areas of concern. Sometimes a teacher's strong identification with the child's perspective may lead to resentment or blaming parents for the child's problems. If left solely to the educators, there may be little contact with parents beyond exchanging greetings in the morning. In some programs, family outreach is delegated to the social worker or family resource person who may not communicate regularly with teachers or the other child specialists. Cultural differences and racial and ethnic biases can further limit staff members' interest in forging partnerships with families.

GETTING TO KNOW FAMILIES

Many mental health consultants face similar barriers in their attempts to establish relationships with families. Despite these challenges, the consultant might be surprised to find that early childhood facilities do offer many informal opportunities to meet families. It is important for consultants to be available during drop-off and pick-up times to introduce themselves and briefly describe their role in the center. Family members may serve as transportation monitors or classroom helpers, or they may spend time in the morning having coffee and chatting with neighbors at the center. Consultants can often join in these conversations while remaining attuned to and respecting more private discussions. Clinicians may, however, have to take the initiative in introducing themselves because strangers in community centers are not always readily acknowledged by the more familiar members.

The consultant gets to know some families through these casual contacts and others when an individual child is referred. Even in situations involving a more intensive relationship with a child and family, the consultant needs to recognize that meeting with families in early childhood centers differs from seeing them in a private office or a clinic. The centers are by nature less formal and more open places where the consultant may be expected to share some details of his own family and personal life with staff members and families. Each consultant needs to determine his own limits of disclosure and to assess how these limits affect his relationship with the center. For many consultants, this less confined role can be a welcome break from the more formal constraints of therapy, and it can add a healthy balance to their working lives.

Boundaries and Confidentiality

Consultants and child care staff need to be aware of boundary issues when presenting educational or treatment recommendations because families are not always eager to participate and may be confused by the on-site presence of a mental health specialist. Typically, children who display signs of behavior or emotional problems in early childhood programs have not been previously identified as needing services. Parents who enroll children in preschool or child care programs are not necessarily seeking support or advice with these issues, as they would, for instance, if they voluntarily came to a mental health provider. It is, of course, well within the parents' prerogative to refuse to meet with the consultant or to seek help elsewhere. Early childhood programs have to recognize their own limitations in meeting all of the children's needs and to respect families who choose not to participate in the center's programs if they are not required to do so.

Often, the need for more family input will arise when a child is having difficulties in the classroom or when her behavior is disruptive. In these instances, centers have a right to ask parents to come in to discuss the situation. If families have already established a relationship with the program, they are more likely to comply with this request. Furthermore, if the staff and consultant assume a nonthreatening stance in presenting the areas of concern, families may react less defensively. Parents should be assured that these meetings are confidential and that the topics covered will only be repeated, with their permission, to staff in direct contact with their children. Sometimes, however, when the concerns are related to problems such as abuse or neglect, the issues will by definition pose a threat to families. If other agencies need to be involved, the consultant and other staff cannot necessarily promise the usual confidentiality and will need to work in unison to maintain communication with the family.

Confidentiality and boundaries are much more easily maintained in a private therapy office or clinical setting, where professional staff share a common tradition of therapeutic parameters and the physical space and appointment structure afford more privacy and time for exploring conflicts. In early childhood programs, the consultant has an opportunity to contribute to the family's sense of security and to help staff draw clear boundaries regarding handling personal details and family history. Sometimes a simple reminder to keep things within the team, or acknowledging families' need for privacy, can help build more trust and openness with families.

Respecting boundaries and confidentiality does not mean giving up the warmth and familiarity that child care workers often enjoy with families or assuming a rigid or distant approach to the children. It does, however, require that staff members and the program as a whole adopt a professional attitude, one that reflects the serious nature of the work they have undertaken. This is frequently difficult in practice, especially in grassroots community centers where parents and teachers are often neighbors or acquaintances. Much of the appeal of child care centers lies in their friendly atmosphere and openness, so preserving these attributes while maintaining a professional demeanor can be difficult.

Again, mental health consultants may have an opportunity to serve as a model for early childhood program staff. Clinicians may initially err in the other direction, being too formal and reserved, and may be seen as detached and uninvolved with the children. If consultants show, however, that they can be active participants in the school—playing with children, cleaning up after them, and spending informal time with staff and families—they can sometimes disprove the notion that being a professional means giving up a sense of warmth or connection with the children and families. Similarly, when teachers and staff express positive feelings about the consultant in the presence of parents, families often feel encouraged to accept the consultant.

SUPPORTING THE EARLY
CHILDHOOD PROGRAM'S WORK WITH FAMILIES

Once the consultant is established as a familiar person in the program, she can begin to play a more active role in reaching out to families and supporting the program's overall family involvement efforts. As the following scenario exemplifies, the first step is to acknowledge which parent outreach efforts have been successful.

> *At a child care center primarily serving African American families, the teachers in a class of 5-year-olds had become increasingly discouraged by the parents' seeming disinterest; as a result, the teachers had grown more reluctant to reach out to the families. During Black History Month, the class worked intensively on a "Diversity Quilt," with each child contributing patches of cloth that were sewn together and displayed prominently in the center's front hall. Having received much praise from other staff, family members, and visitors, the class decided to host a dinner for families to celebrate the completion of the children's work. The event was a resounding success, with families and children attending together and the teachers feeling that their hard work had been truly acknowledged and appreciated.*
>
> *After the event, the consultant had the opportunity to talk with the teachers, and together they identified the key factors that contributed to the evening's success. The teachers found a creative and culturally relevant means to showcase the children's accomplishments, chose a theme that resonated with families, scheduled the event in the evening when most families could attend, and provided a meal and a festive atmosphere that made the evening feel like a celebration of the children, not just another school meeting. Recognizing and recording these ingredients provided a blueprint for future family events and also presented a context in which teachers received support and affirmation from another professional.*

Consistent positive feedback of this sort can help bolster teachers' enthusiasm and their willingness to seek out other venues for involving families.

Many early childhood programs are interested in encouraging family involvement, but the teachers and administration are constrained by the day-to-day functioning of the program and lack the time to commit to this endeavor. The consultant often has more flexibility in setting his schedule and agenda at the preschool and is in a good position to help strengthen the family program. This assistance may consist of facilitating meetings in which staff examine their feelings and attitudes about parents and establish some concrete goals for increasing family involvement. In addition, the consultant can address these issues through formal workshops. The consultant also may help organize events and programs that staff support. Finally, consultants can encourage the program's work with families by participating in parent–teacher conferences. Teachers often appreciate the presence of a mental health professional when meeting with parents to talk about social or emotional issues, and these conferences offer another opportunity for the consultant to facilitate communication and planning between teachers and families.

INTERVENTIONS WITH FAMILIES

The collaborative model allows consultants to work directly with families at many different levels. A key aspect of the model is that consultants are available to meet with caregivers on an as-needed basis.

Brief Interventions for a Family Crisis

Families sometimes find themselves going through a difficult period with their child or coping with an unexpected problem or family crisis. These sorts of episodic struggles generally do not lead parents to seek outside professional help, but they are much more likely to accept the involvement of a mental health professional when such services are available within the context of their child's preschool. This availability is the essence of the preventive approach: The consultant is able to become involved with families before problems escalate and to be a resource for parents who might otherwise struggle in isolation. Sometimes families engage in brief periods of work with the consultant based on the recommendation of the classroom teacher; other times they refer themselves.

The consultant may meet with a parent only once or twice, to address an immediate concern, as in the following example.

> *Jonathan was a happy, a well-liked, and an artistic little boy who was thriving in his neighborhood preschool. His mother, Mrs. Mills, called the consultant, Dr. Reyes, after Jonathan's grandfather died. The Mills were leaving immediately for North Carolina, where the funeral was to take place, and they were having trouble deciding if they should take Jonathan with them. Mrs. Mills felt that Jonathan, who had maintained a close relationship with his grandfather, should be included, but her husband worried that Jonathan was too young to attend a funeral and thought the child should stay with a babysitter at home. Recognizing*

that this sort of decision is extremely personal and that there is no clear-cut right or wrong answer, the consultant talked with Mrs. Mills about the pros and cons of each possibility. Dr. Reyes helped Jonathan's mother to imagine how things might go in either scenario. The clinician also recommended some children's books dealing with death, including a book about the loss of a grandparent. Finally, Dr. Reyes encouraged Mrs. Mills to have Mr. Mills contact the consultant directly; however, he chose not to.

The consultant did not hear from the Mills again until about 2 weeks later, when Mrs. Mills stopped by Dr. Reyes's office to inform him that the Mills had taken Jonathan to North Carolina, and both parents felt that it had been a good decision for everyone. Jonathan attended the funeral with his parents and seemed to handle the experience well. Jonathan's older cousins also loved spending time with him, giving the Mills the chance to focus on their own needs and feelings.

At other times, the consultant may sustain a somewhat longer relationship with the family, and the intervention may focus on helping the child indirectly, through parent contact and checking in with the teacher.

The Sterns, whose friendly and confident daughter, Melissa, attended an early childhood program in their suburban town, had watched their home burn to the ground after some faulty wiring ignited a massive fire. The consultant at the preschool, Mr. Fisher, heard about the fire, but the teacher and school director reported that 4-year-old Melissa was doing well and did not appear to need the consultant's help at school. The family had found a suitable house to rent while their home was being rebuilt, and they all seemed to be coping well.

About 1 month after the fire, Mrs. Stern called Mr. Fisher and relayed that Melissa "seemed fine" during the day but was experiencing difficulties at night. She was having a terrible time falling asleep, insisted on sleeping in her parents' bed, and woke up many times during the night. Everyone was exhausted, and Mrs. Stern felt a mixture of sympathy and anger toward her young daughter.

Mrs. Stern did not want the consultant to see Melissa directly but was extremely eager to talk about how to handle the sleep problem at home. They spoke extensively for the next 2 weeks, and during these conversations the consultant primarily provided a listening ear for Mrs. Stern. Mr. Fisher also made some concrete recommendations: Mrs. Stern and Melissa could "play about the fire," using dollhouse figures and puppets; practice relaxation techniques at bedtime; or have one of Melissa's parents sit in her bedroom as she fell asleep. Mrs. Stern used some of the suggestions and remained in telephone contact with Mr. Fisher over the next several weeks. Melissa's sleep problem gradually improved, and she was also able to talk about the experience of the fire with more ease. Mr. Fisher did not hear from Mrs. Stern again until later in the spring, when she called to let him know how much better things were going at home.

Some parents have multiple needs when they are in the midst of an intense family crisis. Domestic violence is one example of a serious issue that sometimes spills over into early childhood centers, especially when a parent or another family member is in imminent danger. Consultants may become involved with parents in brief interventions when the situation is urgent or volatile. In these situations, the consultant helps to ascertain the safety of all members of the household, to make connections with other supports and services within and outside the school, and to provide immediate emotional and practical support for family members.

Ms. Bryant had lived with her boyfriend for 10 years, and their two children attended an urban child care center. Her two children were sometimes clingy and anxious at school, but this had not come to the attention of the consultant, Ms. Gold. One morning, after dropping off her children at their classroom, Ms. Bryant asked to speak with Ms. Gold. Ms. Bryant looked exhausted and agitated, and she revealed that her boyfriend had a weapon and had been threatening her. Ms. Gold was extremely concerned about Ms. Bryant's safety and, with the center's social worker, arranged for Ms. Bryant and her children to stay at a local women's shelter until her home situation calmed down. Although she was fearful and upset, Ms. Bryant did move out with her children. With the consultant's support, she also convinced her boyfriend to attend couples' counseling, and they continued to live apart while trying to sort through their relationship. Ms. Gold did not maintain an ongoing

therapeutic relationship with Ms. Bryant but was able to stay
in touch with the mother and monitor her children, who
continued to attend the center.

In all of these scenarios, families made use of the consultant in a spontaneous, circumscribed manner, but such brief interventions often carry meaning that goes beyond the immediate situation. Many families report a sense of reassurance and relief in knowing that a mental health professional is on hand, "just in case," to answer questions, listen, and provide an informed opinion when necessary. Just as teachers test the waters with the consultant during the entry period, families also may try out the consultant to see if this is a person who can be trusted, is approachable, and is helpful. Even when their encounters are brief, parents' positive experiences with consultants may make them feel more comfortable with mental health professionals in general and are likely to encourage them to support on-site mental health services by spreading the word to other families.

Approaching Families with Concerns

Establishing contact with families of a child who is aggressive, withdrawn, or otherwise distressed presents a delicate situation for the preschool staff and the consultant. The strength of the relationship between the family and the staff will largely determine the tone of the initial encounter. If there is a healthy rapport, calling caregivers in for a discussion can be a relatively simple process, and the consultant may well be welcomed as another potential problem solver.

When Ms. Patterson was called in to the New Beginnings
Nursery School to discuss her son's behavior problems, she
was not surprised. Three-year-old Andre was going through
a difficult period, and for a time an outside therapist had
worked with the child and his mother. Some progress had
been noted over the summer, but Andre was still impulsive
and demanding in the classroom and at home. At the
meeting, Ms. Patterson openly expressed her appreciation of
the program staff for their dedication to helping her son, and
she had in the past made special gestures of gratitude to his
teachers, including small Christmas presents. She was
anxious for the consulting psychologist to begin working
with Andre and was pleased that the clinician would help
Andre's teachers implement a behavioral system, unlike
the previous therapist who had had little contact with
staff members.

The mother in this case was already well disposed toward the school, acknowledged her son's problems, and was not threatened or alarmed by the notion of psychological intervention. The consultant, the teacher, and the school social worker also had time to discuss the issues in advance and were hopeful that they could work together with Andre and his mother. Often, however, problems are presented in a less coordinated and timely manner to families who are not as prepared to hear about them.

> One inexperienced but well-intentioned staff member, after a particularly stressful day with 5-year-old Cedric, told his mother, "Cedric should see a psychiatrist." Cedric's mother was outraged and insulted and had much difficulty discussing Cedric's behavioral issues, even though she struggled with him at home as well. The consultant at that point had little choice but to work with Cedric's teachers on classroom strategies and to allow for a "cooling off" period before he sought to meet with Cedric's mother in person.

At times the consultant has the opportunity to intervene despite strains in the relationship between the families and the early childhood program. The goal is to improve communication and foster a mutual understanding between families and staff as well as to respond to the current problem.

> Ms. Duncan worked as an administrator at a public prekindergarten program and had her 4-year-old son, Richard, enrolled in the program. Richard was an active and rambunctious boy who was prone to accidents at home and in school. Previous incidents at the school during which Richard had sustained minor cuts and bruises had left his parents angry and suspicious, and they believed that Richard's teachers were not providing adequate supervision and did not particularly care for him. In classroom visits, the consultant, Dr. Vincent, did not find that supervision per se was a problem; nonetheless, the consultant did observe that the teachers were not at ease with Richard and a few other active boys in the class. The teachers ranged from being tentative to sometimes being harsh and overbearing with these students. To help the situation, Dr. Vincent suggested that the teachers establish more active outdoor playtime,

and he had been organizing ball games for these boys.
During one of these games, Richard was tackled by two
other boys and received a fairly serious gash above his lip.
He was taken to the nurse, who administered first aid. The
nurse then contacted Ms. Duncan, whose office was just
down the hall. Ms. Duncan was furious that the teachers did
not contact her directly and by what she again perceived to
be a lack of supervision.

Informed by the director of Ms. Duncan's anger, Dr.
Vincent stopped in the mother's office at lunch. He
explained that he had in fact been supervising Richard and
that the teachers had not been remiss in their duty. He also
talked at length with Ms. Duncan about Richard's high
activity level and shared ideas about how to help the child
channel some of his energy and organize himself both at
home and in school. Dr. Vincent also encouraged Ms.
Duncan to meet with Richard's teachers and raise her issues
with them. She scheduled a meeting for the following week
and seemed to feel that the teachers heard her concerns.
The remainder of the school year passed without any major
incidents, and the consultant observed that the teachers
appeared more attentive and comfortable with Richard.

In the preceding situation, a moment of crisis was turned into an opportunity for the parents and staff to take stock of their relationship and air their disagreements. Rather than contributing to a lingering resentment by both parties, the consultant persuaded both groups to examine their issues through this event. The fact that the clinician was involved in the incident placed him squarely in the center of the dispute for a brief time. Though in an awkward position, Dr. Vincent worked hard not to be defensive with this mother or to shy away from her anger. Being in this position also allowed the consultant to share some of the responsibility with the teachers and to further empathize with their dilemmas in coping with active preschool children.

The Difficult-to-Reach Parent

Unlike the mother in the previous example, families having strained or distant relations with their child's center often keep little contact with staff and may not be cooperative when concerns arise about their children's behavior or emotional state. In the most difficult situations, families remain distrustful and defiant toward the teachers and may seek to undercut their authority as caregivers even while their children continue to attend the center. This behavior frequently indicates that the families themselves are in considerable distress, but it leaves little room for empathy or outreach from child care providers. Typically, programs respond by limiting further attempts to communicate with these families and seeking to handle problems with children "in house," unless they are forced to contact families or social welfare agencies.

Yet addressing a child's problems without involving the family runs contrary to the philosophy of most early childhood programs; it also greatly diminishes the chances that the staff will be successful in negotiating any struggles in the classroom. In these instances, the consultant can play a critical role in helping the program staff better understand and tolerate family behavior, to realistically assess family availability, and to plan together how to involve the family more actively in the program. The following is one case illustration of a difficult-to-reach parent.

Ms. Perkins was known by the staff of Cedar Community Child Care, as her daughter, Chanel, and her son, Andrew, had each spent 3 years there. Both children were extremely bright, but Chanel was defiant and oppositional and Andrew was often sad and withdrawn. Andrew had been diagnosed with severe asthma while at the center and had been receiving regular medical treatments for 2 years. Ms. Perkins was an intelligent and resourceful woman, but she had been largely unsuccessful in coping with her drug and alcohol abuse. She had been imprisoned for 1 year on drug-related charges when her children were infants, and she then lived with them in a number of different apartments in several communities. Though Ms. Perkins clearly cared about her children and was sometimes actively involved with the school, she could also be harsh and neglectful. At her lowest points, she could be irresponsible in caring for Andrew and Chanel, leaving them in dangerous situations or allowing them to witness violence in the home. Her variability was particularly disturbing to the teachers and social workers of the school who felt that Ms. Perkins was capable of consistently providing for her children.

Ms. Connor, the consulting social worker at Cedar Community, had worked with the family for many years and saw both children twice a week in therapy. She helped Chanel cope with her anger over her home situation and encouraged Chanel to use her charm and intelligence, rather than her defiant and oppositional behavior, to get the

*attention she wanted from adults. Ms. Connor also worked
with Andrew as he confronted his sadness over his illness
and helped draw him out of his shell to become a more
active and playful boy. She also endeavored to maintain a
relationship with Ms. Perkins and stuck by the mother
through her many ups and downs over the years. The two of
them formed an open and genuine bond, and Ms. Perkins
was generally honest with Ms. Connor about her successes
and shortcomings with the children. When feeling depressed
or incapacitated, she would reach out to Ms. Connor for
help with food or clothing or to send a message to Andrew
in the hospital.*

*Ms. Connor faced an uphill battle with other staff
members at Cedar Community, who struggled with hostile
feelings toward Ms. Perkins. The consultant explained that
their anger toward and disappointment in Ms. Perkins were
understandable—at times, she also shared these feelings—
but that this mother needed a place where adults that she
trusted could stand by her and reach out to her. This did not
mean that staff could ignore warning signs or not hold Ms.
Perkins responsible for her behavior, and sometimes they
did have to call in child protective services and other case
workers. But as a team they could strive to treat Ms. Perkins
with respect and avoid dismissing her as merely a "drug
abuser" or "bad mother." Ms. Perkins appreciated these
efforts and proudly took part in graduation and other school
activities. She seemed to respond in small ways to the staff's
continued support and outreach efforts, and she was
surprised and relieved that they were not more critical of
and distant toward her.*

Even the most experienced early childhood program staff need
opportunities to express their frustration and to share the stress of coping with these hard-to-reach families. It is easy to feel hopeless and
helpless when faced with such seemingly intractable problems, and
consultants are not immune from experiencing these feelings. Despite
this and the fact that they will often not have clear-cut solutions, the
consultants can provide a forum for discussing the burdens these cases
place on staff and can perhaps help them acknowledge gains in their
work with families. Ms. Perkins often slipped back to drugs, and if that
was the sole criteria for evaluating their impact on this family, the staff
of Cedar Community could only feel they had failed. But she was also

more involved with and attentive toward her children and grew to appreciate the efforts of the teachers and other staff members on their behalf. Ms. Perkins also became much more open and honest with staff, a critical advance in a school where insincerity was often cited as the staff's biggest complaint against parents. A key component of the success of this case was the ongoing and intensive nature of the collaboration. The consultant worked at Cedar Community 5 days per week and had been part of the on-site therapeutic team there for 7 years. The local mental health agency where she worked full-time had established a satellite clinic at Cedar Community, and three to six clinicians were assigned to the school during the academic year. Although such intensive services are nearly unheard of and not warranted in most child care centers, the children in this program had endured an unusual number of traumas and dislocations. Ms. Perkins' situation was an extreme case; nevertheless many families in the community shared a need for clinical and concrete services from the on-site mental health professionals.

Supporting Staff in Their Work with Challenging Families
The needs of the families can justify the level of clinical services at places like Cedar Community, but these families also provide a special challenge to staff members whose own needs are often overlooked. Few preschool teachers or other staff members dealing with frequent crises and high incidences of trauma have an adequate education in these areas. They have not received training in coping with their own responses to traumatic material and in recognizing and ameliorating the impact of trauma on children. When families casually reveal shocking details from their personal histories or current lives or show a threatening or menacing attitude toward their children or teachers, staff can feel unprepared, overwhelmed, frightened, or helpless. They need to know that they can have confidence in another professional who will support them and join with them to face these challenges. This trust can only come through experience and time spent together. It would be difficult, if not impossible, for a consultant to be effective at a clinically intensive preschool with just a few hours of on-site time per week or if he rotated placements every year.

The hard-to-reach family is a challenge to clinicians in all settings; however, the consultant has many advantages within the early childhood program. The resistant family is often most in need of services but is least likely to follow through with a traditional outpatient clinic referral. The reasons are numerous and include logistical and organizational barriers, suspiciousness of mainstream service providers outside their community, distrust of medical settings, and avoidance of mental health labels that stigmatize families. The family is far more likely to engage with consultants who seem less like outsiders and more like genuine community members, who might be seen reading in the classroom, dancing at holiday parties, and singing on the bus. In fact, the greater the strength of the collaboration between the consultant and staff, the more likely these challenging families will form ties with the mental health professional.

> *Ms. Drew was a Caucasian consultant new to a small but well-established early childhood program serving predominantly African American children and their families. It became immediately apparent that the first priority for the consultation was to address the needs of a troubled little girl and her notoriously resistant mother, Ms. Johnson. During a team meeting, the consultant and staff agreed that this family was in need of services, though the teachers doubted Ms. Johnson's receptivity to Ms. Drew. They restated a commonly held belief: "Ms. Johnson doesn't like white people." The African American family worker, a senior and well-liked member of the community, disagreed. She claimed, "Ms. Johnson doesn't like anybody" and suggested it was worth the effort to schedule a meeting. They agreed to invite the mother to a joint conference with the consultant and the family worker. Ms. Johnson agreed to the meeting though she remained quiet and aloof through much of the hour. Toward the end of the meeting, the family worker spontaneously stood up and put her arm on the consultant's shoulder, in view of the reluctant parent, stating "This one's all right." Although the therapeutic gains were indeed modest, Ms. Johnson nonetheless was able to develop an ongoing relationship with the consultant over the school year, a bond that would have been difficult to form without the stamp of approval from the trusted family worker.*

The fact that services in the early childhood consultation model are introduced and supported by well-regarded community members and are embedded within the preschool program maximizes the likelihood that resistant families may eventually sustain a working alliance with a mental health professional. In addition, many families are more comfortable with the notion of prevention, in which interventions are framed as attempts to avoid more intractable future problems that could require special classes, diagnostic labels, and the involvement of outside agencies.

OTHER MODALITIES FOR
ENGAGING AND WORKING WITH FAMILIES

This chapter has thus far presented an overview of some of the issues involved in working with families within the context of the early childhood setting. Much of the consultant's work with families is geared toward the prevention of more serious problems. The consultant may also be involved with families who need intensive therapeutic interventions and schedule regular appointments for families in these instances. In some centers, the consultant may attempt to reach a broader group by offering support groups or workshops. In the next section, two specific ways the consultant can further engage and work with parents are presented—dyadic work, in which parents and children are seen jointly, and parent groups.

Dyadic Work with Parents and Children

In dyadic therapy, the consultant meets with the parent and child together in the same session, instead of seeing each separately. This provides an opportunity for the therapist to work directly with and intensively on the relationship between parent and child (see Carter, Osofsky, & Hann, 1991, and Lieberman & Pawl, 1993, for a full explanation and examples of dyadic therapy). Dyadic work can be particularly effective for the consultant doing on-site therapeutic work. The consultant, the teacher, and the parent become partners in trying to find ways to build stronger relationships with the child. The parent may have discovered ways to help the child at home and can work with the teacher and the consultant to form educational and treatment plans at school. More frequently, the parent is struggling with the child's behavior at home. In this case, the consultant can work with parent and child either in or out of the classroom to understand the meaning of the behavior and to respond in a consistent way to the child's needs.

> *Jennifer came to the attention of the consultant, Dr. Powers, as a severely acting-out, aggressive, and hyperactive 4-year-old girl. She was in a self-contained preschool classroom for children with emotional difficulties, and she was very aggressive with the other children. Her mother and father had recently separated and were embroiled in conflict with each other. They would often argue vehemently in Jennifer's presence. After meeting with the parents separately to help them find ways to curtail their anger in front of their daughter, Dr. Powers began working on site with Jennifer and her mother together in sessions outside the classroom. At first these sessions focused on managing Jennifer's*

frequent outbursts and temper tantrums. Jennifer's mother,
who could be dismissive and was overwhelmed by her
daughter, grew more empathic and slowly learned to play
with her. As Jennifer became more calm, her mother could
enjoy the child's artistic skills and sense of humor. At this
point, the focus of the sessions began to shift to Jennifer's
sadness over her parents' breakup and her wish to get them
back together. Along with these sessions, Dr. Powers also
spent time with Jennifer's teachers, helping them to limit
Jennifer's ability to dominate the classroom and to respond
quickly to her aggression. Jennifer had improved markedly
by the end of the year, and the teachers made plans for her
inclusion in kindergarten.

In dyadic work, it is important to establish goals that are focused on the parent–child relationship. In the previous example, the initial goal was to find a way to contain Jennifer's behavior. This enabled Jennifer's mother to feel more in control, and she gradually came to understand her daughter's anger and pain. In contrast, had Jennifer been in individual therapy, the primary goal may have been to connect her emotional outbursts to her feelings of sadness and anger from the beginning of treatment. Conceptualizing a parent–child intervention can be challenging for the consultant who has not previously engaged in dyadic work because it demands broadening the focus beyond the immediate needs of the child. The therapist must develop an ability to empathize simultaneously with the child and the parent as well as concentrate on the parent–child relationship.

When both a parent and a teacher are interested, it is often helpful for the consultant to work with the parent and child in the classroom. If parent–child sessions are indicated, the consultant needs to decide whether this is feasible. First, the teacher and the program director should be consulted. There is sometimes too much going on in a classroom to consider bringing in a parent to work with her child. In addition, the work may involve the direct exploration of personal and private issues that would not be appropriate to air within the classroom. Occasionally, when other children in the class have experienced loss of a parent or chronic neglect, a parent's presence can be quite stimulating, and care should be taken to make sure that the teacher is willing and prepared to cope with this situation. If the teacher is inexperienced, new to the center, or feeling overwhelmed, it is probably best to consider holding the sessions in a separate space outside the classroom.

When dyadic work can be accomplished in class, the parent benefits from directly experiencing the structure of the room and can test new skills in a supportive environment. The process may be smoother if teachers have stabilized the child's behavior at school. However, this approach can be effective when a child is acting up in the classroom as well. In this situation, the consultant typically needs to play a more active role, either by modeling or problem solving on the spot with teacher and parent, while simultaneously attending to their feelings about the consultant's adopting this stance. Helping a parent better accept her child and not feel humiliated in a public place can contribute greatly to facilitating their relationship.

Three-year-old Daryl was struggling in his new preschool classroom. His teachers were struck by his aggression in the face of not getting what he wanted and characterized him as "spoiled." His mother, Ms. Martin, had expressed her frustration with Daryl to the teachers, and they in turn asked the consultant, Mr. Kim, to speak with her. Mr. Kim listened as Ms. Martin talked about feeling overwhelmed and unable to cope with her active and strong-willed son. She was afraid of providing discipline for fear of losing his love. Mr. Kim decided to ask the teachers if he could bring Ms. Martin into the classroom to show her how the teachers were beginning to help Daryl; the teachers were consistently providing Daryl with much-needed limits and consequences without losing their affection for him. After the consultant and parent jointly observed Daryl in the classroom and discussed what was happening, the consultant set up an appointment to meet with Daryl and his mother together the following week. During this dyadic session, Mr. Kim watched as Daryl repeatedly tested his mother. The consultant encouraged Ms. Martin to try some of the techniques she had seen in the classroom, such as time-out and maintaining a firm "no" with clear ramifications. Although Ms. Martin continued to struggle with her son, to her surprise, he accepted her limits more readily than she had expected, and she began to see how much he needed them. She also began asking the teacher for help and advice on how to handle Daryl.

This vignette exemplifies one of the benefits of dyadic work with parents at their child's school. Daryl's mother was particularly grateful to his teachers for their understanding attitude toward him even after he misbehaved, which then made it easier for Ms. Martin to be receptive of their interventions. As Ms. Martin began working with her son, with support from the consultant, she experimented with techniques she had seen the teacher use. This forged a connection between the mother and the teacher that continued and deepened even in the consultant's absence. In this way, the teacher was able to continue the therapeutic work the consultant had started.

Decisions about when to proceed with dyadic treatment should be based on the needs of the individuals as well as pragmatic issues. If the parent is unavailable or uninterested in attending joint sessions, the consultant's options are more limited. Even when the parent is available, working with a parent and a child together is not always a viable option. The center may not be open to this type of treatment occurring within the early childhood program, or either the parent or child may have too many individual needs.

> Andrea was referred to Dr. Alina by the preschool teacher
> because of the child's emotional outbursts and concerns
> regarding Andrea's mother, Ms. Travers, who seemed erratic
> in her ability to care for her daughter. After meeting
> separately with Andrea and her mother, Dr. Alina decided to
> meet with them together in order to help Ms. Travers learn
> to interpret her daughter's behaviors better and to respond
> more consistently to Andrea's temper tantrums.
> Nevertheless, after two sessions, it became clear that Ms.
> Travers had a severe emotional disturbance that was
> characterized by mood swings and dissociative episodes.
> Sessions became dominated by the mother's recounting her
> own difficulties, and Andrea was left to play by herself. Dr.
> Alina decided to refer the mother for her own treatment and
> to work individually with Andrea to help her understand and
> cope with her mother's inconsistent responsiveness. After
> some weeks in treatment, Andrea was more able to
> verbalize her feelings of anger and confusion. This in turn
> helped Ms. Travers recognize the effect her mental illness
> was having on her child. Ms. Travers became somewhat
> more capable of shielding her daughter from her problems,
> as she became more stable herself.

At times, dyadic work occurs in conjunction with other techniques. The consultant may decide that some relationship topics would be best addressed in joint sessions outside the classroom, with separate individual sessions for parent and child to explore personal issues. The consultant may also recommend interventions with the parent and the child within the classroom to address behavior management and social problems and to encourage parental involvement.

> Naomi was a precocious 4-year-old girl who was having a number of problems in class. She was negative and defiant and at times engaged in dangerous behaviors. The teachers were unsure how to handle Naomi's indiscriminate flirtatious interactions with adults, particularly unfamiliar men. When the consultant became involved with Naomi and her mother, Ms. Carson, it became evident that the family was struggling with many difficult issues. Ms. Carson had only recently regained custody of her daughter following a chaotic history of drug use and prostitution. In addition, Naomi had sporadic and unpredictable contact with her father, who had been inconsistently involved in her care.
>
> The consultant began to meet individually with Naomi's mother. Ms. Carson was able to examine her painful past and make important connections between her former lifestyle and current behavioral concerns for her daughter. These explorations required the privacy and support of the therapist in individual meetings outside the classroom. Next, Naomi and her mother were able to participate in dyadic therapy to address current issues such as reestablishing themselves as a family and setting reasonable guidelines for Naomi's contact with her father. Ms. Carson began to see how Naomi's provocative behavior was at once a replication of what the mother had modeled and also a learned attempt to gain closeness with a largely unavailable father. Ms. Carson began to examine her own difficulties expressing warmth and affection to her daughter, a quality she wished to change, and made important strides in doing so during these joint sessions. In addition, Ms. Carson began to feel more empowered as Naomi's primary caregiver by participating actively in the classroom and working with teachers to set limits and give appropriate rewards. She also increasingly enjoyed her daughter's strengths and abilities, which both mother and daughter were discovering.

As this case indicates, dyadic sessions are often the cornerstone of an effective plan of treatment but may first require an understanding and trust that emerges in individual parent sessions. Often the gains made in joint sessions are then consolidated and broadened by continued parent–child contacts in the classroom.

Parent Groups

Early childhood programs that make families feel welcome and develop multiple opportunities for them to become involved are more likely to forge the type of vibrant program–family integration that creates continuity and support for young children (see McDonald et al., 1997, for an excellent example of this type of program). Parent groups are one of the more effective means of encouraging this involvement in early childhood environments. Consultants are often asked by early childhood centers to assist in developing and implementing a stronger family program. In some cases, the preschool has never had regularly scheduled parent groups, and the administration asks the consultant to establish such a group as a new aspect of the center. In other programs, regularly scheduled parent groups already exist, and the center seeks the consultant's expertise on specific topics at occasional meetings. Although it is tempting to respond immediately to a center's request to initiate a parent group, it is generally a mistake to plunge forward without some preliminary work. Environments vary tremendously in terms of the motivation of families to participate in these groups, the level of support and encouragement given by the staff, and the practical logistics. Understanding these issues as well as the history of family involvement, the specific individuals served, and the level of commitment and support from the center is critical before the consultant attempts to form a parent group.

Koplow (1996) reviewed the basic types of parent groups, which include educative, support, and therapeutic groups. Educative groups focus on imparting information on topics such as child development and practical parenting issues and techniques. They are generally led by a professional who has some expertise and experience in parenting. (See the Appendix for samples of group agendas and topics.) Support groups are generally less structured, exist as a means of reducing caregivers' feelings of isolation, and may or may not be led by a professional (Faber & Mazlish, 1980; Samalin, 1988). Therapeutic groups are led by a qualified professional, such as a social worker or psychologist, and not only focus on the pressing issues that parents have with their children but also delve into parents' own childhood experiences. This type of group explores the links between parents' present behaviors and feelings and those of the past, in an effort to heighten parents' self-awareness and to free them to become more empathic and responsive to their children's emotions and needs.

These three types of parent groups—educative, support, and therapeutic—are not necessarily mutually exclusive. As the following example demonstrates, a didactic presentation on discipline techniques often elicits strong feelings from parents, which the consultant might then use as a starting point for moving into a deeper and more personal discussion.

> *Dr. Frank had initiated a new parent support group at the Little Tots Center, and in the first meeting she asked parents what they would like to discuss in the subsequent meetings. Discipline was the resounding first choice and was the designated topic for the second meeting. As Dr. Frank talked about different ways parents could respond to their children's misbehavior, she noticed that one parent, Ms. Lopez, looked quite distraught. When Dr. Frank asked the parent if she would like to share her thoughts, Ms. Lopez, who was a young mother of two little children, began to talk about how she herself had been disciplined as a child in Puerto Rico. Whenever Ms. Lopez did something "bad" as a child, she was forced to stand outside in her bare feet on a pile of uncooked rice, which was prickly and sharp. Although this was an extremely unpleasant memory for her, Ms. Lopez had recently been tempted to use the same punishment with her 3-year-old because she did not know what else to do. This mother's openness about her own past released a flood of other memories and feelings among the other participants. Dr. Frank picked up on the need to spend some time talking about the parents' own experiences, with the promise that the group would return to the topic of discipline techniques at another group meeting.*

In large part, the emphasis of a parent group will, at least initially, reflect the skills and personality of the consultant. Some consultants feel more comfortable with open-ended support groups, without a set agenda or didactic portion. Others may prefer the educative type of group, which includes a structured informational approach with handouts and a predetermined topic. The successful consultant will be able to use her own abilities and style while responding to the needs of the families at the school.

Regardless of the emphasis and specific format of a parent group, the consultant should bear in mind some overarching principles that typically identify effective parent programs. Five factors identified by the National School Public Relations Association (Ross, 1988) are climate, relevance, convenience, publicity, and commitment, adapted here for use in early childhood programs.

Climate   The consultant aims to create a warm and welcoming atmosphere for all participants. Providing refreshments, greeting parents individually, and establishing expectations about confidentiality and acceptance all convey the consultant's intention to offer a comfortable and accepting climate.

Relevance   There are certain topics that the majority of parents with young children will wish to discuss, such as discipline, eating, sleeping, and sibling rivalry. Nonetheless, the consultant should seek family input about topics to be covered rather than assume that she knows what is foremost on the group members' minds. For example, in one group, the consultant was surprised to learn that parents were feeling extremely anxious about their children "graduating" from the child care center and moving on to kindergarten. Most of these parents were recent immigrants who had little or no experience with public education in the United States. They wanted concrete information about the schools in their community, including which were the best public schools and how they could enroll their children in them. Several parents in a different group lived with extended family members; their priority was to talk about the complications of these relationships, especially in terms of shared child rearing.

Convenience   Many families are burdened with the numerous demands of home and work, and for families who are without economic resources or who have serious problems of their own, the idea of an extra event or commitment is simply overwhelming. Although the consultant cannot change the reality of the families with which she is involved, she can strive to make it as easy as possible for families to attend. In one Head Start program, the meetings were held in the morning, and parents were allowed to ride the bus with their children so they could easily get to the center. In early childhood programs serving primarily working families, meetings are often held in the evening.

Publicity   The consultant should be prepared to communicate with families in multiple ways: fliers sent home with the children, newsletters, notices posted in the building, even personal invitations (see Appendix). One consultant, who worked in a center with many non–English-speaking families, wrote the notices in both Spanish and English. She also enlisted the help of the family worker, who was Latino, in making telephone calls to Spanish-speaking families, encouraging them to attend the meetings and informing them that the family worker would be present as a co-leader and translator.

Commitment   The consultant's commitment to families, a desire to bring parents together to help each other, and consistency in offering an ongoing group will increase the chances that families will over time see a group as an experience that meets their needs. It can be discouraging for a consultant when only a few people attend a group that was painstakingly planned and publicized. In fact, many consultants must adjust their expectations of what a "good turnout" might be and learn to appreciate that, in some centers, it will take months of consistent effort to increase involvement in a parent group. For some particularly stressed families, getting out of the house and participating in an activity beyond the immediate family is a huge step. Others may be marginalized in their communities, due to personal problems such as divorce, substance abuse, or job loss, and find it very difficult to see a parent group as a place for them. Christenson (1995) noted that developing partnerships between families and schools takes a great deal of effort and emphasized that this type of collaboration is "an attitude, not simply an activity"(p. 253). This notion is relevant to the success of parent groups; that is, the specific activity the group engages in may be less important than the consultant's expressed commitment to working with families to create meaningful and enjoyable groups.

Further Considerations
In addition to the factors identified by Ross (1988), there are other relevant issues regarding school-based parent groups that are addressed in the following discussion.

Confidentiality   In any group experience, the issues of privacy and confidentiality are important to address, but in the school-based parent group, there are complications that the consultant should be aware of and address in the early stages of the group. Families who attend a group may be friends, relatives, or neighbors with a history of close connections or conflict. A parent's child may have spoken either positively or negatively about the child of another parent who attends the group. Without seeming naive about the tendency of people to talk about each other, it is highly important to keep private the names and specific situations that are brought up in the group, especially in a group that is composed of friends and neighbors.

Language   Consultants who work in centers where there are many non–English-speaking families will need to consider how to approach the diversity of the population. Some consultants may themselves speak more than one language; others may work in settings with social workers or family workers who are fluent in other languages. An interesting and subtle question emerges for consultants who work in settings with families from many different backgrounds and languages: Should there be separate groups for each dominant language?

One early childhood program served African American, Latino, and Caucasian families. When asked by the center to

*initiate a parent group, the consultant talked with the
administration and other staff members about the issue of
translation during the group; she discovered that there was a
difference of opinion. Some believed that it would be easiest
to have two groups—one in English, one in Spanish. That
way, the English speakers would not have to wait while
everything was translated and the needs of the Spanish-
speaking families would still be met. Others believed that it
would be divisive to separate parents in this way and that
many of the Spanish-speaking families were immigrants who
did not have much contact with parents from other
backgrounds. During her time at the center, the consultant
tried both approaches and, in the end, settled on offering
one group for all parents, with a translator present.
Eventually, most of the parents grew accustomed to the
rhythm of translation. Although there may have been some
parents who did not attend because they did not like waiting
for the translation, on the whole, the group continued to
grow and to reflect the diversity of the center's families.*

When possible, it is preferable to unify families from diverse backgrounds so that they can share this richness of culture and experience
as their children do in the classroom. Similarly, when families work as
one group, they support the cohesiveness of the preschool community
and further the staff's efforts to encourage children from dissimilar ethnic and cultural backgrounds to develop tolerance and friendships.

Encouraging Parent Leadership   As in any group, the participants will be most enthusiastic when they feel that the group belongs
to them and reflects their priorities and needs. The consultant who facilitates parent groups will soon be struck by the extent to which many
parents feel unsupported and unappreciated in the work they do raising their children. In addition, many group members are women who
have little political or economic power and are not accustomed to seeing their experiences and views as worthy of interest and respect. The
consultant should try to find ways to help activate involvement in the
group and to provide opportunities for parents to emerge as leaders.
Parents can be encouraged to tell their friends about the group, to offer
child-rearing approaches that have worked for them, and to recognize
their ability to help other families. Sometimes a specific or unantici-
pated need within the group will push a parent toward greater self-
confidence and leadership.

*The family worker usually translated the biweekly parent
support groups, but on the day of one such group meeting,*

she was absent. The consultant, Mr. Powell, did not want to cancel the group because several parents had already begun to gather in the meeting room, yet he knew that a number of them spoke little or no English. He recognized one of the parents, Ms. Martinez, who was bilingual but had been one of the quieter group participants. Mr. Powell took Ms. Martinez aside, asking her whether she would be willing to translate that day's meeting. Ms. Martinez expressed a good deal of nervousness and doubted whether she was capable of taking on this responsibility; nevertheless, she reluctantly agreed. In fact, she was graceful and quick in translating, and the meeting proceeded extremely well. Mr. Powell noted that Ms. Martinez grew more confident as she spoke, and in future meetings she was more outspoken and assumed a leadership role within the group.

Discussing Emotionally Charged Issues   Whether the consultant facilitates informational workshops or a more informal support group, it is common for participants to reveal personal and sometimes painful feelings and experiences, especially in centers where families have experienced a great deal of hardship. As the next vignette illustrates, parents who share memories and feelings about their own early lives in support groups typically begin to understand their children more fully and feel less isolated as parents.

The consulting social worker, Ms. Robbins, facilitated a weekly parent support group at a Head Start center in a small city. Most of the families whose children attended the center were Latino, and many had recently immigrated to the United States from a variety of locations in South and Central America. One week the discussion turned to sibling relationships and rivalry. Ms. Robbins was struck by the intensity with which many of the parents spoke about sibling issues. They were adamant in their desire for their children to be close, to always treat each other well, and to share everything. It seemed extremely hard for the members of this group to accept the normal conflicts and struggles of most siblings.

These feelings crystallized as one mother, Ms. Vargas, talked about her own early experiences. She had moved with her parents from El Salvador to the United States when she was 6 years old. Ms. Vargas's family could not afford to bring all of their children with them, so her older sister

stayed behind, living with her grandparents. Life in El
Salvador was extremely difficult, due to both political and
economic upheavals, and maintaining contact with the
family in the United States became increasingly difficult. As
a child, Ms. Vargas missed and worried about her only sister
a great deal. Her parents were vague when answering her
questions, and on the surface they seemed matter-of-fact
about the separation. Ms. Vargas ultimately lost touch with
her sister for many years, reconnecting with her when they
were both young adults.

Ms. Vargas was now a young mother of two girls. She
could not tolerate any dissension between her daughters,
punishing them swiftly whenever they fought. By telling her
story in the parent group, Ms. Vargas began to connect her
quick temper regarding her daughters with her sense of loss
about her own sister. A number of other group members had
similar experiences and shared stories of losing loved ones
through separations or early death. As she listened, Ms.
Robbins came to understand the meaning and depth of their
feelings about sibling rivalry and to appreciate the struggles
that marked their early years more fully.

Families are sometimes reluctant to talk about certain topics, although they may also be relieved when the consultant begins a discussion about seemingly taboo subjects. For example, a workshop entitled
"Talking to Children About Difficult Subjects," including topics such
as sex, illness, and death, may be suggested but should not be forced
on families. However, these realities greatly concern most parents, and
they may not have had many opportunities to discuss these matters
with their peers or a mental health professional.

The participants in Dr. Thompson's support group for
mothers had requested a meeting on talking about sex with
children. There was a large turnout but much silence and
squirming on the part of the mothers as the group began.
Slowly the ice was broken, and, with considerable
embarrassment, the women began talking and asking
questions. Ms. Ryan relayed that she had never dared ask
her parents anything about sex when she was little, but just
the other day her 4-year-old son bluntly asked, "What is
sex?" Ms. Evers believed that sex should not be discussed
until her children were much older, but they persisted in

*asking her questions, such as "Where do babies come
from?" Like Ms. Evers, many of the other mothers worried
that once they began responding to their children's
questions about sex, they would have to delve into details
and subjects that did not seem appropriate. They were also
concerned that their children would become too interested
in sex and wished they could just avoid the whole issue. Dr.
Thompson did not deny the discomfort and confusion felt by
the parents, and she offered her perspective on the subject.
Her experiences with preschoolers had shown her that
children typically are satisfied with brief factual answers to
questions about sex and that such discussions did not
generally stimulate an intense interest in sexual matters. The
mothers still had many questions and conflicts, and this
meeting was only a first step in giving them a chance to
share their concerns about this delicate subject.*

Consultants should be attuned to their own comfort level in talking about issues that may emerge in parent groups. In addition, they
should strive to maintain a balance in the emotional intensity of topics
that are discussed and to resist adopting an overly therapeutic or didactic stance with families. The consultant's ability to create a relaxed
and trusting atmosphere generally develops gradually, and his skill in
leading discussions about controversial subjects grows as he gains experience and comes to know the families in the center.

Closing Rituals   Most mental health and educational professionals recognize the importance of closure when completing a group.
In facilitating school-based parent groups, there are several unique features the consultant should bear in mind. Typically, the groups follow
the schedule of the school calendar. The end of the school year is a time
when it seems to be harder for everyone to stick to a structure, and
most staff feel end-of-year fatigue and loss of motivation. The consultant may also feel some "June burnout" herself and wonder if it is worth
the effort to mobilize the parent group at a time when motivation
seems to be fading. It is important for the consultant not to give in to
these feelings of malaise and to encourage families to attend a last
meeting. Reflecting on the group's importance, the efforts of those who
have attended, and celebrating the growth of the participants are all
ways to affirm the vital work accomplished in a parent group.

Finally, the consultant may want to combine the last group meeting with some sort of graduation ritual and party to celebrate the families. Providing a concrete token, such as a certificate of attendance that

acknowledges participation (see the Appendix), is another way to convey the consultant's respect for families as well as to symbolize the end of the group. This type of graduation ceremony often has special meaning for parents whose opportunities or motivation for taking part in groups has often been limited and whose own educational experiences may have had mixed results. Decorating the room or organizing a special meal that the families can share are other ways to bring the group to a close with an air of pride and enjoyment. It is frequently the families themselves who will take on this responsibility, sometimes to the surprise of the consultant.

> June had been hot and humid, and the hallways and classrooms at the child care center felt sticky and thick. The teachers were tired, looked forward to the summer break, and tried their best to make it through each day. Attendance at the center was dwindling. At the previous parent group, one participant suggested having a lunch to celebrate the end of the year, but the consultant, Dr. Bertrand, now wondered if anyone would show up and if it was worth the effort. Several days before the final group, Dr. Bertrand and the family worker, Ms. Chavez, called parents to remind them about the meeting, but it was hard to tell who was actually going to attend.
>
> On the morning of the meeting, Dr. Bertrand was surprised to see a number of parents arriving early, each with some food to share. By 9:30 A.M., it was clear that the turnout would be quite good, and the atmosphere in the room seemed both expectant and subdued. The table was loaded with wonderful dishes, many of them Latino specialties. Someone sent homemade flan even though she was unable to attend the gathering. Another parent had bought a beautiful layer cake.
>
> Dr. Bertrand spoke briefly about the year and also acknowledged the contributions made by Ms. Chavez, both as a translator and a co-leader. Dr. Bertrand and Ms. Chavez then gave parents certificates that proclaimed their attendance in the group and celebrated their efforts to learn and share with one another. This symbol seemed to mean a great deal to the group members, who accepted their certificates proudly. The parents also received booklets, prepared by the center, describing summer activities for children. The rest of the meeting passed quickly and was more like a social gathering than a structured group.

As the meeting drew to a close, Dr. Bertrand looked around the room and realized how fond she had grown of many of the parents as well as how much she had enjoyed the group experience. There were still gaps between the consultant and the parents, in terms of language, class, and culture, but there was a sense of closeness too. As the cleanup began, one of the parents turned to Dr. Bertrand and said (in Spanish), "We are happy today and also sad. We leave with full stomachs and happy hearts!"

This anecdote illustrates the importance of the closing ritual for both families and group facilitators. In this case, the good turnout and lovely food signified that the parent group had indeed held meaning for many parents. A consultant may mistakenly underestimate the significance of the group if attendance has been inconsistent or if he has not received much verbal feedback from the participants. Thus, it is important to give parents an opportunity to share with each other through both words and actions.

CONCLUSION
This chapter presents a range of possibilities representative of the many ways in which mental health consultants can come to know and work with families in early childhood settings. The goal in strengthening and expanding existing parent services is to form meaningful connections with the people who are most important to children—their families. In doing so, the implementation of a preventive model that extends the reach of the early childhood program creates links between families, schools, and mental health services.

chapter six

Observing and Assessing Young Children in the Early Childhood Program

It was early September, and the consultant had been at the preschool for 1 week. One morning, as she entered the building, a teacher quickly approached her saying, "I have to talk to you about one of my kids, Lorenzo! He's driving me crazy! He won't listen to me, he won't share, and he runs everywhere! I can't keep up with him. He's a cute kid, he's funny, but the only thing he wants to do is sit in my lap. Can you come and see him?"

It may be the first hour, first day, or first week, but it is certain that the consultant will soon be asked to respond to a teacher, an administrator, or another staff person who has concerns about a particular child. Often this is a child who is disruptive or unruly and hard to handle in a classroom. Sometimes it is a child who is having great difficulty entering into the routines and relationships of the group. Maybe a child's behavior seems puzzling, odd, or disturbing to a teacher. This chapter examines the process of referral and assessment as it is conducted in the model of on-site mental health consultation. This topic is approached by describing each step taken, from referral to observation, assessment, and designing interventions. Case examples illustrate the range of referrals and the contrasting paths taken in response to the initial request for help.

ON-SITE REFERRALS AND ASSESSMENT

Mental health professionals who work in clinical environments are accustomed to getting referrals and conducting intakes through relatively standard procedures. There is generally an established process by which information is obtained about a child and family, and often the reason for the referral is fully explored before the therapist ever meets the child. A referral to a therapist in a mental health clinic generally reflects a serious enough problem to warrant at least a short-term intervention. In contrast, referrals to a preschool-based mental health professional represent a wide continuum of issues. The referral may be the result of mild problems that can be addressed relatively easily and quickly. For instance, a teacher may ask for help in dealing with a young child who is having difficulty separating from his mother, crying every morning, and taking a long time to get involved in activities. This type of adjustment problem usually can be handled within the school setting, without the involvement of outside clinical professionals. At times, however, the initial referral may indicate serious and complex issues that need in-depth and long-term responses and may require the ongoing involvement of the mental health clinician. Optimally, the model encompasses this wide range of concern so teachers feel comfortable bringing both small and large problems to the attention of the consultant.

A second important difference that distinguishes the on-site assessment model is the opportunity to observe and assess both the child and the everyday environment in which that child spends so much of his time. The consultant can watch the child at circle time, in the playground, and during transitions. The mental health professional sees how the child functions alone, with peers, and with adults. The clinician can also observe the style, structure, and tenor of the classroom. In other words, the on-site consultant has the ability to understand the child through multiple direct observations in a familiar, natural, and comfortable setting. Furthermore, the clinician gains insight into the child's relationships with his teacher, his peers, and the school program. This allows the mental health consultant to formulate a much richer understanding of the transactional nature of the child and his environment and guides recommendations toward interventions with the child and his school.

On-site referrals and assessment also offer the consultant a chance to approach parents from the position of a school team member. As discussed in Chapter 5, many families avoid using mental health centers because of logistical or psychological barriers. Yet it is often much easier for a parent to interact with a mental health professional who is recognized as part of the community, someone seen playing with children in the classroom and interacting directly with the child's teacher.

In this model, assessment is intertwined with the ongoing collaboration with the early childhood education staff. Through the assessment process, consultants can readily gain access to the many resources available within the child's preschool—teachers, administrative staff, the family worker, an in-house translator, even the bus driver—and they have the chance for repeated contacts over time with all of these staff members. For example, some children who function well in a classroom have problems on the bus ride home when they may encounter difficult social situations at a time of day when their ability to cope is diminished. It may be the bus driver who first notices a change in a child's behavior and recognizes shifts that no one else in the early childhood program has observed. It is unlikely that this type of information would reach an outside clinician, whereas the on-site consultant is in an ideal position to receive the important day-to-day concerns of staff who perform varied roles in the child's life—concerns that may lead to a more broad-based referral. On-site consultants offer professional perspective and expertise when trying to understand a child, but they also have the opportunity to rely on the everyday knowledge and experience of those who know the child best, an opportunity that is rarely afforded in traditional off-site clinical practice.

SOURCES OF REFERRAL

As previously noted, referrals come from multiple sources in the preschool environment. Most commonly, teachers will raise concerns about a child. Yet at times the referral will come from an administrator whose knowledge about a family situation suggests that the child should be closely monitored.

> On one of the consultant's first days, the Head Start director made a point of speaking to her about Chandra, a 4-year-old child who was new to the program. During the school intake process, which occurred in the summer, a number of issues emerged that were of great concern. A social worker,

Mr. Delgado, had called the center, urging the director to take Chandra even though the center was nearly full. Mr. Delgado described an extremely turbulent family situation. Chandra's mother, a chronic substance abuser, had lost and then regained custody of her children, and Chandra's father was incarcerated. During periodic home visits, Mr. Delgado had found the children without any food and under little supervision. During the intake process, the family worker, Mrs. Williams, met Chandra's mother, who seemed moody and impatient but was adamant in her desire to find a good preschool for her child. Chandra herself had struck Mrs. Williams as an extremely thin, silent, and sad-looking child who did not interact with anyone during her visit to the center. These observations confirmed the need for the on-site consultant, Dr. Dawson, to observe and help monitor Chandra during the first weeks of school and to make contact with the mother during this time.

This case exemplifies a situation in which prior knowledge of a child, combined with the staff's firsthand observations during the intake, confirmed the need to involve the consultant promptly. It should be emphasized, however, that children with impoverished, unsettled, or stressful home environments will not necessarily require the consultant's involvement. For many children, the experience of attending a good early childhood program, with teachers who respond adequately to their needs, will sufficiently nurture their overall development and emotional growth. The consultant should therefore not presume that a child's adverse history will inevitably lead to the need for assessment or intervention.

Occasionally a family may initiate a referral, although this is rather unusual. Once the children become familiar with the consultant, they may even "refer" themselves by approaching the consultant and telling her they want to talk. Sometimes the consultant suggests focusing on a child, based on observations and interactions in a classroom, as in the following case.

It was wintertime, and the consultant, Ms. Cooper, had been at the child care center for several months. Four-year-old Juanita, a sweet, quiet Latina girl from a Spanish-speaking home, seemed to fade into the background of the busy classroom. One day Ms. Cooper observed a math lesson for a small group of children. The lesson involved identifying and labeling numerals. The consultant's attention was drawn to Juanita, the only child who seemed unable to follow the lesson or comprehend the task. When it was her turn, she smiled sweetly and consistently gave the wrong answer. The teacher, Mr. Hernandez, was bilingual and provided explanations to Juanita in both Spanish and English, but in both languages Juanita remained befuddled. Her delays did not appear to be related to limited English skills. Ms. Cooper watched Juanita more closely during other activities that day and noted that the child's language was extremely meager; Juanita also seemed lethargic, especially during the more structured activities. However, she did have friends to play with and was an openly affectionate child who loved to sit in the teacher's lap.

The previous vignette illustrates how the consultant may notice children whose difficulties are less evident in the classroom because they are compliant, quiet, and socially appropriate. It is difficult for any teacher to ignore an aggressive, loud, or domineering child, but the child who recedes into the background and does not make demands on the teacher will naturally be noticed less often. Again, this does not imply that all reticent, solitary children require mental health interventions. Instead, it suggests that the consultant, who does not have to manage a classroom of young children, is sometimes able to use a trained clinical eye to detect in children a developmental lag or other problem that should be explored.

The fact that referrals come from multiple sources is one of the benefits of this model; nonetheless, it also presents new complications for the consultant who is more accustomed to the structure of clinic- or office-based services. For example, suppose the consultant brings up questions and concerns about a child not raised for discussion by the teacher. Some teachers may feel appreciative that the consultant has drawn attention to this child, but others may feel threatened and become defensive or annoyed. It is possible that a teacher would perceive such a referral as an implication of her inability to handle the child, even if this is far from the consultant's mind. A teacher may feel protective toward the child if she believes that the consultant is overstating the child's problems or labeling him as damaged or abnormal. Others may suspect that the consultant's referrals are influenced by ethnic or racial biases. In the case of Juanita, the consultant's observations reverberated with the teacher, and once they began to talk, the teacher's own concerns about this child emerged. Another teacher might be more defensive or territorial, erecting barriers that the consultant would have to address before being able to have a productive discussion about the child.

Conversely, if a consultant does not respond to a teacher's referral with a compatible degree of concern or alarm, the teacher may feel misunderstood, angry, and alienated. For instance, a teacher may be upset by aggressive or unpleasant fantasy play that the consultant believes is developmentally appropriate. The clinician may not always share the teacher's level of concern, yet if she does not find a way to understand and respond to the teacher, the consultant may inadvertently appear unreceptive or detached. These dynamics are manageable and are part of building relationships with educators, but the consultant must be aware that the need for communication with school staff is essential throughout the referral process, especially in the early stages of the collaborative relationship. The consultant will need to create ample time for this communication, viewing it as a priority when responding to teachers' requests for intervention.

UNDERSTANDING THE REFERRAL

When a referral is made to the consultant by a teacher or other staff member, the first task is to understand its nature and meaning. Is the teacher wondering whether a child's behavior is "normal"? Does the teacher seem angry with the child? Is the teacher looking for reassurance, support, suggestions, or services? Does the teacher want this child out of her class? What are the teachers expectations vis-à-vis the consultant? When the referral is initiated by the consultant, it is incumbent on him to engage the teacher in a discussion about the child, explaining concerns and asking questions that may either confirm or contradict the clinician's perspective.

Ideally, a referral serves as the foundation for developing intervention strategies. The consultant helps the teacher feel more able to understand, relate to, and teach the child. In some cases, all that may be necessary is for the consultant to observe and offer reassurance about the referred child. In other situations, those preliminary observations will be only the beginning of a multifaceted plan. One of the consultant's first tasks in the early stages of the referral process is to make decisions, along with school staff, about what sort of assessment, if any, is needed. In addition, are there other immediate steps that should be taken? For instance, a child who is referred because he threw a rock at another child's head requires more immediate attention than a child who is impulsive and has a short attention span but has not behaved in an overtly dangerous manner. In the first situation, the child's parents should be contacted without delay, and a plan should be quickly formulated with the family and school. In the second case, the consultant has more time to explore the meaning of the behavior before taking action.

Understanding a referral from a teacher involves asking questions that help the teacher describe concerns in detail. Preschools are busy places, and teachers have little time to talk about their students. Often teachers initially describe a child in broad strokes, such as "I'm really worried about Joey." By asking questions that enable teachers to talk more specifically about the child, the consultant can help clarify the referral with the teacher and begin to make decisions about next steps. These questions might include

- What does the child do that makes you say he's acting . . . (e.g., "bad," "crazy," "strange," "different," "upset," "distracted")?
- How often do you notice this behavior? Has it changed recently?
- What do you like about this child? What are his strengths?
- What are the cultural and ethnic traditions of this child's family?
- What is his home life like?
- In what kind of community does he live?
- Is the child doing anything that is dangerous to himself or others?
- Is the child able to express himself verbally?
- How does the child socialize with peers and with adults?
- Has the child ever been in an early childhood environment before?
- Do you know of anything new or unusual that has happened in this child's life?

Teachers are keen observers, and these early conversations about a referral will give the consultant a fuller sense of both the child's functioning and the teacher's perspective and personality. However, the consultant must be careful not to spend excessive amounts of time amassing information about a child before taking any action. In a clinical setting, there is generally an extensive intake completed before decisions are made about appropriate interventions to try. In contrast, the on-site consultant tends to compile information more gradually and through a more dynamic process that involves listening, observing, and playing—all as an active participant in the school. Even as the assessment process continues, the clinician may begin a prompt intervention, such as recommending and helping to implement a classroom management plan.

BEGINNING THE ASSESSMENT

After an initial conversation with school staff, it may appear that further assessment is needed in order to understand the child and begin to make decisions about how to proceed. The first step the consultant generally takes is to make some informal observations of the child and, equally important, of the classroom environment. In conjunction with the staff, the consultant should also decide whether the child's parents should be contacted at this point or if it is better to gather more information and make some preliminary observations before engaging the family.

The consultant should ask the teacher about optimal times to observe the child. This conveys respect for the teacher and also will make the observation time more targeted. If the child has problems participating appropriately at circle time, the consultant naturally will want to coordinate his observation to include that activity. The consultant may also want to observe during other times of the day to get an overall sense of the child and to note changes in the child's behavior. When possible, it is best initially to monitor the targeted child without interacting. The child may behave differently or feel uncomfortable if she is aware that she is being observed, so the consultant must be discreet and sensitive, shifting his focus between directly watching the child and engaging in other classroom activities.

Observing as an on-site consultant presents distinct advantages. The clinician benefits from his presence as a known, trusted figure to teachers and children. Once viewed as someone who is part of the school, his visit to the classroom will not signal alarm or disrupt the group. Because the consultant is not a stranger, the children usually accept him as part of their school experience, and they will not be too distracted by wondering who he is or what he is doing in their class.

Another advantage of observing children as an on-site consultant is the ability to see a child in multiple contexts and times. It is rare for outside mental health professionals to be able to visit a child's school and almost unheard of to visit more than once. Yet the on-site consultant can be available throughout the school day to monitor the child and can follow up with subsequent observations over time. Suppose a child who is consistently aggressive on the playground is referred to an outside therapist. In trying to understand this behavior, the therapist must rely on secondhand information and, in unusual cases, might visit the school. When a therapist meets a child in a clinical setting, he must extrapolate the child's social conflicts, although there may be no evidence of these problems in the confines of the office. In contrast, the on-site consultant has the advantage of seeing the child during the time when problems are occurring. This is especially helpful when, as in the example of aggressive behavior on the playground, the child's problems emerge in social environments. The consultant can look for triggers to the child's aggression and can also see the child at other times of day, comparing behavior on the playground with that during other activities. The clinician can observe how the child's aggression is handled and surmise whether the reactions of the adults appear to be helpful as they respond to the child's behavior. Finally, the consultant can see how this child fits in with the rest of his class. Perhaps he is one of many active, physical boys whose energy seems to ignite aggression. Or maybe he lacks play skills and resorts to physical contact as a way to gain attention. Such differentials are extremely helpful in understanding the referral and are achieved with much greater ease by an on-site consultant than by an outside clinician.

These advantages clearly enhance the on-site consultant's ability to understand a referral early in the process—the opportunity to observe the child in multiple contexts and times, in a natural environment that includes interactions with peers and adults, by an adult who is a familiar member of the school community. Yet at times the consultant's familiarity and accessibility are disadvantageous when his aim is to observe a child quietly without being drawn into an interaction with other children. The consultant may wish to watch a given child without actively participating in the classroom, to recede into the background so he can fully concentrate and attend to the referral questions. If, however, the consultant is well known to the children, they are likely to draw him into the life of the class and to seek his active involvement. This is less likely to happen to a visitor, such as an outside professional, who is clearly established as someone who is there to watch but not participate. If the consultant removes himself from the activities of the classroom and does not respond to children who approach him, this distance may unintentionally increase the children's anxiety or confusion. In sum, the consultant needs to be aware of how his presence affects the group at any particular time and to remain flexible. The clinician may accomplish a lengthy, informative observation the first time he tries, or he may need to make several attempts before completing the observation.

Although the advantages of conducting observations as an on-site staff member far outweigh the disadvantages, there are some other obstacles that should be noted. The fact that the consultant performs multiple roles in the school setting can be confusing to young children. For example, if the consultant works individually with a child in a classroom, that child could develop a special attachment and may have difficulty understanding or accepting that the consultant is connected to other children in the room as well as the group as a whole. Depending upon this child's issues and personality, she may feel possessive and may not like the consultant to pay attention to anyone else. The child's still-evolving sense of time may add to her confusion, so that whenever the consultant enters the classroom, the student might expect to be taken out for an individual session. If the consultant is in the room to observe, he must be aware of these types of reactions from the children. In a manner that will not disrupt established bonds with individual children, the clinician needs to let them know that he is there for another purpose.

Observing the Classroom Environment

As already noted, on-site mental health consultation generally requires an informal, flexible approach to work. This becomes immediately clear when the consultant begins her observation. Young children are curious about and often uninhibited in their responses to a new adult who enters their classroom. The consultant should be prepared to be noticed by the children, greeted, and perhaps asked why she is in the room. An effective consultant is one who can shift between being an active participant in the classroom and an observer of the targeted child, and at times she will conduct these activities simultaneously. The consultant may find herself sitting at a table with four children who are using clay although the child she has come to observe is painting at the easel nearby. While engaged and active with the group, the clinician is also unobtrusively watching the solitary child.

When entering a classroom, the consultant should be sure to greet the teacher, to ask if it is a good time to visit, and to be aware of how her entrance may interrupt the flow of class activities. The classroom is the teacher's dominion, and the consultant must be mindful of this. The consultant should take her cue from the teacher as to whether she should sit quietly by the side or become more actively involved in what is going on in the room. Some questions the consultant should keep in mind when observing the classroom include the following:

- How many children are in the room?
- What is the ratio of adults to children?
- What is the physical setup in the room?
- Does the day allow for balance between active and quiet periods, structured and free play times?
- How are transitions handled?
- What qualities comprise the teacher's style (e.g., energy, patience, voice quality, affection, use of language, discipline style, sense of humor)?
- If there is more than one teacher, how do they get along?
- Do they have different styles, strengths, and responsibilities in the classroom?

When gathering information about the classroom, the consultant tries to understand how the identified child responds to that environment. To do this, the consultant should be open to what is actually seen as opposed to relying on assumptions about how a child may respond to a given teacher or setting. Suppose the consultant notices that a classroom is quite unstructured, with plenty of time for free play and relatively few teacher-centered learning activities. She cannot conclude how this environment affects an individual child without observing this interaction firsthand. Limited structure may add to one child's sense of disorganization and restlessness; another child may easily immerse himself in extended pretend play with other children and may thrive in the fluid, open-ended atmosphere. While observing, the consultant seeks to assess the fit between a child and a classroom environment, which can best be accomplished through multiple, direct, and unfettered observations.

Observing the Individual Child
When observing young children, the consultant offers the perspective of a professional whose knowledge of child development enables her to make informed judgments about what she sees. Preator and McAllister (1995) discussed the skills required for effective observation and assessment of young children. These include a knowledge of the range of typical development; the ability to distinguish delays from atypical development; an understanding of early childhood curricula; an awareness of related concerns, such as medical issues, and familiarity with a variety of instruments; and techniques for assessment and observation.

This section emphasizes the aspects of observation that are unique to the consultation model rather than reiterating practices that are elaborated elsewhere (Greenspan, 1992; Preator & McAllister, 1995; ZERO TO THREE: National Center for Infants, Toddlers, and Families, 1994b). It may, however, be helpful to highlight and review some basic areas that the consultant should keep in mind when conducting a classroom observation (see Figure 2). It is, of course, essential that the consultant also take into account a child's ethnic and cultural background, especially as it may differ from that of other children, teachers, or the consultant.

SHARING INITIAL IMPRESSIONS
AND PLANNING INTERVENTIONS
After the consultant has completed initial observations, he attempts to make a preliminary formulation about the child. This includes integrating the information he has culled about the child based on observations and discussions with staff, articulating the child's apparent strengths and weaknesses, and posing some working hypotheses about the presenting problem. At this point, it is important to share his thoughts with the teacher. Soon after observing the child, the consultant should set up a brief meeting with the teacher to discuss his impressions. It is impor-

1. *Overall first impressions*—Is the child playing alone or with others? Does she look happy, sad, or angry? Does the child look healthy? How is the child dressed? Does she appear alert and engaged? Does the teacher seem to like this child?

2. *Cognitive functioning*—Does the child have the expected concepts, such as early math skills and the beginning ability to use logic? Does the child have object permanence? Does the child ask questions?

3. *Large motor skills*—How does the child walk, run, and jump? Does he seem comfortable with his body? How does he sit in a chair? Does he fall down often? Is he cautious, bold, or overly risky with his body? Does the child observe physical boundaries (i.e., conventional space between himself and others)? How does he communicate with his body? Does the child seem to grab, hug, bump, hit, or lie down more often than the other children?

4. *Fine motor skills*—Does the child enjoy using her hands? How does she hold a crayon, a brush, or beads? Has the child established hand dominance? Can she manipulate zippers and buttons and tie her shoes?

5. *Language*—What language(s) does the child speak, and how does this compare with the classroom teacher's native language? Can the child be understood? Does the child use language to make his needs known? Does he seem to understand multistep verbal directions? Does the child appear to hear normally? Does he speak in one- or two-word sentences or use more elaborated language? Does the child appear frustrated by difficulties in verbal communication?

6. *Social/emotional*—Does the child tend to play alone or with others? Is the child able to share? To compromise? Does the child follow classroom rules? Does the child focus on the adults in the room or on other children? Does the child express a range of feelings? Can the child express feelings through words? Compared with the other children, does this child seem excessively aggressive, timid, anxious, or quiet? Does the child approach the teacher for help when needed, and how does the teacher respond? Do other children seem to like this child? How does the child relate to others? What is the level of relatedness?

7. *Play behaviors*—Does the child appear to enjoy playing? Can the child use her imagination? Is there evidence of symbolic play? How organized is the child in play situations? Does she create play sequences with more detailed narratives? Does the child prefer solitary or interactive play, and is she flexible in shifting between the two? Are there strong themes apparent in the play? Is there evidence of repetitive, anxiety-driven play?

8. *Temperament*—Is the child active and energetic? Quiet and low key? Does the child dive into new experiences, or is he cautious and slow to approach novel situations? Does the child seem to need a lot of interaction with others? How does he handle routines and alterations in those routines? How does the child respond to transitions? Does he eat and rest? Is the child unusually reactive to sounds, touch, or taste? Is she even-tempered or moody? Is the child strongly expressive of her emotions or more restrained? Can the child sit still for long periods, or does she need frequent changes in activities? Is the child impulsive and driven? Does the child's attention span tend to be long, short, or dependent upon the activity?

Figure 2.   Factors to consider when observing a child in the classroom.

tant that the consultant give these impressions in language that is clear, respectful, and supportive. The consultant may recommend some beginning strategies and schedule a time to follow up. This is also the time to determine subsequent actions, which may range from watching and waiting to initiating a multifaceted intervention plan.

By the time the consultant meets with the teacher, the original problem sometimes has resolved itself and does not require any further immediate action. This was the case with the student, Lorenzo, who was mentioned at the beginning of this chapter.

> *The consultant, Mr. Liu, and the teacher, Ms. Marshall, met to talk about Lorenzo, the boy whom Ms. Marshall had described as "driving me crazy!" Mr. Liu observed Lorenzo and noticed several things, which he then shared with Ms. Marshall. Lorenzo was an exuberant, bright-eyed 3-year-old who was physically active, extremely affectionate with his teacher, and quite accustomed to getting his own way. Lorenzo did not join the class during circle time on the day that Mr. Liu was in the room; instead, the child quietly played with puzzles in another part of the room and did not appear to disrupt the group. He seemed to enjoy many of the other activities, but his attention span was limited. Lorenzo found every possible opportunity to fling his arms around Ms. Marshall, squeezing her in a giant bear hug. This embrace was always returned, and the teacher generally seemed to enjoy this active, independent child. She was often able to cajole him into following the routines and rules of the room. As they talked, it became clear to both Mr. Liu and Ms. Marshall that Lorenzo was still adjusting to his first structured group experience and was already doing much better since the beginning of the school year. It was too soon to jump to conclusions about his activity level or attention span, and Lorenzo was lucky to have a teacher who had sufficient energy to keep up with him. The conversation ended with an agreement to keep in touch about Lorenzo but to take no further action at that time. Ms. Marshall seemed satisfied and somewhat relieved by this decision as well as pleased that Mr. Liu's findings concurred with her own.*

At other times, the teacher and the consultant may both agree that further assessment is needed. They should also decide whether the child's family should be contacted at this point, who should first make contact (teacher, consultant, or director), what should be said, and whether it would be best for the consultant or teacher to meet alone with the parent or whether they should organize a joint meeting. This concept is illustrated with the continuation of the vignette involving Juanita.

> Ms. Cooper met with Mr. Hernandez to talk about Juanita's progress in class. They talked about Juanita's slow pace in learning letters and numbers and her limited ability to listen to stories and answer questions about them. Also, Mr. Hernandez acknowledged that because Juanita was such a sweet and quiet child who did not demand much teacher attention, he had not realized how little Juanita seemed to be absorbing and how she often seemed "spacey" and "out of it." The child would be starting kindergarten in the fall, and Ms. Cooper was concerned that Juanita might need some form of special education support. The consultant recommended a full developmental evaluation, which would include a speech-language assessment, a psychological evaluation, and educational testing. Ms. Cooper and Mr. Hernandez then discussed how to broach the subject with Juanita's mother, who was a single parent from Central America with limited education and knowledge of English. They decided that Mr. Hernandez, who was Spanish-speaking, would invite the mother into school to talk about Juanita. Ms. Cooper would join them to explore with Juanita's mother the idea of testing, with the support and translating expertise of the teacher.

Sometimes the teacher and the consultant may agree that it is best to begin some sort of intervention, such as including a given child in a socialization group, while continuing to gather information about the child and making contact with the family. This point is shown in further exploration of Chandra's situation.

> The staff at the Head Start center continued to feel great concern about Chandra, whose solemn face and almost total lack of communication had not changed much since the beginning of the school year. When Dr. Dawson observed Chandra, she saw that although this child did not participate in any group activities, she was neither disorganized nor unmotivated in other ways. She often chose to play with highly structured materials, and she was able to complete

*puzzles appropriate to her age. Chandra also liked the
housekeeping corner, but only if she could play there alone,
gently holding, dressing, and feeding the dolls, without
uttering a word. After observing her several times, Dr.
Dawson met with Chandra's teacher as well as the school
director and the family worker. It was easy to feel
overwhelmed by the depth of Chandra's sadness and the
many needs and problems of her family. Nevertheless, they
came up with a place to begin. Everyone agreed that
although it might be difficult, it was important to attempt to
reach out to Chandra's mother, Ms. Vaughn. The family
worker, Mrs. Williams, relayed that Ms. Vaughn came in
fairly regularly to pick up bags of groceries that were donated
by a local charity and that they had talked casually several
times. The school team decided that Mrs. Williams would
make the initial contact with Chandra's mother, asking Ms.
Vaughn to meet with her, as well as the teacher and the
consultant, about Chandra's adjustment to the center. Dr.
Dawson would also use this meeting to talk about the
"Friendship Group" she was starting and to obtain written
permission from Ms. Vaughn for Chandra to participate.*

After the next steps are determined, the consultant and the teacher
should agree on a time frame for checking on the child's progress. This
may range from an informal moment to touch base (e.g., "Let's talk in
2 weeks and see if Lorenzo is able to sit a few minutes longer at circle
time") to a more structured meeting (e.g., "Let's invite the mother in to
talk about Chandra by next week"). Written notes that describe the observations and any initial recommendations can be given to the teacher
to help both the consultant and the teacher monitor their discussions
and future plans.

STANDARDIZED
INFORMATION-GATHERING TECHNIQUES
After the consultant and the teacher talk, they may conclude that to
better understand the child's behavior and issues, it would be benefi-
cial to do a more in-depth assessment, using some type of standardized
measurement tool. The consultant may also wish to do another observation using a more systematic approach. (An excellent summary of
systematic observations can be found in Hintze & Shapiro, 1995.) The
various assessment tools include behavior rating scales, developmental screenings, and psychological tests. Behavior rating scales are ques-

tionnaires completed by teachers and parents to obtain more information about behavioral and emotional functioning. Screening measures are administered by consultants, teachers, or other early childhood staff who have been appropriately trained. These brief tests of cognitive, language, and adaptive behaviors are designed to identify potential problems and gain a broad look at a child's functioning. (For an excellent discussion of early childhood screening, see Gridley, Mucha, & Hatfield, 1995.) Most Head Start centers and some prekindergarten programs are now required to administer a developmental screening to all 4-year-olds, so the consultant working in these environments will have easy access to screening information and may even participate in their administration and interpretation. Psychological tests of cognitive, perceptual, and personality development, used when children undergo full evaluations, are more thorough and must be administered by a trained psychologist or psychometrician.

Early childhood standardized assessment tools have both positive and negative features. One advantage of standardized measures is that they are useful in gaining a broader perspective on a particular child relative to the larger population. When one is immersed in a particular preschool community, it is often difficult to maintain an awareness of the severity or frequency of a child's problems respective to children outside the community or compared with local norms. Another positive component is that these measures cover a broad range of relevant behavior that can be missed by informal evaluations. Finally, standardized measures can be critical for documenting the need for special education services and for tracking a child's progress.

There are, however, a number of drawbacks of standardized assessment tools. Many behavior rating scales emphasize negative behaviors and do not tap strengths that may be part of the foundation for approaching problems constructively. Questionnaires may also intimidate teachers and parents and may erect barriers based on their feeling that the consultant is an "expert" who is detached or judgmental about the child and his family. Finally, although questionnaires may add some useful information, they cannot adequately capture the essence of any child's unique personality in the context of their particular family, culture, and school situation.

With an understanding of these advantages and disadvantages, the consultant may decide that in some cases he would derive some useful information about the child by using a rating scale or behavioral questionnaire. If this is the case, the clinician should not flood teachers with numerous questionnaires but should pick measures that pertain directly to the referral question and evaluate how cumbersome a given questionnaire is relative to the information it may yield. In addition, the consultant should carefully explain the purpose and limits of the questionnaire to the teacher and family. That way, those filling it out will understand that this is one way for the consultant to perceive the child from the point of view of the people who know that child best. The consultant should be familiar with a number of rating scales so he can choose the appropriate tool. A list of several frequently used behavior measures follows.

1. Behavior Assessment System for Children (Reynolds & Kamphaus, 1992)
2. Child Behavior Checklist (Achenbach, 1991)
3. Conners' Teacher Rating Scale–Revised and Conners' Parent Rating Scale–Revised (Conners, 1997)
4. Early Screening Project (Feil, Severson, & Walker, 1998)

After the consultant digests the information obtained from a rating scale, he should provide feedback in a timely manner to the teacher and the child's family. It is important to connect this feedback with intervention plans so the people who live and work with the child do not simply end up hearing confirmation of what they already know or leaving with a greater sense of pessimism. Some questionnaires, such as the BASC, do include questions that highlight the child's strengths, and these can be mentioned both to balance any negative information and to capitalize on positive aspects of the child when designing interventions.

In certain circumstances, the consultant may want to recommend that a child be given a complete developmental evaluation. This recommendation may emerge from the consultant's observations and discussions with teachers, from a review of the screening results, or from a request by the family. The consultant may suggest a full evaluation for children who might have language or learning delays, whose emotional challenges seem to be posing developmental roadblocks, or whose behavior and learning style remain puzzling and enigmatic over a period of time.

Evaluations are generally conducted by a private clinician or at an approved mental health agency or educational testing site. If the consultant is a psychologist, she is qualified to conduct a psychoeducational evaluation on site. Full evaluations typically include the following components: a cognitive and psychological assessment battery, perceptual testing (visual and auditory), speech-language testing, gathering developmental and family history, and a structured interview with the parent or caregiver to assess adaptive functioning. At times the psychological evaluation also includes assessments of emotional functioning via projective tests (special tests that reveal the child's internal emotional life) and a play observation. Less frequently, the consultant may also recommend testing by another specialist, such as a neurologist, a psychiatrist, an occupational therapist, or an audiologist. These types of professionals are most often contacted after completion of an overall developmental evaluation or when a child presents either a significant medical history (e.g., a head trauma, chronic and severe ear infections) or dramatic behaviors (e.g., hallucinations, serious motor impairments, persistent tics).

Evaluation Results and Recommendations

The evaluation process can be stressful, confusing, and mysterious for families, especially those who are less knowledgeable about testing, child development, and educational bureaucracies. Many families are unaware of the services for which their children may be eligible. Although there is variability across economic groups, generally the most educated and affluent families have greater access to information and learn to navigate the special education system, obtaining the most comprehensive services for their children. The consultant holds roles as both an "insider" and an "outsider"; therefore, he can be a vital link in leveling the playing field, acting as a liaison between a family and an agency and supporting the notion that all children who are eligible deserve thorough and professionally conducted evaluations.

Another important role the consultant serves during the evaluation process is to help both teachers and parents understand testing results once the evaluation is completed. Again, a useful approach is to think in terms of articulating the child's strengths and weaknesses as well as giving ideas about how the school, the family, and, in some cases, specialists can help the child. This point is demonstrated in the following scenario.

After Anthony's school received his test report, the consultant met with Anthony's mother, teacher, and the program director to discuss the findings. The clinician began by elaborating the good news, which was that Anthony's overall level of cognitive development was right on target for his age. Also, he had some impressive strengths, such as his visual-motor ability, his strong effort and motivation, and his artistic ability. The testing also clarified why Anthony was having so much trouble sitting still during circle time, listening to stories, or following the teacher's directions: It revealed a lag in his language development of over 1 year, a significant gap for a 4-year-old. These results helped the teacher and Anthony's mother understand that this little boy was not being intentionally oppositional or inattentive, and

*Anthony's mother was eager to learn how to obtain help for
Anthony through the preschool special education program.*

When testing confirms or delineates emotionally based problems, the consultant is faced with a particularly sensitive job of helping families understand the test findings and translating the results into practical applications. Resorting to the use of diagnostic categories (e.g., Oppositional Defiant Disorder, Generalized Anxiety Disorder) is almost always intimidating and frightening to parents and may be confusing to teachers. Using simpler explanations in language that is nonjudgmental is much more helpful, such as "Charisse's pictures and stories show how angry and helpless she feels. This might be why she has trouble concentrating and gets into fights with other kids." As an individual with an understanding of testing as well as an ongoing relationship with the preschool, the consultant is in an excellent position to help implement test recommendations and, in some cases, advocate services. In many programs, the recommendation for therapy will result in a referral to a therapist outside of the early childhood program. Consultants who offer on-site therapeutic services have the opportunity to both conduct the assessment and provide therapy within the school day.

CONCLUSION

On-site mental health consultants have an opportunity to expand the vital process of understanding children's needs and observing the interplay between the individual child, family, and school staff. Referrals come from diverse sources and typically encompass a wide range of issues and questions. When the consultant is a consistent presence in the preschool, it is more likely that the staff will raise both serious problems and less significant concerns, making it possible to address children's difficulties when they are milder and less entrenched. The on-site model also allows for in-depth assessments that reflect the child's functioning in multiple situations over a period of time. Both informal and standardized assessment methods are used, and there is room for flexibility and creativity in tailoring recommendations and collaborating with teachers to devise interventions. The on-site version of observation, assessment, and designing interventions is dynamically intertwined with the consultant's collaborative efforts with staff and families; in addition, it can demystify a process that teachers and parents often find overwhelming and confusing in more formal clinic-based practices. Rather than removing the child from his everyday setting for the purposes of evaluation, the on-site consultant is able to bring the assessment process to the child.

chapter seven

Therapeutic Interventions with Young Children

The early childhood consultation is designed with one central goal—to enhance the mental health of young children and their families. The interaction between consultant and child affords the most direct opportunity to meet this objective. The theoretical orientation, professional background, and individual style of mental health professionals may vary substantially within the field, but early childhood consultants typically share a number of objectives and values that form the basis of their work with young children. These include a recognition of the importance of the emotional development of children, a respect for early childhood education, a belief that educators have an important role in promoting the emotional well-being of young children, and a commitment to early intervention and the prevention of mental illness.

Within this generally accepted value system, consultants may possess a wide range of viewpoints regarding the most effective means to achieve these ends. This is just as true for the educational staff as it is for the mental health practitioners. Some teachers place greater relative weight on the importance of discipline and acquiring academic skills; others focus more on social and emotional development. Similarly, some consultants emphasize behavior modification and cognition when intervening with children whereas others give priority to understanding the emotional lives of children and developing relationships with them. This collaborative model is built on the belief that a child's behavior reflects his experience and expresses underlying feelings and conflicts. The model also strives to assist both children and staff in recognizing this connection. However, this approach does not preclude the use of behavioral interventions and psychoeducation, essential tools when intervening with preschool children and their families. The aim of interactions with children and staff is to promote a healthy emotional environment, with strong bonds between the adults and children in the community.

When working in early childhood settings, consultants have an opportunity to intervene on a variety of levels, through a broad range of modalities. They may conduct play therapy, behavioral treatments, parent guidance, family therapy, psychiatric evaluations, and psychological testing. The specific nature of the direct contact with children is determined by the needs of the center as well as the professional expertise of the consultant. Although all consultants should be trained therapists, equipped to assess and treat children, only psychologists are qualified to administer testing batteries, only psychiatrists are medically trained to prescribe medications, and social workers may be most competent in service coordination and community outreach. The consultant's profession will therefore influence the treatment methods she is able to offer and should be taken into account when an early childhood program selects a consultant or consulting agency. It is often in the best interest of the program to collaborate with an established mental health agency, well versed in the full range of mental health services, to ensure access to a broad range of professional disciplines. Regardless of their field, consultants should be committed to the goals of early childhood education and child care, have experience in family and child therapy, and have specialized training in the mental health needs of young children.

Direct therapeutic intervention with children is typically a central arena of the mental health consultant. This intervention can take on a multitude of forms, depending on the beliefs and qualifications of the consultant as well as the needs of the program. Consultants work both within the classroom—with the children as a group or with selected individuals—and outside of the classroom with small groups, individual children, and family members. At times, the consultant focuses on the identification and treatment of existing problems, whereas in other instances she works in a preventive manner with the whole class.

These are not, of course, mutually exclusive domains; therapy with individual children certainly includes the goal of prevention, and interventions in the classroom may address existing problems as well. In general, however, the consultant works with children in the classroom to facilitate positive emotional development by supporting the children's mental health and by addressing concerns—the normative and expected issues (e.g., separation, aggression) in addition to special problems that may emerge. The class may sometimes face particular challenges because of the group's shared exposure to a loss, a trauma, or another crisis situation. The role of the consultant in addressing trauma and crisis is examined extensively in Chapter 8.

PREVENTION IN THE CLASSROOM

The mental health consultant performs more than one service in the classroom. At times, she observes or intervenes with a particular child; in other instances, she engages with the classroom as a whole. This section examines the goals and activities of the consultant working with the classroom as a group. As discussed in Chapter 4, the consultant and the teaching staff join forces to develop a collaborative relationship in which they can define a mode of classroom interaction that best supports the mental health needs of the children. The form of this endeavor is, by definition, unique because it emerges from the individual needs and qualities of the teachers, the consultant, and the children. Some consultants tend to function as quiet observers with little or no participation in group activities; others become central players in classroom activities, focusing on group discussion and process. The roles of the consultant and the teacher also shift over time as needs change and trust develops.

Once a comfortable collaboration has been established, the consultant and the teacher begin to interact with the children as a group with the intent of supporting emotional strengths while addressing psychological concerns. The consultant and the teacher address these issues in a number of ways during free play and other unplanned interactions as well as in planned activities, such as circle-time discussion, storytelling, and puppet and dramatic play.

Informal Exchanges

Consultants can promote the goals of prevention in the classroom through spontaneous and casual exchanges with children and staff. By being available to discuss issues as they arise, the consultant is often best able to address the concerns that emerge directly from the children. The following vignette shows how mealtimes present an excellent opportunity for such informal exchanges.

Ms. Larson, a head teacher at a preschool, found that meals were most efficient when the children were encouraged to share in the preparation, serving, and cleanup, all the while keeping conversation to a minimum. The center's director, however, had recently suggested that informal conversing during meals could support language development. The consultant, Mr. Singh, felt that such group discussions could also nurture emotional growth. He believed that the group focus during meals was a natural time to help children express themselves verbally, articulating their own feelings while responding appropriately to the expressions of others. Mr. Singh therefore offered to join the class for meals. The eager and animated young children lost no time volunteering to participate in group discussions. Teachers and the consultant typically followed the lead of the children with discussions that ranged from the smell, sight, taste, and feel of the food they were eating to events that occurred at home and reflections on classroom activities. At times, Mr. Singh initiated discussion about a topic of some particular relevance to the classroom, such as feelings about a teacher's unplanned absence or an impending holiday or vacation. Despite Ms. Larson's initial reticence, she soon found that these little chats were enjoyable to all and also improved the classroom's atmosphere without causing breakdown in its carefully cultivated order.

Some teachers express the understandable concern that the unstructured nature of such conversation will contribute to disorder in the classroom; indeed, depending on the content, this can occur. Although verbal expression of negative feelings can lead to a more expressive, less controlled atmosphere, this short-term consequence is far outweighed by the long-term benefit of gains in understanding and support. In fact, opening such themes for discussion often has the opposite effect: Children can become unruly and disruptive when their feelings remain unaddressed but continue to lurk beneath the surface, and they are usually calmed when given the chance to express themselves and to be understood by an adult who listens to them.

Of course, it should be noted that these group discussions are not meant to be biased toward more difficult or painful emotional content—the children are free to express both negative and positive thoughts and feelings. The open sharing of joy, excitement, and other warm and loving feelings is an equally important part of establishing a therapeutic environment in the classroom. Young children, especially those who live in difficult home environments, need the opportunity to experience happiness in the classroom as much as they need the chance to freely voice their problems and concerns.

Michael loved music and dance. He would particularly come alive when his teacher, Ms. Santos, played one of his favorite tapes. Not only did Michael experience pleasure from the simple joy of expressing himself through dance, but he welcomed the notice and praise he received when his skilled and graceful movements were observed by classmates and teachers. Fortunately, Ms. Santos was someone who loved music and dance and spontaneously integrated musical activities into the class routine. Although more reserved teachers seemed less comfortable joining in the free-flowing dance, Ms. Santos's obvious enjoyment was infectious, leading to full participation and laughter that echoed down the hallways. It was not until sometime later that the consultant fully understood the value of these experiences for Michael. At home, Michael's mother was suffering from severe depression, insisting on darkness and quiet for much of the day as she tried to sleep away the hours. Michael struggled through this trying period at home, turning to his classroom for laughter, dance, and song.

Joyful self-expression in music, art, and play can, in itself, be therapeutic for children. The consultant can communicate these achievements directly to teachers who may not always be aware of how valuable such activities are for children, particularly for those from more depressed or less enriched home environments. In addition, informal group discussions very often lead to warm, humorous exchanges. These moments afford the opportunity for a good laugh, improving the mood of the children and boosting morale of the staff. Of course, the laughter is only therapeutic when children feel they are laughing with the adults, not being laughed at or ridiculed.

Ms. Toby was leading the children in a circle-time discussion about their free-play activities. She had noticed that James was intensely engaged in the dramatic play area, meticulously dressed in men's clothing and carrying a briefcase. She commented on his activity, asking him who he was pretending to be. The reserved youngster responded that he was Daddy. "And how is Daddy feeling today?" Ms. Toby asked. "Good" was James's curt response. Ms. Toby continued to draw him out by asking, "I wonder what made Daddy feel good today?" Without missing a beat, James responded, "The Dow Jones is up 10 points." Though the humor may have been lost on the children, the laughter of the adults was infectious, causing James to grin widely at the merriment he had produced.

Laughter is, at times, the best medicine, lifting spirits and contributing to group cohesion in the classroom. Again, it is often the role of the consultant to remind teachers of the value of such exchanges, which can be taken for granted or overlooked in the course of a busy school day.

Planned Activities

Consultants and teachers collaborate to build a therapeutic emotional environment during informal group discussions as well as in planned special activities and within the daily routine. Most early childhood programs incorporate some time during the day when the children join as a group to be greeted, sing songs, read stories, and have lessons and group discussions—this is commonly known as circle time. This important group activity is an excellent means for the consultant to join the teachers in addressing emotional issues.

Storytelling   As the teacher devises the curriculum and thus sets the agenda for circle-time activities, the consultant typically follows the lead of the teaching staff, participating in activities when appropriate and contributing to group discussions as indicated. When the teacher reads a story to the children and initiates discussion of its meaning, the consultant may raise related themes that address meaningful emotional issues. These themes can be special topics evoked by the story (e.g., scary feelings, saying good-bye, the birth of a sibling), or they may simply attempt to help the children recognize the emotion portrayed, label it verbally, and consider this feeling within themselves. In fact, storytelling is a way to promote the emotional health of the classroom, and consultants often find themselves particularly involved in such activities. Consultants may volunteer to read books to the children, and many acquire their own library of books with thematic relevance to current classroom issues and activities. They may themselves read the books and discuss them directly with the children or offer their resources to the teacher, providing suggestions for appropriate use in each instance.

Personalized Books   Some consultants find that they can create books around special topics to enhance therapeutic aspects of the classroom. This allows them to address subjects that have a timely relevance for a particular class. Children typically respond well to this approach, as they are eager to recognize themselves, their environment, and their feelings in a story that was custom made for them.

> *Dr. Lind was preparing the children for her impending maternity leave. She decided to use this as an opportunity for the children in the Head Start program to say good-bye to her and to express their feelings about separation and loss. In addition, they would be able to articulate other concerns that are often stimulated by the birth of a child, including issues of sibling rivalry, maternal preoccupation, and the wish to be babies themselves. Dr. Lind decided to create a storybook with pictures that would explain her upcoming absence in simple, understandable terms. This book would also communicate her own feelings of sadness and address some other related issues that might be incited by her pregnancy. Dr. Lind read the book to each classroom during circle time and left a copy with a photograph of herself in each room. The children commented on the story as it was told, asking pertinent questions and offering information about their own experiences, and, finally, expressing sadness at saying good-bye. One child asked to "keep this book right here in the room so we can look at it whenever we get sad that you're gone."*

Not only do homemade books articulate issues of particular relevance, they also exist as concrete items with meaningful pictures that children can hold and touch. In this way, books can function as transitional objects, helping young children hold on to representations of people, even when those people are not present. A variety of homemade books can be used to achieve this goal; some classes create group picture books that document activities over time and become a record of people who have left the class. In addition to writing and illustrating an original story, teachers and consultants can use carefully selected literature, photo albums, and videos to highlight and elaborate on important emotional themes, to document the preschool experience, and to create a lasting visual presence of absent friends and teachers.

Dramatic and Creative Arts   Similarly, puppets, dramatic play, and creative arts are excellent vehicles for expanding the range of emotional experience in the classroom. Whereas most educators typically incorporate these activities into their curricula, the consultant can provide a useful contribution, as he is trained to understand the meaning of children's expression and to make use of these interpretations in a therapeutic manner. Most preschool children love to enact stories, ideas, and feelings through puppets or other theatrical activities. These activities can be particularly relevant when issues of special concern are addressed.

> In a therapeutic classroom for children with emotional problems, the consultant joined the teacher in using puppets and fairy tales to address important themes. Two puppets, one with a sad face and the other with a happy face, were used to introduce "talking time" and became central figures for the class as the children recognized and expressed their own feelings. In addition, enactment of fairy tales became favorite activities designed to address key issues and worries. For example, the children repeatedly enacted "The Three Little Pigs" as a means of communicating their experiences with residential instability. In this way, they were able to articulate their worries about lack of shelter and their fears about the dangers they faced in their daily lives.

In the presence of safe and responsive adults, the children could identify, lend voice to, and strive toward mastering their painful feelings by acting them out in dramatic form.

Music Activities   Depending on the consultant's special skills or interests, he can also use his own artistic or musical abilities to enrich the therapeutic nature of the classroom.

> Dr. Douglas enjoyed singing and guitar playing as a hobby. When consulting at an early childhood program, he would bring his guitar for special holidays and school events. He typically played the classroom favorites but would also add some of his own selections that were particularly aimed at recognizing and labeling feelings. He developed his own version of "If You're Happy and You Know It" to encourage children to imagine a wide range of emotions and to describe them verbally. When he completed his internship at the program, Dr. Douglas compiled a songbook with words, music, and photos that had particular meaning to each classroom.

Again, music activities are central to any good program in early childhood. The consultant typically has an understanding of its therapeutic uses that can complement the teacher's curricula in the creative arts, even when he or she lacks any specialized abilities in the area.

Special Themes   In addition to these creative arenas, the consultant can contribute substantially to organized discussions about important themes, such as planned holidays and vacations, as well as unplanned events, such as illnesses or sudden absences. As mentioned previously, the consultant usually follows the formal agenda set by the teacher, although there are instances in a well-functioning collaboration when the consultant initiates such conversations on her own.

> *Dr. Berg entered Ms. Jefferson's classroom and was surprised and saddened to learn that Joey was no longer attending school. There had been no advance notice, and the children and staff did not have an opportunity to say good-bye. The consultant observed that Joey's sudden absence was not discussed with the other children. It soon became evident that this pattern of abrupt withdrawal from school was not an isolated event, as the children at this program for homeless families were often placed in new housing without warning. The teachers were struggling with this themselves and were becoming increasingly frustrated with the lack of foresight and planning. They found themselves feeling both angry at the system and upset about their own feelings of loss regarding the child's unexpected departure. Consequently, the teachers were unwittingly compounding the class' struggle. They avoided confronting their own feelings and, in so doing, left the children to cope with this sudden loss without preparation or reflection. Dr. Berg therefore took it upon herself to address Joey's absence during circle time when attendance was taken. She asked who was missing today and was surprised to be answered not only with Joey's name but also with a long and accurate list of every other child who had suddenly vanished from their classroom family. Dr. Berg then initiated a discussion of what happened and why, offering the children and staff the occasion to voice their feelings about losing their friends and allowing them the freedom to voice any associated concerns that were stimulated by these abrupt departures.*

It is often particularly difficult for teachers to start these discussions because they may find themselves close to the painful feelings the children are experiencing. When consultants initiate such explorations, teachers and children are usually relieved. Although consultants often become integral members of the school family, they often have a role that is akin to that of a more distant relative: They are a little further from the intensity of feeling experienced by the nuclear family and, as a result, are better able to initiate such difficult discussions.

The "one step removed" position of the consultant often helps him observe classroom events from a different perspective that can be useful to teachers and children. He can encourage children to examine and verbalize their feelings as they prepare for significant events and changes in their lives. This is true when confronting major transitions, such as absences, new arrivals, illnesses, and injuries, and when preparing for adjustments in the classroom as well. When, for example, the class is actively engaged in the practical preparations for their impending graduation, the consultant can remind the children about the reality of the transition, encouraging them to express their feelings about this momentous ending. Although the busy preparations do have value in helping the children to master the transition, they can also obscure the reality of the event and may limit opportunities to process the meaning of saying good-bye to teachers and friends. The consultant can help the group confront these topics, giving children a way to explore and voice their emotions as they prepare for new situations. The consultant, by virtue of his training as well as his position in the classroom family, can address themes that are salient to the class as a whole but may be difficult for teachers to acknowledge.

In addition to differences in training and his "family role," the consultant is unencumbered by the practical academic and caregiving activities of the teachers and is thus free to engage with children in a different way. All good teachers are adept at listening to children and hearing what they have to say, but the consultant is often able to spend more time focused on this critical activity. Not only does the consultant listen closely to the wide range of preschool communication, he also is particularly inclined to hear the meaning behind these often cryptic expressions. The teacher may be the first to pick up on the emotional content and to demonstrate compassion; the consultant then has the time to allow the child to discuss concerns, joining the child as she experiences these difficult emotions. Ideally, the consultant's training and experience allow him to tolerate ambiguity and emotional distress and have expanded his ability to adjust to the amorphous, atemporal, and, at times, disjointed quality of a young child's communications.

Similarly, the consultant must have or develop a comfort with the physicality of young children. As most teachers are well aware, preschool children typically engage the world tactilely and are eager to have physical contact with their caregivers through hugging, sitting in laps, and other forms of touching. They also have a healthy interest in natural body processes and often express these interests without censor—a quality that can be endearing or unsettling, depending on the content of a child's communication and the responses of the adults. Although careful to observe appropriate boundaries, the effective consultant is open to children's natural curiosity about physical processes and strives to understand their communications and to respond to their concerns.

Over time, young children become remarkably capable of recognizing the therapeutic function of consultants and eventually come to see them as classroom therapists, enlisting clinicians when they feel the need for extra help or discussion about important issues.

> *Dr. Perez was the consultant for a large nursery school program. One of her duties was conducting individual therapy sessions with a select number of children. While participating in the routine circle time, the consultant observed that Mia, a 4-year-old child who had not yet been seen individually, was becoming upset during a group discussion about families. She became increasingly agitated and, before the teacher or the consultant could address her feelings, she raised her hand and said, "I have a lot on my mind; can I have an appointment with Dr. Perez?" Mia did get the opportunity to "consult" with Dr. Perez and, as problems continued to emerge and as her mother was eager for assistance with Mia's difficulties, Mia began individual therapy with the consultant.*

It is unusual for such a young child to make such a specific and appropriate self-referral for psychological treatment, yet children do tend to recognize the role of the consultant and, when feeling particularly distressed, actively seek increased contact. More typically, however, it is the consultant who becomes familiar with the children and then identifies certain individuals who may need psychological services. In addition, parents, teachers, and other staff members often develop concerns about particular children and refer them to the consultant for evaluation. One of the great strengths of this collaborative model is the availability of the therapist to provide emotional support to all and to work more intensively with those having special mental health needs, many of whom have no access to formal clinical settings. Likewise, teachers, parents, and staff have a known, trusted, and available professional to whom they can turn when they believe a child is in distress.

ESTABLISHING THE FOUNDATION FOR TREATMENT

Whether initiated by the consultant, a parent, a physician, a teacher, or the child herself, once the referral has been made and the assessment indicates a need for psychological intervention, the consultant can then lay the groundwork that supports the treatment process. In traditional settings, a primary caregiver must physically transport the child to the clinic or private office, which serves as an implicit agreement to treatment. Eventually, this implied permission becomes explicit consent when the parent signs a formal agreement or treatment plan. By contrast, when working with children on site, the consultant may identify a child for evaluation even before the parents indicate concern and well before they start the evaluation process. When the preschool staff believe an assessment is necessary before the family does, the staff must present this matter to the primary caregiver and seek to engage the family in the process. In these cases, there is a risk that parents may choose not to have their children evaluated, as the process may have begun prior to their direct involvement, and they may not share the viewpoint of the consultant and teaching staff.

A parent's acceptance is of course required for the treatment to proceed, and ongoing involvement is a fundamental aspect of any therapeutic intervention. It is therefore essential that the consultant and early childhood staff involve the family as soon as they determine that therapy may be warranted. The staff and the consultant may observe the child and have an initial discussion about an evaluation, but the primary caregiver should be contacted and must grant informed consent before proceeding further. Family participation is contingent on their level of concern and acceptance of treatment: The parents may become immediately involved as caring, active participants and allies in the process, or they may resist treatment until they concur that their child needs therapy, they feel safe in the school environment, and they trust the consultant's competence and intent.

Yet engaging a child in effective treatment requires more than the family's permission. The consultant must also be supported by the teachers and the director as well as key staff members, such as social workers, speech-language therapists, and other specialists. Just as the parents require varying degrees of engagement, depending on whether they initiated the treatment or agree with recommendations, so too does staff participation depend on whether they made the referral and if they share the clinician's level of concern. In addition, the staff member's degree of involvement with the child will have a significant effect on the nature of the engagement with the consultant. Although the director may do little more that acquiesce to the intervention, the specialists may contribute to the evaluation and treatment planning, and the teachers may be involved in the therapeutic process on a daily basis.

Designing Interventions

Once the need for treatment has been established, the consultant can collaborate with parents, teachers, and specialists to design an intervention plan that best meets the needs of the child and his family. As previously discussed, the form of the treatment will, in part, be determined by the philosophical orientation, training, and discipline of the consultant as well as the needs, beliefs, and physical space of the early childhood environment. One of the strengths of this model is the expanded opportunity for interventions that emerge when the therapist is an integral part of the preschool community. It may, for example, be determined that a child who has experienced a serious trauma would benefit from twice-weekly individual play therapy outside the classroom as well as monthly family therapy sessions. In contrast, a child with a circumscribed behavior problem, such as enuresis during naptime, might not need individual treatment but may be helped indirectly through consultation with teachers to determine appropriate management in the classroom. Similarly, once the consultant is an established member of the community, parents might seek her out for advice and support, even when formal therapy is not indicated. The traditional therapist rarely has the freedom to design this range of interventions. Furthermore, the clinician often has the opportunity to work with individual children within the classroom and, when such an option is available, to conduct formal therapy in a separate, dedicated space that is still within the familiar surroundings of the early childhood program.

The location of the intervention has clinical as well as programmatic implications. Some programs adhere to a strong inclusion mandate, which demands all services be conducted within the classroom, whereas others make allowances for individual counseling. The collaborative model supports the belief that the needs of young children should be addressed in the least restrictive manner and that they should be integrated in the classroom to the greatest extent possible. Nonetheless, there are instances in which the clinical requirements of the child and the classroom are best met when individuals are pulled out for special services and, in rare cases, placed in a smaller classroom where teachers and staff are specially trained to meet particular therapeutic needs. In this way, children can obtain necessary services at this early and critical juncture, increasing their readiness for inclusion when school begins. A variety of matters can be successfully explored within the classroom, yet some children need intensive play therapy that requires the space, supplies, and privacy of a separate room. Just as family therapy would not be indicated in a bustling classroom, neither should all of the intimate psychological concerns of young children be addressed in such a public forum.

INTERVENTIONS IN THE CLASSROOM

For some children, therapy begins in the classroom as a means of making the transition to the outside space. For others, it has been determined that treatment will only occur in the room. For still others, there may be a combined approach in which some issues are addressed in the classroom while the more individual psychological concerns are attended to in the separate space. In general, the classroom provides an ideal environment for consultants to focus on issues that are predominately social or academic in nature. Consultants trained in assessment and remediation of learning difficulties can collaborate with teachers to identify and address academic delays. In this way, the consultant has the opportunity to observe firsthand over time how the child functions at school and, when indicated, to participate directly in academic activities with the child. With the exception of school psychologists, this is in contrast to the experience of most therapists, whose involvement with schools is limited to isolated observation and infrequent teacher consultation that is usually structured around crises.

Children with peer difficulties or other social problems can also benefit from classroom interventions. Again, consultants can observe the children's "real-world" environment over time and in many social contexts. Clinicians can intervene with social issues as they emerge, having an immediate impact, rather than dealing with concerns through secondhand reports after they have occurred. For children whose problems are circumscribed, treatment may be limited to such interventions within the classroom. Those whose needs are multidimensional, affecting a variety of areas, may get help with social and academic matters in the classroom while more emotional and familial problems are addressed in therapy sessions outside the classroom. The latter method is demonstrated in the next example.

> Maria was a shy 4-year-old Latina girl who appeared to be behind in her academic skills. It was, however, difficult for her teacher to identify the child's particular weaknesses because Maria refused to speak in class. It was unclear whether this refusal was a result of difficulties with English, general problems in expressive language skills, or emotional concerns. It was soon agreed that the consultant, Dr. Joseph,

would evaluate Maria. As a result of her assessment, Dr. Joseph discovered that Maria was animated and highly verbal in both English and Spanish at home. Maria's mother described a number of family problems and expressed an eagerness to address these concerns in therapy. Maria's withdrawal did appear to be emotional in origin; nevertheless, her prolonged shyness in class had caused her to fall behind in learning. Dr. Joseph set up a plan of intervention that included individual play therapy with Maria as well as family therapy and parent guidance in the on-site therapy room. Dr. Joseph also visited the family at home several times. Although she examined the issues underlying Maria's withdrawal in sessions outside the classroom, Dr. Joseph worked with the child's shyness on a behavioral level in class by encouraging social interactions with peers. In addition, the consultant used puzzles, books, and drawing to help Maria attain the skill level that would be expected for her age and cognitive abilities. This multifaceted approach resulted in Maria's full classroom participation and acquisition of age-level skills by the end of the year.

In this case, addressing the child's needs across a wide range of contexts achieved a primary goal of collaboration—the amelioration of problems at an early age so that children are able to enter kindergarten at grade level without additional educational or therapeutic services.

Special Considerations for On-Site Therapy

Whether occurring in a private office, a clinic room, or an off-site space, the actual work of individual and family therapy is shaped primarily by the skills and beliefs of the therapist and the needs of the child and family. In general, the interventions that take place outside the classroom proceed in a manner comparable to that occurring in any other therapy setting. Nonetheless, there are significant differences in context that affect the substance of treatment, including the nature of engagement, the shape and duration of the process, and the role of the therapist in assisting transitions before and after the clinical hour.

As noted previously, conducting therapy within the preschool community tends to support the engagement process for children as well as their parents. Families need not face logistical barriers and travel to an unfamiliar medical or institutional setting to obtain treatment. Furthermore, as they become accepted in early childhood programs, consultants have the opportunity to help families navigate external systems, such as special education providers, social service caseworkers, child protective agencies, adult intervention services, and other organizations providing mental health or social services.

However, the very community context that supports the process for most can be disconcerting to some families. Communities tend to be familiar and comfortable but they are also, by definition, quite public. A clinic or office environment may seem distant and unfriendly to some, whereas others welcome the anonymity provided by such settings and the reassurance that treatment will proceed in a private manner. It is therefore incumbent on the consultant as well as the early childhood staff to recognize the public nature of their center and to protect families' privacy to the greatest extent possible. In general, the individuals involved in the process should maintain confidentiality, discussing the relevant aspects of treatment only after obtaining permission and only with those directly involved with the child. It is often best to allow the family to set their own parameters around the degree of privacy they require. Some families will disclose little to anyone besides the therapist. Others will openly discuss their child and the treatment process in highly public settings.

Unlike in a clinic or a private office, on-site treatment depends on a number of program variables. Whereas appointments in traditional settings usually occur at the same time and in the same place, therapy in preschool environments tends to be far more variable, occurring on irregular days, at various times, and in different spaces, subject to the physical constraints of the center. Although this inconsistency can be a barrier to the treatment process, it does offer some advantages in its inherent flexibility. For less organized or cooperative families, the task of arriving at scheduled clinic appointments in a regular and timely manner may not be possible. As most clinicians are aware, it is often these families who are in greatest need of such interventions. A therapist who works on site more than once a week is likely to see the child with even the most erratic attendance on the days that child is present, without waiting for an anointed day and time.

Nevertheless, the timing of therapy in early childhood settings is contingent on the center's hours of operation. Typically, there is little opportunity for evening family appointments. The length of treatment can be constrained by the program's calendar; long vacations and summers can impose limits on occasions for intervention over time. When therapy ends with the school year, preschoolers are often faced with a number of difficult endings occurring simultaneously. Consultants can, however, often navigate their way around these limitations. Some centers offer flexibility in available hours, so consultants can meet with families in the early morning or late afternoon when the program is not in session. Many therapists find that school closings afford an excellent opportunity for home visits, a useful adjunct to ongoing treatment on site. Alternatively, consultants may continue to see families at their host agency or private office during school holidays and summers and may provide treatment after the child leaves the program if continued intervention is indicated. For many children, a year of therapy that parallels their preschool experience can be an appropriate amount of treatment, allowing them to enter kindergarten at grade level without the need for further intervention.

Another key difference between individual or group treatment in traditional environments and on-site therapy is the child's need to make the transition between the therapy room and the classroom. It is the role of the therapist to support this process by carefully choosing appropriate times to remove the child for treatment and by spending time in the classroom after the clinical hour is complete. At times, consultants may deliberately guide the treatment process in such a way that the child has the chance to back away from difficult clinical material at the end of the session so that he can better manage the return to the classroom routine. In the clinic, a therapist may choose to push a little harder, encouraging the child to make clinical gains even if that results in some short-term distress, as the child will not be immediately faced with the demands of a formal school setting. Therapists cannot ensure that all transitions will go smoothly, but they can remain aware of the need to support a child's return to the classroom and to manage difficulties in transitions as they arise.

Communication with Teachers

When a clinician sees a child for group or individual therapy in a clinic setting, she may occasionally speak with the child's teacher, but when conducting therapy within an early childhood program, it is imperative that communication be much more frequent. Although there is a need for ongoing dialogue between the teacher and any specialist who takes a child out of the classroom, it is especially important for the mental health consultant to do so. First, many teachers feel mystified and perhaps intimidated by therapy, and without ongoing communication, the barrier between teacher and consultant may grow wider. Second, in contrast to other specialties, such as speech-language or occupational therapy, the nature of psychotherapy elicits strong feelings and can sometimes make the transition back to the classroom more complex for the teacher as well as the child. Unless the consultant talks with the teacher about goals, observations, and the therapeutic process, the teacher may feel resentment and confusion when a child returns to class appearing more fragile than he was before he left. Conversely, the consultant needs to listen to the teacher's observations about the child to assess the therapy's impact and to adjust the tempo and intensity of the work when necessary. Finally, it is typical that the behaviors and issues seen in therapy will mirror what the teacher sees in the classroom. Sometimes, however, a child may behave quite differently in therapy, and this can be confusing or alarming to a teacher if it is not discussed and understood.

On the surface, it would appear that frequent communication with teachers would not be difficult; nevertheless, it takes a concerted effort on the part of the consultant. It is optimal for the therapist to talk briefly with a teacher immediately after the therapy session, giving some feedback about what he noticed about the child. Even a brief comment, such as "Mark was having a lot of trouble sharing in the sandbox in group, but he worked really hard on waiting," gives the teacher some sense of the child's behavior. Equally important is the fact that the child senses that the consultant and teacher are working together on his behalf and are openly sharing their observations of him. Often, however, a teacher is busily engaged with other students when the child returns to the classroom, and it is not an opportune time to speak. Similarly, the consultant has constraints on his time that make it difficult to meet at other times during the school day. The best approach is to ask the teacher when she can meet and to try to connect at least weekly to share information about a child's progress. Some teachers may prefer that this occurs in a quiet corner of the classroom during a time when an aide can supervise the children. Other teachers will opt for a meeting during a break, before or after school. Once again, flexibility and the avoidance of rigid protocols are vital to finding ways to communicate with teachers.

> Steven was a bright and active 4-year-old who seemed
> highly distressed about separating from his mother in the
> beginning of the preschool year. He had run out of the
> classroom, attempting to leave the building several times,
> which concerned his teachers. As time passed, Steven
> settled in nicely to the routines of the class. Ms. Crosby, his
> teacher, referred him to the therapeutic group because she
> felt that Steven's self-esteem was shaky; he sometimes would
> erupt in unprovoked anger, and he had much trouble
> sharing. As the year progressed, Steven became calmer and
> happier in the classroom, and this change was reflected in
> the group sessions as well. Near the end of the academic
> year, however, Steven began to show in the group some of
> the same problematic behaviors he had displayed in the fall,
> although he remained quite contained in the classroom.
> During one group session, Steven suddenly became

*oppositional and angry, tried to run from the room several
times, and finally lay on the floor crying, "I want my
mommy!" He was not able to talk about what was upsetting
him, although the consultant, Mr. Shaw, was able to return
with Steven to his classroom. By this time the child was less
emotional but still clearly upset. As Mr. Shaw walked into
the room with Steven, Ms. Crosby exclaimed, "He wasn't
like that before!" Mr. Shaw stayed with Steven for several
minutes in the room where the child was able to reorganize
himself slowly. It was clear that, in this situation, the teacher
perceived that the consultant had somehow made Steven
"worse," and this needed to be addressed immediately.*

*Later that day, Mr. Shaw sought out Ms. Crosby, and they
talked about how sometimes children regress temporarily or
act out when their feelings have been evoked. They also
discussed how Steven's anxieties about separation were
escalating as the end of the school year approached, and
they tried to think of positive ways to help him cope with his
fears. Mr. Shaw reassured Ms. Crosby that he would work
with Steven to contain the child's feelings and would assist
in the transition back to the classroom.*

INDIVIDUAL THERAPY

Once the consultant, teachers, social services staff, and parents agree
that individual treatment is indicated, the consultant can begin the
process of forming an alliance with the child. Unlike clinic-based interventions, the therapeutic process may have already begun, as the consultant is typically known by all of the children in the classroom. Most
commonly, this familiarity is an advantage because the child is eager to
have his own special time with this well-known adult, who is, ideally,
well regarded and trusted. In addition, the work can begin, and may
continue to take place, in the comfort of the child's own classroom
where she is secure in her familiar environment, surrounded by teachers and peers.

When intervening with individuals within the classroom, the therapist engages the child as she would in any other context but with certain variations. A major difference is that the direct clinical activities and
those related to indirect work with teachers tend to blend so that both
occur within the same session and, sometimes, the same interaction.

*Keisha was an obese preschooler who was being seen
individually for her depression as well as for family work
related to parental conflict, illness, and drug histories.*

During snack time, Keisha began to eat at a feverish pace. Her teacher had difficulty disguising her disgust and abruptly instructed, "Stop stuffing yourself," urging Keisha to use her napkin, slow down, and "eat like a big girl." The therapist turned to Keisha and said, "You must be so hungry." Keisha, who seemed distressed by her teacher's reprimand, nodded sadly. The consultant then added, "I think that sometimes when you're sad, you feel very hungry inside; it must be hard to ever get full." Again, Keisha agreed. The consultant then turned to the teacher and said, "I think you're right— the grown-ups do have to help Keisha slow down when she eats. Maybe we can help her feel better inside so she won't need to go so fast."

In this example, the consultant intervened in a variety of ways: She joined the child by affirming Keisha's affective experience without judgment and interpreted the child's behavior by suggesting that her need to overeat was connected with feelings of emotional hunger and emptiness. Simultaneously, the clinician attempted to support the teacher's actions while reframing the command in a less punitive format. In this way, a single exchange can have a therapeutic impact directly with the child and indirectly, by influencing the people caring for her.

The consultant also has the opportunity to intervene at multiple levels when a child has peer difficulties. In the classroom, the consultant can address social issues as they arise, influencing the targeted child and his peers. In general, children with social difficulties tend to cluster into two groups—those with externalizing or acting-out difficulties and those who internalize and withdraw from social contact. As required by their role in the classroom, teachers frequently address these concerns in terms of behavior. When a child acts out and breaks rules, limits are set and consequences are devised. Conversely, teachers try to facilitate entry into the peer group for a withdrawn child who suffers social rejection, encouraging prosocial behavior in others and helping the quiet child make contact. Consultants may participate in these behavioral interventions, but they also try to help the struggling child recognize and understand his behavior, become aware of patterns, and devise his own alternatives. A teacher may appropriately place a child in time-out for hitting someone. The consultant, either alone or in concert with the teacher, may then ask the child to think about the feelings of the victimized child, to understand why she was hitting, and to help her find a more positive, verbal way to express her underlying feelings. In addition, the consultant may have the opportunity to take the child aside and explore the event further, examining the broader individual, classroom, and perhaps family context surrounding the behavior.

When working with withdrawn children, the consultant may choose to engage the child in a one-to-one activity in the room and gradually admit other interested children into the activity, encouraging an interactive process. Alternatively, the consultant may join a small group in free play and attempt to interest the child in participating. The consultant may also try to address social matters indirectly by intervening individually with the child to focus on issues that underlie this withdrawal. Depending on a child's needs, the consultant can implement a number of strategies and can vary these over time.

> Brianna was an extremely shy little girl with large, sad brown eyes. Her teacher became concerned about Brianna's withdrawn behavior so she asked the consultant, Ms. Kilmer, to observe the child. Ms. Kilmer first contacted Brianna's mother, who was quite surprised by this report, stating that Brianna was "an animated little chatterbox" at home. She nonetheless agreed to an evaluation. Ms. Kilmer found that, despite her well-rehearsed clinical techniques, Brianna would not leave the room and remained silent and taciturn. The consultant therefore began to engage the child in the classroom; Brianna continued to avoid Ms. Kilmer, refusing to participate in any direct conversation. It was eventually decided that Brianna would benefit from therapy.
>
> Ms. Kilmer continued to work with Brianna in the classroom, more by default than design, as Brianna simply would not cooperate in any other modality. Gradually, the consultant began to interact with Brianna during free play, engaging her in small-group activities in the dress-up corner. Ms. Kilmer began to see glimpses of the happy, expressive child described at home. Brianna became more playful and responsive; she began whispering quietly to friends and actively involving the consultant in her play. Ms. Kilmer later included the child in a small socialization group. Brianna soon became not only a full group participant but also a leader, selecting the activities and assigning children their roles. The consultant began to meet with Brianna's mother and learned of a number of family concerns that likely contributed to Brianna's withdrawal and sadness, which, though less marked, persisted. Eventually, Brianna

*was able to participate in individual treatment and express
her feelings and worries verbally and through play with
the consultant.*

   Although many in-class interventions tend to be public and group
related, there is the opportunity for more private and individual exchanges as well. This typically occurs during free play, when the child
and the therapist can find a moment to converse discreetly at an unoc-
cupied activity table, in the drama corner, on the circle-time rug, or on
the playground. The supplies in the room can often be used for play
therapy as children express themselves either through dramatic play,
books, music, drawing, and painting or with small manipulatives, such
as dolls, trucks, blocks, and other items commonly found in a preschool.
The process is, nevertheless, influenced by its context—it tends to be
more flexible, shifting gears as other children join in or disrupt the
play. The consultant must expect these interruptions and modify her
interpretive responses to be appropriate to this public context. Care
should be taken to protect the child's privacy; he should never feel exposed or humiliated.
   Specific issues, particularly those involving family problems, are not
usually aired in this setting. In general, when a consultant initiates more
in-depth examination of individual and family issues, she is most likely
to do so in private. Of course, young children are notoriously uncon-
cerned with confidentiality and may spontaneously discuss these matters publicly with consultants, teachers, or peers. In these instances, the
consultant and the teacher must rely on their judgment, taking care to
address the child's comments while limiting further probing that might
elicit additional public disclosure of more personal family concerns.
   When children struggle with deeper issues, they often welcome
the intimacy and privacy of a separate space for individual treatment.
Children who receive on-site individual services do, however, face a
number of challenges in sharing the therapist with others. For young
children in treatment, the therapist is often a child's "special person";
they may struggle to share the clinician with others, a reality with
which they are confronted far more often than in traditional settings.
As treatment intensifies, it can be difficult for children to see the consultant arrive at the classroom without offering to take them out for individual sessions. To make matters more difficult, the consultant may
even take the hand of another child and escort her to the therapy room
for an individual session. Fortunately, young children tend to have
flexible representations of people and can usually accept others' diverse roles. With the help of sensitive teachers and clinicians, children

can accept that it is not always their turn. The inability to tolerate this structure suggests high levels of stress or pathology and may, on rare instances, indicate the need for more intensive services.

Nonetheless, the need to share the therapist with others presents a difficulty for children who, in other environments, would not be confronted with this troubling situation. This is particularly true for children who may end therapy while continuing in the early childhood program, as illustrated by the next vignette.

> *Dr. Fitzgerald began evaluating Peter, a bright, verbal young boy, following concerns that his language was dominated by themes of violence and aggression. It was unclear whether the child was able to differentiate his violent fantasies from reality; in addition, there were implicit worries regarding past and current exposure to violence, though Peter presented no behavior difficulties in school or at home. Peter loved to join the consultant in her office for extra individual contact and soon proved to be highly intelligent, and the concerns about his reality testing seemed to be unwarranted. He also had a secure home environment and caregivers who provided stability, safety, and nurturance. After his guardians agreed to eliminate exposure to violent movies at home, Peter's aggressive verbalizations ceased and it was decided that treatment would be terminated. Peter was quite saddened by this news and asked for an explanation as to why he could no longer visit Dr. Fitzgerald's office when she still came to his class and let others have a turn. Dr. Fitzgerald tried her best to reassure Peter that they would continue to remain friends and see each other in the classroom, but now other children needed the private time that he did not need anymore because of all his growth and positive gains.*

Although the explanation was couched positively, Peter was still faced with termination as a loss made all the more poignant by the daily reminders of his therapist's continued presence and availability to others. The structure of on-site therapy forced this young child to confront a reality that would be difficult for even adults to acknowledge. Nevertheless, Peter was able to maintain ongoing contact with the therapist in the context of her classroom visits; this allowed the relationship to continue in a less intimate context, which is an option rarely available to children in treatment. Most important, Peter's high level of functioning, his healthy attachment to school and to a number of available adults, and his supportive and loving home life all gave him the tools to express his feelings and to successfully navigate this difficult transition.

GROUP THERAPY

Group therapy is a rewarding and challenging modality for the on-site therapist. Preschool groups can have a variety of purposes: socialization, development of empathy, and growth of interpersonal skills through play and group discussions. They provide another way to reach young children whose development may be negatively affected by stressful life events, reflected in maladaptive behaviors such as withdrawal, aggression, or hyperactivity. By observing and working with children's issues in the small-group setting, the therapist can do the following:

- Observe firsthand and deal with social and emotional problems that teachers see in the classroom
- Interpret and address problems in peer relationships
- Intervene to improve adjustment to transitions, listening, and turn-taking

In clinical settings it is often difficult to coordinate the logistics of group therapy programs, but the early childhood program offers an exceptional opportunity to incorporate therapeutic group participation into the child's everyday experience. There are, however, a number of important differences between the two environments. First, there is the critical issue of transitions in and out of the classroom, discussed previously in this chapter. Second, there may be more fluidity in terms of membership for on-site groups than for those in clinical settings because of the mobility of some communities and inconsistent attendance patterns. These changes in group membership can be better accommodated through the on-site model. Third, communication with teachers about what transpires with their students outside of the classroom is both paramount and more easily accomplished in program-based interventions.

Preparing for Small-Group Work

Before beginning an on-site therapeutic group, the consultant needs three things: space, referrals, and parental permission. The practical challenges involved in organizing and running preschool-based groups require flexibility and persistence on the part of the consultant. Problems with space and scheduling vary according to the resources of the particular early childhood program but, in general, remain among the greatest challenges. Rooms are usually multipurpose in preschool settings; the consultant may enter a room thought to be scheduled and discover that the room was already in use. In addition, the program schedule may change from week to week, often in ways in which the consultant may not be aware. For example, the consultant might arrive at a classroom to pick up the children for a group and find that the children have gone on a class trip. Communication with teachers and administrative staff as well as versatility are keys to running successful groups. Frequently, the consultant must take the initiative in establishing as much consistency as possible in scheduling groups, checking out classroom and schoolwide schedules, and communicating with staff about the use of space during group time.

After a meeting time and place are established, the next task is to consider how to equip the room. Again, working in an early childhood center means the consultant cannot always prepare rooms to her specifications. In general, providing a few basic items that encourage interactive play is most conducive to therapeutic goals. These items might include puppets, a dollhouse, a sand table, a few "housekeeping" items (e.g., a telephone, pretend food), markers, and paper. At times, the clinician may have to move toys and equipment out of a room to prepare for the group, either because there is too much or not the right type of equipment. For instance, one room might be full of gross motor equipment—a slide, tricycles, and an indoor basketball hoop. These can certainly become vehicles for interaction, but they do not suit the group's purposes as well as items geared toward creativity. Of course, the need for flexibility exists even when thinking about setting up a room. If a consultant is working with children that respond well to large motor and other gym equipment, she should have the freedom to set her room up accordingly.

Selecting Children for Small Groups

This section briefly discusses the selection of children for therapeutic groups, although many more general issues of communication with teachers about students are applicable to group selection. Sometimes the consultant suggests that a child participate, based on classroom observations or prior knowledge of the child's home situation. Yet referrals most often come from the staff members who know the children best—the teachers. Teachers refer children to groups for many reasons, which can be separated into two main categories: those related to the needs of the children and those based on the dynamics of the classroom and the chemistry between the teacher and her children. Both are important to consider.

It is common to include in groups children who are quiet and withdrawn in the classroom. Although they do not necessarily stand out as having difficulties, these children seem overwhelmed in a large

class, even after several months of school. In these cases, the group
serves an important diagnostic function. Does the child appear more
relaxed, verbal, and well related in the small group? If so, a number of
questions naturally emerge. For instance, is the child's behavior primarily a reflection of her temperament and personality style? Is there
something about the classroom that is making the child uncomfortable? Is the child developmentally ready for preschool? One might
have different and perhaps more serious questions if the child remains
nonverbal, elusive, and unengaged with other children, even in a group
of three or four: Does this child have a language impairment? Has this
child experienced traumatic events or circumstances of which the early
childhood program is unaware? Is this child depressed or frightened
and, if so, of what? When the consultative process is working optimally,
these sorts of questions and diagnostic hypotheses can be discussed
with educators consistently and in depth, which is not generally possible when one works outside of school.

A second and very common reason teachers refer children to
groups is that they are finding a particular child extremely difficult to
manage in the classroom. These are the children who do not follow
classroom routines, who constantly demand the teacher's attention,
who get in fights, and who cannot sit still during circle time. If a
teacher has three or four such children in her classroom, she may feel
overwhelmed and desperate for help of any kind. On one hand, a child
who is difficult for a teacher is not necessarily a candidate for a therapeutic group. The consultant should take the time to think through and
talk with the teacher about how best to meet the needs of a child who
is acting out. On the other hand, when taking referrals for groups in a
preschool environment, consultants may have to extend their judgment about group membership beyond the usual clinical boundaries.
Therapists may indeed consider "difficult" children for the group not
only because they may have needs clinicians can address, but also because it demonstrates that consultants take teachers' priorities and
needs seriously, want to respond to their needs for relief and support,
and are not afraid to take on challenging children. Incidentally, when
teachers observe that consultants do not possess a magical ability to
change children and can become just as frustrated and overwhelmed,
it can sometimes provide a breakthrough in the consultant–teacher
relationship.

In sum, selecting children for groups is ultimately determined by
a combination of logistical realities and clinical choices. Mental health
consultants strive for some balance in groups in terms of verbal ability, activity level, and degree of symbolic play. Safety must always be

seriously considered, especially because therapists generally run small groups alone. In a clinical setting where groups are sometimes co-led, it is possible to take on a greater number of children with serious problems. In a preschool environment, it is important that the consultant does not overestimate his capacity to handle too many children on his own. Above all, the process of group selection should ideally be a collaborative process, involving discussion among consultants, teachers, and administrators.

Another critical step that the consultant must take before beginning a therapeutic group is to obtain parental approval and written permission (see the Appendix). Once again, the consultant should discuss with administrative staff how to approach parents rather than assume this task as an independent agent. In some settings, it may be best for the child's teacher or the family worker to contact a potential group member's family initially, followed by a call or a letter from the consultant. In other cases, the consultant may be the first person to approach the family. The description of the group will also vary, depending on its goals and whether it is to address general socialization issues or specific clinical concerns, such as bereavement or divorce. Regardless of the type of group being considered, it is best to introduce the idea to parents with a straightforward description that avoids stigmatizing the child and emphasizes that the group experience will help the child in his daily school life.

The Process of Group Therapy

As with any clinical intervention, the style, format, and method for running small groups will vary according to each consultant's training, theoretical orientation, and personality. Some consultants may prefer a tightly structured, behaviorally oriented group, whereas others may run an open-ended play therapy group. In addition, groups may be based on topics, such as separation, or they may be more eclectic. Rather than review the pros and cons of the different techniques and approaches the consultant might choose, this section presents a general approach, recognizing that each group will develop its own character, themes, and format. In general, the collaborative model incorporates a dynamic perspective, viewing the child's individual issues and life circumstances as central to understanding her behavior in preschool. This method tends to blend group rituals and child-initiated play. The following descriptions present an overview of a typical group.

Opening Ritual   Often the children burst into the room, eager to play, but it is important to gather them together into a circle for an opening ritual. This allows the consultant to acknowledge the purpose of the group verbally: "We're here to learn more about _____ [how to be friends, how to talk about feelings, how to talk instead of fight]." It also focuses the children's attention on the consultant and each other and helps them make a more conscious shift from the classroom to the therapy room. Puppets are useful tools for the opening ritual because they are attention-grabbers and are nonthreatening. For example, the puppet may greet each child, shake hands, and perhaps ask if anyone wants to discuss something he or she has been doing or feeling. The length of the opening ritual will vary considerably, typically lasting anywhere from 5 to 10 minutes. Before moving onto open-ended play-time, it is helpful to make a verbal transition for the children, saying something like "Now we're going to play and talk together for awhile."

   Playtime   The therapist plays a variety of roles during this seg-ment of the group. At first, he may recede from the action and closely watch what, how, and with whom the children play. Often the clinician simply narrates what he sees, asking questions and trying to under-stand the meaning of the children's behaviors. For instance, if a child is playing alone the therapist might say, "I'm noticing that Gary is play-ing by himself. I wonder if he wants someone to play with him?" As one gets to know the children better, themes and patterns emerge; the consultant tries to highlight these for the children. The next vignette demonstrates this technique.

> In one group of boys attending an urban child care center, the children often played "fathers." The consultant was aware that, in reality, many of the boys' fathers were absent from their lives. These children continually pretended to be truck drivers, construction workers, and dads going shopping. They used the telephones to make "calls" to their fathers and often assumed self-consciously macho roles, which at times included aggressive or provocative behaviors. The therapist attempted to bring the emotions and thoughts represented by this play into the verbal arena, making simple comments such as "You boys really think a lot about your dads" or "I wonder if George misses his dad." These play sequences and narrative comments eventually stimulated a more direct discussion of the children's feelings of disappointment and their longing to connect to adult male figures.

Sometimes children respond to the clinician's words, elaborating the play or making a revelation about their lives. At other times, children do not necessarily reply to what is said. However, even when children are not yet able to use interpretations or even simple invitations to talk about their lives, they benefit from the opportunity to act out their feelings and issues in the supportive group milieu.

On some occasions, the therapist switches out of the role of narrator or questioner and adopts a more active role. This usually occurs when conflict arises in the group. The successful therapist needs to be prepared to cope with aggression and anger, especially when working with traumatized children. How a therapist handles conflict and verbal and physical aggression is an extremely complex topic, particularly when one works in an early childhood environment. (This issue is discussed in greater detail in Chapter 8.) The following description illustrates the issues and behaviors the mental health consultant may encounter in working with children whose anger and hurt are expressed in the group setting.

> Seven boys, ages 4 and 5, were referred to a group in a
> preschool program for homeless children. The intensity of the
> boys' distress quickly became apparent in the therapeutic
> group. Though engaging, the boys were extremely active and
> impulsive, displaying hostility and sadistic behavior toward
> the therapist and each other. The boys often pretended they
> were dogs, with one as the master who brutalized the others.
> They often wanted to be turned into monsters, lest they be
> eaten by one. As the group evolved, hostility gradually gave
> way to more varied and positive play. For example "good
> dogs" could be differentiated from "bad dogs" by their
> behavior, a "good drink" could turn the monsters back into
> normal boys, and the therapist was seen as a "superhero"
> who could protect everyone.

In this situation, the therapist had to set limits on the boys' aggressive behavior while trying to facilitate a narrative process that allowed for more varied emotions and hopeful themes. When meeting with the boys' teacher, the clinician also had to be mindful of how aggression and conflict were handled in the classroom. The teacher and the consultant discussed how and why the approach was somewhat different in this therapeutic group, and they explored ways of explaining these differences to the children.

Closing Ritual   The ending is one of the most significant times of each group meeting. It is extremely important to allow enough time to focus on the end of the session, and it often takes practice before the consultant gains a sense of pace and timing in the closing moments. Creating rituals that mark the end of the group session helps to ease what can often be a difficult transition for the children. The components of the closing ritual generally include cleanup time and a brief good-bye in a closing circle. The end of the group is frequently a time when the children's emotions escalate, and feelings about separation and abandonment are often enacted. Children in the group may refuse to help clean up, try to run out of the room, or suddenly become sullen and withdrawn. These behaviors signal a child's distress and can be important focuses of the therapeutic work.

> *In one preschool group, David, a 4-year-old boy who was the second of five children, would begin to throw the toys around at cleanup time and sometimes tried to leave the room. The consultant consistently interpreted David's behavior in light of his tremendous difficulty with transitions and the reality of how little individual attention he received in his life. Significant progress was noted when, after weeks of this sort of interpretation, David looked sad during cleanup and spontaneously declared, "I want to stay!" This was one of the first times that this child was able to substitute chaotic behavior with a clear statement of feelings. It represented a new stage in his ability to experience and communicate his emotions in a way that gave adults an opportunity to respond to him.*

In addition to interpreting children's behavior verbally, the consultant may use other therapeutic approaches to work through the closing ritual, such as creating positive incentives and rewards. For instance, in one group, the children were very attached to the bear puppet that always said hello and good-bye to them. One of the reluctant cleaners was often roused to action when told that "Bashful Bear" wanted the child to be the first to get a good-bye hug and song.

Once the room is tidied, the children gather into a circle for a few minutes. This time offers an occasion for the consultant to put into words the feelings and themes she has observed. The language skills of preschool children are still emerging, and they may not have been exposed to words that describe and mediate feelings. A few simple concluding statements model the use of language as a way to convey feelings and also help organize the group experience for the children. The consultant might say, "Today you played about scary monsters.

Sometimes you feel afraid." Other concluding statements can be directed toward specific children, focusing on a particular struggle, gain, or question. For instance, in one group, Willie, ordinarily an extremely passive child, finally spoke up for himself when another child grabbed a toy from him. Willie took the toy back and, in a loud voice, insisted, "I'm using it!" At the end of the session, as the consultant acknowledged Willie's ability to assert himself for the first time, the boy beamed proudly.

After the concluding statements, a good-bye song or phrase helps add closure to the group and prepares the children to return to their classrooms. Sometimes the children themselves create ending rituals that ease the transition. In one group session, the children began to dance spontaneously during the good-bye song. This dance time grew into a regular part of the weekly good-bye, one that was special because it originated from the children.

As previously indicated, the transition back to the classroom can be difficult despite adequate time, thoughtfulness, and the inclusion of structures for ending the group. Children may refuse to return to their classrooms, cry when it is time to leave, or suddenly dash wildly around the room after having been quiet for the rest of the session. As in any therapeutic encounter, the consultant must use her creativity and clinical techniques to get through these critical moments. Some children need concrete transitional objects to ease them back into the classroom. For example, one child needed to hold the puppet's hand all the way to her classroom and to have her teacher greet the puppet. Another child wanted the consultant to remain in the classroom for a few minutes, bridging the therapeutic session and the return to her classroom.

Many teachers will make an effort to greet the children warmly as they return, but some teachers may not do this spontaneously. It is not uncommon for an array of specialists to come and go during the course of the school day, and it is difficult for teachers to negotiate the frequent disruptions and breaks in their rhythm. Acknowledging the annoyance of classroom interruptions while also emphasizing the importance of helping children reenter the classroom is vital to the success of conducting therapeutic groups in the early childhood context.

When Children Leave the Early Childhood Program
In any preschool environment, children are sometimes withdrawn mid-year. However, in some environments, abrupt departures are not uncommon and are often related to adverse circumstances, such as family instability and loss of residence. Often the realities of the child's home life have an effect on the goals of the preschool in general and on

the therapeutic work in particular. For example, a group can be started
for children who only engage in parallel play, and the therapist will
seek to encourage their ability to play interactively and to form relationships. A specific child's sudden withdrawal from the program will
have a strong impact on the nature of the group and its goals, especially in a center with a high turnover rate. Sometimes teachers have
difficulty confronting a student's departure and, in an effort to protect
themselves from feelings of loss, may avoid classroom discussion on
the topic. Although this is clearly a schoolwide issue, the focus here is
on how it may be expressed in the therapeutic group.

> The consultant, Dr. Young, had worked with a group of
> three boys for approximately 6 weeks when one of the boys,
> Justin, was suddenly removed from the child care center.
> Little was known about the circumstances of Justin's leaving,
> and the consultant did not realize Justin had been
> withdrawn until she arrived to pick up the three boys for
> group. During the opening ritual, Dr. Young asked the
> children what they knew about Justin's departure and
> attempted to elicit feelings about and responses to the loss of
> their friend. The boys were noticeably silent on the subject.
> During playtime, however, they expressed their feelings
> quite clearly. At first, the two boys played entirely
> separately, as if they were deliberately avoiding contact with
> each other. When the boys did engage with each other, their
> interaction was much more aggressive and hostile than had
> previously been the case. One boy suddenly grabbed the
> neck of Mitchell, the other child. Mitchell became very
> angry at cleanup time, refusing to help. He swayed back and
> forth on a small rocking toy, saying repeatedly, "I can't stop;
> help me stop." These boys did not easily respond to Dr.
> Young's efforts to talk about how Justin's absence had made
> everyone feel sad, a little worried, and angry. In the
> meantime, a new child entered the group, and it took a
> number of weeks and much discussion before the boys
> appeared to have adapted to losing Justin.

The consultant's clinical training helped her view the changes in
the boys' behavior therapeutically so that she was not merely responding to their more provocative actions. The fact that this group met during the school day allowed Dr. Young to share her perspective with the

teacher and to hear whether the teacher had also noticed any alterations in the boys' conduct or feelings. They also discussed ways to follow up in the classroom on what had emerged from the therapy group.

When Children Talk About Possible Abuse

Another situation faced during group work with children is their verbalization of harsh and possibly abusive treatment at home. This sort of revelation can occur in the classroom as well but is perhaps more common in the small-group or individual session, in which children sense the appropriateness of talking about home and family in an intimate setting. Many therapists have to deal with the issue of reporting possible abuse, but there are important differences when disclosure occurs in an early childhood environment. First, although the consultant still has ethical and legal reporting obligations, she must take into consideration the school's policy for handling abuse. In short, the consultant does not respond individually but, rather, approaches suspected abuse as a member of the preschool team. These issues are taken up in much greater detail in Chapter 8.

A second, more complex issue lies in the problem of how to interpret children's play in light of possible abuse. When does a child's play reflect evidence of abuse? Should this be dealt with in the group or individually? How do issues of confidentiality affect the handling of reports of abuse in the early childhood program? Although it is beyond the scope of this chapter to determine when a child's report of harsh treatment suggests abuse, this issue will likely arise at some point in therapeutic group work and is worthy of serious discussion and clarification among the consultant, the director, and the teachers.

> Bernice and Robbie were siblings who attended a
> therapeutic group together at their child care center. Robbie
> was outgoing and playful, although his language was quite
> delayed. Bernice was extremely quiet, withdrawn, and had a
> look of fear on her thin face. In the classroom, Bernice was
> essentially noncommunicative; she did not participate in
> most activities, was silent, and had made no friends.
> Although she was initially reticent in the therapeutic group,
> Bernice began to open up slowly, often through interaction
> with her little brother, whom she tended to boss around. She
> had never shown any aggression toward any children,
> including Robbie. During the closing ritual, in which the
> bear puppet said good-bye to each child, Bernice never
> responded or spoke to the bear, seeming to ignore him and
> the therapist.

*One day, during the good-bye song, Bernice suddenly
reached out and grabbed the puppet, hitting it repeatedly on
the head. She was unable to say anything about what she
was doing and feeling. Only two children attended the next
group session; the others were absent, including Robbie.
Bernice played on her own, becoming interested in a
musical ball that rolled around and jingled as it moved. She
played silently, then loudly stated, "It's gonna get me!" After
a few moments she grabbed a paper towel roll and began
smashing the ball and yelling repeatedly, "Shut up! Shut
up!" The consultant stopped her after a minute and tried to
elicit more from Bernice. Bernice then spoke more than she
ever had before, spilling out a confusing story that was
difficult to follow. She exclaimed, "Robbie screams. Doug is
in the bath and then he hurts Robbie and Mommy sleeps but
Robbie screams and wakes her up." The consultant reported
this conversation to the preschool's director, and together
they decided that the consultant would closely monitor
Robbie and Bernice's behavior and observe them in the next
small-group session.*

*Both children attended the next session, in which they
were extremely active and agitated; they ran around the
room, flitting from one activity to another. When the
therapist attempted to talk with the children about what they
were doing, Robbie began chattering, using language that
was fragmented and hard to understand. He talked about
being hit by his mother's boyfriend and watching his mother
and her boyfriend fight "till there was blood." Neither child
was able to elaborate further or describe a clear sequence of
events. The consultant and the program director again
discussed the situation and decided that the director would
call both the mother and Child Protective Services.*

It is notable that at no time did either Robbie or Bernice speak with
their teacher about any problems at home. Perhaps the classroom was
a place to get away from their troubles and to find a respite, whereas
the therapeutic group, with the stated goal of talking about feelings,
was a place they could discuss such worries. It is also possible that a
child such as Bernice, whose silent and fearful demeanor was heartrending to all, needed the safety and intimacy of a small-group experience to begin conveying her troubles.

CONCLUSION

As described in this chapter, the collaborative model emphasizes the prevention of mental health problems by using both indirect services and direct contacts with children. Enhancing the therapeutic nature of the classroom through a range of activities and dialogues with teachers and children is one of this model's innovative aspects. On-site group and individual interventions extend the boundaries of traditional therapy when they are interwoven with the other aspects of the family–preschool–consultant collaboration, addressing developmental concerns as well as the mental health needs of children.

chapter eight

Interventions for Young Children Affected by Trauma

This chapter concentrates on a group of young children who may experience considerable pain and suffering and pose a great challenge to the preschool system—children exposed to trauma. They require an intense commitment from the adults who work with them, and the mental health consultant will often be called on to support and collaborate with the early childhood staff to minimize the impact of painful events in children's lives. Childhood trauma tends to occur as either long-term and chronic stress or intense but short-term crises. Although some early childhood centers have relatively few families experiencing chronic stress, most have to confront the rare and sometimes extreme crisis that can cause great upheaval in the child, the family, and the school. Other programs have a large number of children affected by trauma of both types, particularly in communities where a disproportionate number of families struggle with the ongoing effects of poverty, violence, and residential instability.

Through the seminal work of Terr (1991) and other researchers in the 1990s, it has become evident that trauma can have strong repercussions in children's lives. This chapter reviews the symptoms of trauma typically observed in early childhood programs. For the consulting clinician, the trauma model, which emphasizes the importance of addressing underlying risk factors and reducing the impact of multiple stressors (Rutter, 1979), presents a helpful diagnostic framework as well as a language for communicating with teachers and parents. Young victims of trauma need not be seen through a psychopathology lens or be labeled as having severe emotional disturbances, though they may at times exhibit severe symptomatology. This model instead highlights the deleterious effects of the disruptions in children's relationships and sense of security following acute traumatic events or chronic stressors. The goal of the early childhood program is to provide a context in which the child's development can continue unfettered while maintaining the working assumption that young children in healthy and stable environments can overcome most stressful events. The consultant and early childhood staff have the opportunity to work in concert toward this end.

Although this optimism typically prevails in preschools, it is challenged on occasion by faulty notions that children with traumatic early experiences, chronic deprivation, or biological vulnerabilities inevitably have poor outcomes. It is often said, for instance, that a child's disruptive behavior can be explained by his exposure to drugs in utero, as if the fact that he was a "crack baby" accounts for any current behavior concerns. In reality, there is a paucity of research directly linking later behavior problems to early exposure to cocaine, in part because of the methodological difficulties in differentiating between the effects of prenatal exposure to toxins, overall prenatal and postnatal care, and early environmental insults (Griffith, Azuma, & Chasnoff, 1994). Yet there is a commonly held belief that these children are destined to suffer from developmental delays and neurological impairments (Lyons & Rittner, 1998). Similar presumptions may beset children identified—often without a thorough differential diagnosis—as having attention-deficit/ hyperactivity disorder (ADHD) or, worse, those termed "project kids." Little damage would result if such concerns were translated into a redoubling of efforts to reach out to these children and provide them with additional supports. Unfortunately, the reverse often occurs: When biological risk factors or traumatic histories are seen as destiny, expectations are lowered and, in some situations, interventions reduced. In case conferences and other clinical discussions, educators and social workers sometimes question whether clinical or classroom interventions will be successful for children who were prenatally exposed to alcohol or other drugs. Yet it is often not the drug exposure itself but the associated risk factors, including the chaotic environments in which many of these children live, that pose the greatest challenge to them. Although therapists cannot alter history, they can directly address the current risk factors that continue to threaten the children's development.

It is typically the mental health consultant's role to foster hope in the face of this pessimism, to provide teachers and parents with practical suggestions and encouragement, and to increase families' and educators' knowledge base about how young children can recover from trauma. One consultant found it useful in workshops for teachers working with children under chronic stress to point out the ratio of a year in school to the age of their students. She presented the opportunity teachers have to influence development—in a way that their peers working with older children and adolescents do not—by reminding them that they had students in their care for one quarter of the children's lives. Remarkable things can occur in children in the course of one preschool year: a 4-year-old girl who had witnessed severe violence and did not speak at all in September communicated openly with teachers and classmates by the following spring; an extremely aggressive boy, abandoned by his mother, learned to take pride in his work and to respect his peers and his teachers. Each occurred without major clinical intervention.

Consultants often need to communicate these success stories to counteract images of "problem children" who disrupt classrooms and seem impervious to adult instruction or counseling. Except for a small percentage of children with extensive therapeutic needs, the vast majority of young children can be served in general early childhood programs within their communities that adopt the team approach, combining the clinical and educational expertise outlined throughout this book. Children under stress may well need individual or family counseling and support from a mental health professional as they adapt to the routines of the school day. In addition, their teachers require much training and support not only to recognize the signs and symptoms of stress, but also to meet the challenges of caring for these children. However, rather than focusing on the etiology of children's current behaviors and possible long-term effects, the consultant can help child care staff embrace a new conviction: A solid preschool experience can help children build resilience and overcome the developmental insults that have marked their early years. For many children with a history of trauma, this is their best hope to get back on track.

THE IMPACT OF TRAUMA
AND CHRONIC STRESS ON YOUNG CHILDREN

Terr (1991) described a common pattern of trauma symptoms in children of all ages that includes visualization, specific fears, persistent memories of the events, repetitive play, reenactments of the trauma, and diminished expectations about the future. Children exposed to chronic stress also tend to engage in denial about their experiences and, in extreme cases, withdraw into a "psychic numbness" in which they avoid all emotional interactions and responses. These children are also prone to rage reactions, and their anger is at times turned against themselves in the form of self-abusive or risk-taking behaviors.

Although covering a wide range of behaviors, this symptom list is a useful starting point for the consultant and the teacher observing children who may have been exposed to any of the following traumatic events or chronic stressors: separation from a parent; foster care placement; being a witness to or victim of violence, abuse, or neglect; death of a family member; hospitalization or illness; mental illness in a parent; or loss of a family home through fire or eviction. It is particularly important to note which children display more than one symptom and do so consistently over time. Of course, not every child who is angry and plays roughly with dolls or other toys has been the victim of abuse or other trauma, but these behaviors do warrant careful attention and monitoring over time, and the early childhood staff should listen closely to these children's stories. When participating in the day-to-day activities of the center, the consultant can help the staff differentiate typical behaviors and play from those that suggest more serious concerns.

The trauma model also draws attention to behaviors that may be easily overlooked. The withdrawn child may be seen as shy or quiet and indeed may be a welcome presence in a classroom of otherwise active children. But when this behavior persists for several weeks or months, well beyond the time when most children in the room are comfortably engaged with each other, further observation and assessment are necessary. Severely limited responsiveness in the classroom is perhaps the most reliable predictor of which children have been the victims of intensive and long-term trauma. One 4-year-old girl whose family had been homeless for most of her life, and whose parents had been cited for neglect on several occasions, was described by her teacher as "just there," almost unnoticeable in the classroom. This child was not referred for assessment for several months, even though a psychologist was on site in her Head Start program and available to observe her. She was not difficult to manage and could be pleasant enough, and it was not easy for her teacher to identify or describe what was wrong. Eventually the impact of this stress became more apparent; the student was referred to treatment and gradually became more involved with her peers and engaged with her teachers.

Likewise, the overly active child is commonly viewed as exuberant or perhaps hyperactive. Although these are plausible explanations, repeated instances of children putting themselves at risk—climbing on tables, jumping from high places, or darting in the street—all warrant closer observation and a more careful review of the children's histories. If these behaviors continue or escalate after appropriate limits are set in the classroom, the mental health consultant should begin a more formal assessment process, including a discussion with parents about possible exposure to trauma. Self-abusive behaviors, including head banging, tearing at one's skin, and hair pulling, deserve immediate attention, as do apparent life-threatening behaviors.

> In class sharing time, 4-year-old Anna reported lying down in the street outside her house. She explained that she was saddened by the death of her former neighbor, "Aunt" Debbie, whom she and her mother had discovered dead a few months earlier. Anna wanted to join Debbie in heaven and, like most children her age, did not understand the finality of what she was proposing. In addition to intensifying her ongoing psychological treatment, Anna's mother was immediately contacted and agreed to put strict limits on the child's activity outside the house. A psychiatric consultation was also recommended to address Anna's impulsivity, and she was medicated for a brief period. The therapist and the teachers explained to Anna that although she loved Debbie, Anna would be killed and could never return if she followed through on her plan. They helped her to share more details of discovering the body and to mourn the loss of this family friend. Although she remained visibly saddened by Debbie's death, Anna began to find other ways to remember her and began to speak of Debbie more frequently. Anna's risk-taking behavior and wish to hurt herself diminished considerably in subsequent months.

It is important that early childhood professionals recognize the symptom clusters and isolated behaviors associated with trauma, but they should also understand that trauma's impact on young children often expresses itself in a more global manner, affecting their ability to achieve age-appropriate developmental tasks. Young children under chronic stress, especially maltreated children and those exposed to violence, often fail to develop attachments to their caregivers and do not have a sense of basic security or trust in the world (Osofsky, 1995). They may be wary of strangers and hypervigilant, noticing minor deviations in their immediate environment that could portend danger. These children frequently have extreme difficulty separating from their parents when coming to school and cannot readily carry an image of their caregivers through the school day. They may be exceptionally clingy and appear anxious when their caregivers are absent. Transitional objects can be useful in helping them bridge the gap between home and school, and teachers can encourage parents to send a favorite stuffed animal or toy, pictures, or another reminder of home.

Children with a history of trauma often fear and expect rejection, especially from adults. To limit possible rejection, they may avoid establishing a connection to their teachers or forming meaningful relationships with other children. Others may act out aggressively and actively push people away from them, fulfilling their own prophecies of their unworthiness and protecting themselves from the potential loss of affection from a significant adult figure. Some bright children refer to different adults simply as "teacher," even after several months in the same class, choosing not to differentiate or form any special bonds. Even in early childhood, these children may begin to abandon dreams or aspirations and come to believe that the future holds little promise for them.

In addition to their hesitance in relationships and limited aspirations, preschoolers with a history of trauma commonly have delayed cognitive skills that further hinder their growth in the classroom. Young children living in tumultuous or stressful environments typically have had little time for quiet, exploratory play, and many have not had available adults who could encourage their use of symbols and early language. As a result, their symbolic play and dramatic skills, cornerstones of most early childhood experiences, often lag behind those of their peers. Their spontaneous speech may also be limited. Furthermore, trauma-induced delays in the development of object constancy and a sense of security can hinder young children's ability to delay gratification in school. They fear that their turn will not come, and their frustration tolerance and ability to wait are often limited.

Research has shown that older children who are abused display only limited motivation and are less likely to respond to challenging material (Aber & Allen, 1987). Preschoolers who have been abused can seem similarly disinterested, and many are unfocused and inattentive. Young children coping with stress often are impulsive and have high activity levels, and they are sometimes hastily given a diagnosis of ADHD without a full exploration of the stress and anxiety that may be driving their behaviors. Some children express their fears by raising their level and intensity of activity in school, especially if they do not have sufficient words or feel safe enough to express these concerns.

Young children under chronic stress often learn to limit their movements as well as their words. Fearful or unable to establish independence from their caregivers, they may develop a "sensory muting" in which they remain molded to adults (Craig, 1992). They can look clumsy and awkward and appear to have limited orientation in space. They may also have difficulty establishing boundaries between themselves and others. These children may be diagnosed with a primary sensory disorder without adequate consideration of environmental stressors and family functioning. Likewise, lags in language development may also be recorded in children who have learned to monitor their verbal and nonverbal messages closely for fear of reprisal. In extreme cases, a victim of trauma may be mute and withdrawn, mimicking the symptoms of autism or other developmental disabilities.

DIAGNOSIS AND TREATMENT

Determining the etiology of symptom patterns in young children with a potential history of trauma is critical to establishing an appropriate course of treatment. Often a young child is referred for services due to an apparent disability, and the impact of trauma or possible family stressors is not considered; planned interventions frequently focus only on discrete learning issues. In Head Start, for example, the majority of children (67%) who are referred for services are identified with speech-language delays, whereas only a small number (4%) are referred for emotional or behavior problems (Knitzer, 1996). Although many of these referrals represent a legitimate first step and may be the most agreeable point of entry for families, treatment and intervention plans derived from subsequent evaluations are often circumscribed and discipline-specific and do not allow for a more integrated approach to the child.

Early in the school year, the child care center referred 4-year-old Byron for speech-language and special education services, as he had articulation delays, was easily distracted in group situations, and appeared unable to process much of the material presented in class. Initial work with his special education provider, Ms. Palmer, proved to be extremely difficult; Byron became aggressive and resisted all of Ms. Palmer's efforts at skills work. Byron's behavior had also deteriorated markedly in the classroom around the same time. Ms. Palmer was clearly exasperated by Byron, and she told the director of the center that Byron "could not be helped" and would likely need to be in a much more restricted setting.

The following week, Dr. Cruz, the consulting psychologist, spent time with Byron and gathered more recent history. Although Byron was initially defiant and

angry with Dr. Cruz, the child responded to limit-setting and
soon grew very distraught, sobbing that he missed his
mother and wished to see her. It turned out that Byron had
had little opportunity to see his mother in recent weeks
because she had taken on double shifts at work to save
money for a new apartment. He was spending weekends
with his father who was estranged from his mother at that
time. All Byron could focus on in school was his mother's
absence. The child's volatility was exacerbated by his
teachers' talk of his moving on to kindergarten and the head
teacher's vacation, as suddenly school was also a less
reliable and consistent presence in his life.

Although Byron clearly needed help, the prescribed
itinerant services were destined to fail if they did not include
accommodations for his current life circumstances. Dr. Cruz
worked with the early childhood staff to help Byron
integrate his home and school experiences. The child first
needed to feel that his attachment to his mother was secure,
so plans were made to have her visit the center during her
lunch hour. Byron also needed to feel reconnected with his
teachers at school, and Dr. Cruz recommended that the
additional learning and speech services occur within the
classroom. Most important, Byron needed to know that he
was understood by all of the adults working with him and
that they would encourage and support him while
recognizing the difficulty he was having focusing in school.

The mental health consultant can often play a role in helping teachers and specialists adopt a more holistic approach to a child's functioning in the classroom, including an appreciation of a child's history of trauma and ongoing family stressors. Language difficulties can be influenced by several physiological factors, including hearing loss, immature musculature, and processing delays; environmental factors can also play a significant role in language acquisition and expression. In addition to inquiring about the level of stimulation in the home and elsewhere, clinicians need to ascertain if children are reticent to speak for other reasons. Some of these children suffer from depression and have learned too well to be "seen and not heard." Others have learned to monitor their speech closely to not reveal anything about their family lives. In some extreme cases of neglect or abuse, children remain mute, unable to repeat the "unspeakable" things they have witnessed or endured. Speech-language therapy may be indicated for these children but it needs to be delivered within a therapeutic context of nurturance and safety and with an eye on children's overall self-concept. Unless there are additional interventions with their families to reduce or eliminate the stressful experiences and to enhance these children's coping skills, the remedial help they receive will likely fall far short of its goals.

EXPOSURE TO VIOLENCE

The following section examines specific stressors that influence young children's development, beginning with exposure to violence, an issue of great concern to many early childhood educators. Demographic research in the 1980s and the 1990s has documented the prevalence of children who have experienced violence as either victims or witnesses. In one study at Boston City Hospital, 10% of the children in a pediatric primary care clinic had witnessed a stabbing or shooting by age 6 (Groves, Zuckerman, Marans, & Cohen, 1993). A study of children living in high violence neighborhoods in New Orleans reported that 51% of the fifth graders surveyed had been victims of violence and 91% had witnessed some type of violence (Osofsky, 1995). Reports suggest that at least 3.3 million children nationwide have witnessed parental abuse, ranging from hitting or slapping to murder (Jaffe, Wilson, & Wolfe, 1988).

Although researchers struggle to identify the differing effects of domestic and community violence and the impact on children who are abused or experience violence (Knitzer, 1995), there is much convergence in their findings. Symptoms of anxiety are common in school-age children exposed to violence, including sleep disturbances and nightmares (Osofsky, 1995). Young children living amidst violence tend to be more anxiously attached, fearful, aggressive, inattentive, and uncertain about an adult's ability to protect them (Knitzer, 1995; Osofsky & Fenichel, 1994). They may display symptoms of posttraumatic stress disorder (PTSD), including withdrawal and depression, disruptions in sleeping and eating, disassociative behaviors, disorganized attachment patterns, difficulty focusing and paying attention, and reexperiencing the trauma. Preschoolers who observe violence are less likely to explore their environments freely or seek opportunities for mastery (Osofsky, 1995).

Young children who have witnessed or experienced violence are particularly vulnerable to developmental lags and emotional disturbances. Children who are physically abused have a much more difficult time establishing a stable representation of self and maintaining a positive self-image (Koplow, 1996). They also struggle to retain benign images of adults, especially if the perpetrator is a caregiver or family member. They often have little faith that relationships can be trustworthy and dependable, making it more difficult to form connections with teachers or peers. In the classroom, they may mimic the immediacy of the violent responses they have seen or endured, fighting for turns in games or activities, with little frustration tolerance, impulse control, or ability to delay gratification. Children living amidst violence may engage in dramatic play that is repetitive and motivated by the trauma; they may, for instance, smash dolls and play violently with pretend guns or knives. Although these reenactments may not seem so different from typical aggressive play in early childhood and appear to offer a release, they do not help children exposed to violence develop mastery over their experiences or control over their own impulses. Instead, they tend to be a replication of the trauma that can act as a call for help; however, if left untended, such behavior may also perpetuate the impact of the violent events.

As previously mentioned, the withdrawal and "psychic numbness" to which Terr (1991) referred are key indicators of severe trauma in young children, often associated with chronic exposure to violence. Fearful of what they see around them, these children choose to turn inward, away from contact with others and the potential pain that it might bring. One 4-year-old girl always cowered in front of adults in her class and was described by her teacher as having a "wounded animal" look. In extreme cases, this defensive posture can take on a disassociative quality, and children can appear to go numb and to be disconnected from their current experiences.

> Five-year-old Jasmine had seen her father repeatedly
> threaten her mother, witnessing her father holding a gun to
> Jasmine's mother's head and breaking down their apartment
> door in the middle of the night. Enrolled in a preschool
> therapeutic nursery, she would often come in with a blank
> look on her face and stare straight ahead at meals or in
> group time. Jasmine would sometimes crawl on the floor or
> curl up in a fetal position, ignoring all contact with adults.
> Although cognitive testing indicated she was of average
> intelligence, she often spoke in gibberish and appeared silly
> and disorganized. Jasmine would sometimes emerge from
> her trance-like state and suddenly fly into a violent rage for
> a brief period, only to return to her shell after adults
> intervened to calm her. At other times she would
> intentionally try to punch or otherwise hurt herself.

Many young children affected by violence follow a more direct pattern of imitating and identifying with the behaviors they have witnessed or experienced. They often side with the aggressor in an attempt to gain control in a situation in which they have little or none, and they do not believe they have any real power to alter their environment or to stop the violence from occurring. Biting, spitting, hitting, cursing—all are familiar ways in which these children seek to make their presence felt with other children or adults. Although preschoolers, their behavior and language often mimic the adolescent swagger and adult bravado that is familiar to them.

> *Three-year-old Max lived in a turbulent household that included much verbal and physical violence. The day Dr. Murphy visited his class, Max was playing quietly by himself with dress-up clothes, pretending to be a cowboy. When he saw Dr. Murphy playing with his friend Annette, Max strutted across the room in his best John Wayne style, approached Dr. Murphy, and punched him square in the shoulder, knocking the clinician over. Max stated simply and triumphantly, "She's my girl!"*

Such behavior can be particularly difficult in the classroom. Consultants who have direct experience with these children have an opportunity to empathize with teachers' frustration and stress and to work with educators to contain outbursts and prevent their recurrence.

Young victims of aggression will frequently provoke confrontations with adults. They will test limits and pick areas of vulnerability in the adults who care for them. This pattern of behavior in young children contains at least three meaningful communications. First, by acting out aggressively, these children confirm their own self-representations of unworthiness and deserving punishment or scorn. Second, by striking out at others, they keep people at a distance and avoid forming more intimate relationships that could ultimately cause them more harm or disappointment. Third, and often overlooked in the heat of their outbursts, violent children are telling adults that they are fearful and in pain and feel out of control. On the surface they seek to gain control and inflict pain or damage, but most aggressive young children are searching for benign adults who can handle them and help them master their impulses. If they are uncertain on this count, these children may continue to test perceived weaknesses in their classroom team or intensify their behavior; nevertheless, most have not yet lost hope that they may meet their match. In this way, their behavior is more related and developmentally advanced than those who withdraw and remain isolated from peers and adults.

This last message is the one that educators must appreciate and respond to if they are to make headway with children who are difficult in the classroom. The consultant's role is often to reveal this meaning hidden in aggressive outbursts, not as a way of licensing the behavior but as a possible point of entry for teachers who may otherwise feel little empathy or hope regarding these children. Consultants can help teachers understand that aggressive children frequently long for comfort or solace, and they actually feel vulnerable and scared. This point was demonstrated dramatically by one preschool class that included several aggressive boys with tough exteriors. On the day they were to have their blood lead level screenings, these boys were the most frightened by the prospect of having their fingers pricked. Many needed to be carried to the nurse's room; then, when the technician tested them, the boys had to be held by their teachers. This minitrauma poignantly displayed how vulnerable these children were feeling and gave their teachers a new appreciation for the boys' internal experiences that were masked by their outward bravado.

Classroom Interventions with Children Who Have Experienced Violence

More than anything else, young children with a history of exposure to violence need to feel that their school is a predictable setting in which they can safely play and learn. Consistent, caring teachers who treat these children as individuals and value their ideas and imaginations can do much to reduce the impact of the violent events they have witnessed or endured. Frequently, the consultant must remind teachers that their role in creating this warm and secure environment is invaluable, particularly when they are confronted with children who are difficult to manage and seem incorrigible. For some of these children, school is the *only* place they feel safe, especially if their families are unstable or threatening or if they live in dangerous neighborhoods or shelters.

This background of safety and security allows children to begin reaching out to their teachers and to develop hope in relationships, often after first testing adults. In most cases, patient teachers can help timid and withdrawn children eventually feel comfortable enough to try out new toys and to explore the room enough to expand their repertoire of cognitive activities. With proper limits, children who act out violent episodes can learn to play with puzzles, blocks, and other dramatic materials in more adaptive ways. They generally come to welcome the opportunity afforded them in the classroom to enjoy the rites and rituals of childhood free from external intrusions or fear of disturbances. These are no small achievements for children exposed to violence, including some who fear that Santa Claus is a killer and others who can only relate to Martin Luther King, Jr., as "the guy who got shot."

Establishing a Nurturing Environment

Creating a reparative milieu for children living with violence involves an acceptance of their experiences and a willingness to talk about what they have seen or heard. Affirming children's perceptions and feelings about events that they have witnessed can greatly reduce their symptoms and help them feel less isolated and alone with this knowledge (see Pynoos & Eth, 1986, for a more detailed description of a clinical interview technique for child victims of violence). Yet many teachers shy away from these discussions, fearing that they will open a Pandora's box of feelings and private family details that should not be discussed in the classroom. As a start, however, most teachers are willing to let a mental health consultant talk to the child privately.

On arriving at the Rainbow Center on Monday, Dr. Edwards learned that Alan's mother had been murdered the previous week, apparently by her boyfriend. Although he lived with his aunt, Alan saw his mother frequently and had a fairly good relationship with her. The school had reached out to the aunt immediately, sending food and offering to help in any way possible. Alan told his teachers what had happened when he arrived at school the next day, but he had not discussed it since then. However, his demeanor had changed markedly. He looked wan and tired and was noticeably upset and sad. Alan frequently complained of headaches and stomach pains and asked that his aunt be called to take him home.

Dr. Edwards had known Alan for 2 years, and they had a good rapport despite infrequent contact during that academic year. The consultant explained to Alan that she had heard about the news, was sorry, and wondered if Alan wanted to talk about it. Though reluctant at first, Alan told Dr. Edwards that nobody at home was talking about his mother. He related some details about the funeral, most notably that he was surprised to see all the adults crying and that he and his sister, Sara, a year older, were two of the few people who did not. Dr. Edwards talked to Alan about feeling mixed up, not knowing if he should cry or where that was allowed. She also told Alan, "Sometimes our bodies hurt when we have hurt feelings." Alan's eyes slowly welled with tears while they were talking, and he seemed visibly relieved to have someone with whom he could talk about this tragic loss.

In the subsequent weeks, Dr. Edwards visited with Alan on a regular basis. She also encouraged one of his teachers to

spend time with Alan each morning and to check in
regarding how the child was feeling. Dr. Edwards suggested
that every teacher be aware of Alan's grief symptoms,
including his body pains and his increasing oppositional
behavior in the classroom. When one teacher suggested that
the boy should be "getting over" his mother's death and was
now using it as an excuse to act out in class, Dr. Edwards
offered to meet with the classroom team to discuss Alan's
behavior and to provide some instruction on the normal
grieving process for young children. After the meeting, the
teachers seemed more compassionate toward Alan. They
began to remind him that he could talk about his feelings and
that he did not have to act out to call attention to his plight.

Group Discussions of Violence

Young children exposed to violence and other trauma often actively look to share their experiences with adults and their peers. This openness and lack of defensiveness separates them from latency-age children who have been socialized not to speak freely about their home lives and may have heard the implicit or explicit message to keep things private. Although respecting young children's and their families' right to privacy is essential, preschoolers can benefit greatly from the opportunity to report their experiences to adults (Pynoos & Eth, 1986).

The notion of preschool group discussions as a cornerstone of the early childhood experience garnered interest in the 1990s and has a direct bearing on children affected by violence. In her review of Japanese methods of preschool instruction, Lewis (1995) was particularly impressed with the daily group meetings that helped children develop a sense of community and shared responsibility. A report by the Center for Preventive Psychiatry on the clinical impact of group discussions with young children in a therapeutic nursery suggested that preschoolers can develop a shared empathy for their peers' traumatic life experiences (Lopez, Balter, Howard, Stewart, & Zelman, 1996). They observed that child witnesses to violence who disclose their stories become noticeably relieved and display fewer signs of alienation and isolation. Other clinicians have noted a reduction in children's acting-out behaviors, denial, and other defensive maneuvers when they are encouraged to openly talk about their lives. The goals of these group discussions include 1) recognizing the reality of the children's experiences, 2) normalizing their responses to the threatening situations to which they are exposed, and 3) helping them develop strategies to cope with their environment (Donahue, 1996).

Most preschool classrooms are not, of course, designed as therapeutic milieus, nor do they seem to have a place for intense group discussions of traumatic material. Yet more and more children are coming
into their classes and relating stories of violence to their teachers and
friends. Avoiding these issues typically raises more questions in the
children and increases their anxiety and confusion. Young children
need to believe that significant adults can handle any topic that is
broached, even seemingly intolerable material, and this can give the
children a sense that they can survive and cope with this knowledge.
Teachers sometimes fear that they will show their own feelings in these
discussions or may not be as strong as they would like. The point, however, is not for adults to be omnipotent or to suppress their own reaction to frightening stories. It is allowing the stories to be shared that is
key, giving children license to "speak the unspeakable" and supporting their efforts at making sense of it. Adults are not forbidden but,
rather, encouraged to share their own emotions as a means of freeing
the children to do the same. This may mean simply saying, "That sounds
scary" or "It makes me sad to hear that story."

Teachers are often hesitant to respond for other reasons. They may
wish that the painful realities of the children's lives would somehow
disappear and come to believe that if they avoid speaking about violence and other trauma, they might mitigate the impact of these events.
Some adults ignore children's stories because they are overwhelmed
by the details (a legitimate concern that is addressed later in this chapter) or because they might have to assume the uncomfortable role of
mandated reporter to keep children from potential harm. Certain early
childhood staff are less comfortable with group discussions of emotional material; they may need reassurance that they will not be expected to handle these issues on their own or that they may do so on
an individual basis with the affected child. After encouraging an openness to painful emotions and stories in the classroom, the consultant
should remind teachers that they only have to follow the children's
lead and can allow the children to relate their stories at their own pace.

In the previous story about Alan, the boy's teacher was able to talk
to the class before Alan returned to school. She told the children that
Alan's mother had been killed, which many knew already from the victim's relatives or newspaper reports, and that he would probably be
feeling sad when he rejoined them the next week. She did not provide
details about the killing but rather talked mainly about how upsetting
it was to hear this story. The class got together to make a card for Alan
and went out of their way to welcome him back when he returned.

In many cases, teachers are more comfortable having the consultant join them when talking to the children. In one urban Head Start

program, 4-year-old Brandon reported that his mother had been stabbed over the weekend in a dispute with another mother. After meeting with Brandon individually, the mental health consultant clarified the important details for the class together with Brandon and his teacher: Brandon's mother was not seriously injured and was at home, he was frightened but reassured now that she would recover fully, and he was angry and confused about why this had occurred. The children in the class took this situation seriously, asked a few questions, and mostly sought to reassure Brandon that things would be all right. Some spoke of their own experiences with violence in their families or in the shelters where they lived. Brandon knew also that his teacher and the social worker would follow up with his mother and report back to the child on their discussion.

Discussions of violence, either in the home or the community, can be among the most problematic in the preschool classroom. In addition to worries regarding confidentiality and the appropriateness of the violent material, teachers may grow fearful for their own or their students' safety, and they may be reminded about their own experiences, current or past, with violence or abuse. In one class, a discussion of children hitting each other in class led to several children sharing incidences of being hit by their parents at home. The teachers were unsure of what to do next and looked to the on-site therapist, Dr. Noon, to focus the discussion. She highlighted the empathic comments from the children regarding their shared dilemma—that they cared for their parents yet feared their anger. Plans were then made to contact individual parents, and Dr. Noon told the children she not only wanted to help them maintain strong relationships with their parents but also wanted to ensure their safety.

Intrusions of community violence into preschools can do severe damage to the image, created by teachers and shared by students and families, that their programs are havens from the dangerous and chaotic world that sometimes lurks just outside the door. Some inner-city early childhood programs now restrict use of playgrounds for fear of stray bullets, and teachers and parents report that they are afraid during the walk to and from the centers. Violence close to home is often the most devastating.

During a modified summer session, Nancy, a teacher at the Archway Child Care Center, was murdered. She was the unintended victim of a drive-by shooting. The consultant, Dr. Davis, received a telephone call from the director of the program on Saturday evening alerting him to this event; the director asked for Dr. Davis' help on Monday morning in breaking the news to the children. The teachers at the center were asked to come to school early for a group discussion with Dr. Davis and Ms. Smith, a colleague of Dr. Davis.

Many of the teachers were close to Nancy; some had grown up with her. They were distraught and not sure they could immediately carry on with the children. They spoke angrily about the senselessness of the killing and how a person like Nancy could be so unjustly struck down. Some recalled other violent incidents in their lives and how this compared to them. Many of the teachers wept openly and feared they would continue to do so throughout the day. The consultants assured the educators that they did not have to hide their feelings from the children, who would be having their own reactions to this tragedy.

When the children arrived many were already talking about Nancy. One 4-year-old boy walked up to Dr. Davis and said simply, "Nancy got shot. She's dead." Ms. Rice, the head teacher in Nancy's room, was visibly shaken at group time and deferred most questions to the consultant. The children had many: Why was Nancy shot? By whom? Is she coming back? Are we going to get shot? Dr. Davis tried to answer these as honestly as possible and also addressed their fears regarding safety of the other teachers, their families, and themselves. Like the other staff members, Dr. Davis was also overwhelmed by the volume and intensity of these questions and needed the support of his colleagues at the Head Start center and at his home office throughout the day.

Nancy's death continued to have a major impact at the school for some time. The community quickly rallied and turned out in force to support her family and each other at her wake the next two nights. The funeral, at a nearby church, was especially emotional. Many parents, some who had been quite friendly with Nancy, attended with their children. A former student sang a stirring hymn that released much emotion within the church. The staff seemed to form closer connections with each other and the consultants, bonds strengthened by having endured this tragedy together.

By September, the teachers had turned their attention back to their classes and were able to talk with the children more openly about Nancy and what she had meant to them. They decided to honor her memory with a plaque dedicated in a ceremony that was attended by the staff and students of

Archway, Dr. Davis and Ms. Smith, and Nancy's family.
Nancy's sister had grown quite close to the staff and families
of Archway in the intervening months and was touched by
their dedication to and appreciation of Nancy. She decided
to volunteer in the program and subsequently became a full-
time staff member.

Random incidents of community violence affecting early childhood centers are perhaps the most intolerable. Teachers, administrators, and mental health consultants are doing well if they are able to
continue to function in some capacity in their jobs and support each
other and the families in their care. Teachers and other staff members
sometimes need reassurance that they do not have to confront the
tragedy with steely resolve and that the children can benefit from seeing them and the consultant have expectable, human reactions. Well-
intentioned efforts to try to avoid pain or to protect children can be
confusing and can inhibit the questions and expressions of sadness that
these events naturally arouse in them.

The staff can be encouraged to seek solace and comfort from each
other, and some may need to have explicit permission from the administrators to share their feelings and reflections about violent events.
The effects of experiencing severe violence often linger for some time
and, as with many stress-induced reactions, may not completely take
hold until well after the event. For these reasons, it is important that the
staff continue to have a means of sharing their reactions. At Archway,
the teachers' meetings with the consultants gradually coalesced into a
support group addressing a range of stresses and personal concerns.
The memorial they dedicated served as a means of keeping the memory of their friend alive; her sister's new role as a staff member was an
even more tangible way of maintaining her presence in the program.

Violent Behavior in the Classroom

As discussed previously, young victims of violence often imitate the
aggressive behavior they have observed and bring their experiences
directly into the classroom. Many are provocative and challenging
toward adults and seek to gain control of their environment. An understanding and appreciation of the causes of aggressive behavior in
young children is important for maintaining a connection to them, and
it may ultimately lead to a means of diffusing their anger. Although
many young children exhibiting violent behavior have a history of
trauma, some aggressive children are physiologically prone to active or
impulsive behavior and still others are asserting their opposition to
classroom rules that are in contrast to the more limited structure in

their home environments. Whatever the etiology of a particular child's behavior, teachers need to know that the consultants can help them with concrete strategies to stop aggression in the classroom. In the United States, systematic efforts to reduce classroom aggression have been attempted, most notably the Choosing Non-Violence curriculum developed in Chicago as a guide for creating "violence-free zones" in preschools (Parry, 1993).

Structured Limit-Setting   As a first task, teachers who confront aggressive behavior and language must clearly demarcate the rules of the classroom. The message must be straightforward: Hurting anyone in the room, verbally or physically, will not be tolerated. Teachers also need to make evident the consequences of such behavior: being separated from the group, missing some free play or group time, and so forth. It is the clarity and consistency of these consequences that is important, not their severity. The mental health consultant may help teachers review their expectations and discuss them with the children, and this may be especially relevant after a major outburst in the classroom. Sometimes a word of caution is needed regarding the possibility of reprimanding the children too harshly or with too many moral overtones. A reminder that this behavior may not be unexpected, given the children's life circumstances, can help educators. Although teaching respect for their peers and the adults in the room is part of any consequence, early childhood staff can sometimes be appalled by a child's behavior and implicitly or explicitly label him as "bad."

The child who is physically aggressive or acting out presents a great challenge to preschool teachers. Children may punch, bite, and kick classmates and their teachers; others throw chairs, break toys, and otherwise aim their destructive impulses in the classroom. One such child in the classroom can create chaos and threaten to undermine the learning environment and structure of the room. Intervening in these moments is rarely an uncomplicated event. In the midst of a tantrum or physical outburst, young children often escalate when adults first attempt to stop them.

These are among the most emotionally wrenching and draining aspects of a teacher's job and may not have been what they bargained for when they decided to work with young children. Many early childhood educators are struck by the discrepancy between their expectations of providing consistent care and a warm environment for children and the reality of having to manage problem behavior on a regular basis. Yet many young children need healthy doses of both structured limit-setting and caring acceptance, and the challenge for teachers is to intertwine the two. Teachers may need consultation time to discuss this dilemma and to learn that if they ignore aggressive behavior, they do so at their own peril. Too often the hope that ignoring violent behavior will lessen its incidence has led to more dangerous situations in which a child puts himself or others at risk. In one child care center, the teachers of 5-year-old Jackson responded to his throwing chairs in class by removing the rest of the other children "so nobody would get hurt." Although they accomplished that goal, Jackson got the message that he was in charge and could control the adults and the children, and his behavior continued to escalate.

Physically Intervening   Although sometimes necessary, physically intervening with young children in the classroom is, of course, no easy task. Many preschool teachers could benefit from practical, hands-on demonstrations of how to stop aggressive behavior and contain children, much like the training required of most child mental health professionals. Early childhood staff members also need to have a clear understanding of their school's limits regarding physical restraint and the criteria for when they should seek outside help or refer an aggressive child to a self-contained or therapeutic program. Obviously any intervention needs to be reviewed and approved by parents and, ideally, the same techniques (e.g., time-out, physical removal from an aggressive situation) can be used at home and in school. In order for these techniques to be implemented successfully, teachers also need to observe their effectiveness in curbing behavior over the long term and may need careful supervision both in how to employ these strategies and in charting how a child responds to them. Paying attention to the frequency and intensity of a child's aggressive behaviors is crucial. Reducing a child's daily outbursts from three to one may not seem to be a real advance if she still causes a major disruption in the room, but it does indicate that she is headed in the right direction.

To set limits effectively, teachers have to realize that containing aggressive students can help those children achieve developmental gains in self-control and can enhance their self-image. If adults can handle them and are not repelled by their behavior, perhaps they are not as "bad" as they often think they are. A strong but benign adult figure gives these children another kind of role model for managing aggressive urges and can help them process the feelings of rage and sadness with which they often struggle. Adopting a punitive tone in the classroom can instead give children who act out the impression that they should be ashamed by their actions and their aggressive fantasies, and ignoring the violent behaviors can make children feel more frightened and out of control.

Helping Young Children Express Themselves   In addition to needing assistance maintaining control, aggressive children also need to hear that they can use other means of expressing their helplessness and despair. Teachers of young children frequently employ the phrase "use your words," but children who act out especially need to know that the classroom offers a forum in which they can translate their experiences in other less threatening ways. Verbalizing their fears or what they have seen can be helpful, as can drawing pictures, acting out stories, or reading fairy tales that touch on their life themes. (See Howarth, 1989, for a discussion of the universality of fairy tales and their usefulness in helping children deal with violent urges and aggressive impulses.) The moments after an intervention to calm a child are often the most fruitful in this regard. Aggressive incidents typically follow a dramatic sequence of outburst, intervention, climax, and, finally, a denouement in which a child experiences a physical and emotional release and may cry or seek physical comfort. This last stage offers a good opportunity for teachers and consultants to offer reassurance and to empathize with the children, using plain language rather than interpretive comments. Simple statements, such as "You were feeling out of control just then and needed our help" or "You seem pretty upset; I know a lot of rough things have been going on lately," can give children solace and let them know that, even at their worst, they will not be rejected by these adults.

Regardless of the rationale, some teachers will not be comfortable with either the physical or emotional demands of containing aggressive children; for personality reasons or because of their own history, others might not be so well suited to this task. In classrooms with a team of three teachers, two might assume an active role with these children while the other might focus on more traditional classroom education. Although not ideal, this model can be effective if all teachers agree to the arrangement, are part of strategy sessions, and explicitly approve the interventions used. A teacher with less direct physical involvement might participate in the discussion following an outburst or have more responsibility for designing a curriculum to address aggressive behavior in and out of class. (See Koplow, 1996, for specific curriculum suggestions for addressing violence and other trauma in the classroom.) Much like in two-parent families, there is a danger if one teacher takes on the role of limit-setting to the exclusion of other staff. Aggressive children respond best when they feel that all of the adults can handle them and that each can also maintain a rapport with the children in the face of outrageous behavior.

When encouraging teachers in this role, mental health consultants must realize it is a challenging one. Clinicians should give teachers and other staff members an opportunity to express their ambivalence and other feelings. Aggressive children can be extremely provocative, and teachers need a place to release their emotions without feeling guilty. The support group model discussed in Chapter 4 can serve as one such place, and often it is a relief for teachers to hear how their colleagues are similarly exasperated, angry, or despondent. While acknowledging these feelings, the consultant can also facilitate a discussion about the critical role that teachers play in children's development. The gains children can make in establishing internal control and reassessing their self-image can be the most important gifts they receive in preschool; these skills may ensure that the children are more openly received by the adults who will care for them as they move on to elementary school.

CHILD ABUSE AND NEGLECT

There is perhaps no other issue in preschools that stimulates as much discomfort as a suspicion of child abuse or neglect. These reactions in part reflect the growing awareness in the larger culture of the preponderance of abuse as well as increasing concern regarding the allocation of responsibility for reporting, investigating, and adjudicating these cases. Child care centers have been at the epicenter of some of the most controversial child abuse investigations and, as such, have to be hypervigilant in looking for signs or symptoms of abuse or neglect. Preschool teachers are also frequently the first line of defense for detecting indicators of trauma and have the best opportunities to intervene early and prevent multiple or cumulative trauma from occurring. Yet they are also working with young children who are still learning to express themselves verbally, are not developmentally prepared to consistently distinguish reality and fantasy, and can be more easily intimidated, coerced, or otherwise swayed by adults. Young children also require regular physical ministrations from adults: Many need help with dressing, toileting, or physically containing themselves, each of which poses potential dilemmas for their caregivers at home and in school.

As explored in Chapter 3, the mental health consultant can serve a useful role by being another professional on board to consider and assess signs of abuse and to share the psychological responsibility that these deliberations require. Often it is the latter support that is most helpful. Whether it is hearing stories of physical or sexual abuse, having children show burn marks or bruises, or calling in child protective services and parents to discuss these issues, all take their toll on the professionals involved. Specific support strategies are presented later in this chapter, but the key is for staff to be able to discuss their feelings about the cases, to share their inclinations in strategy sessions, and then to act in a unified and consistent manner. This process, simple on the surface, is rarely a smooth one.

Four-year-old Elissa was aggressive and defiant in her Head Start class. She often refused to follow rules and dared her

*teachers to set limits for her. However, as limits were set
and Elissa grew more comfortable in her class, she began to
reveal the details of her mother's drug use and its impact on
her. One day she told her teacher anxiously, "There are
crack vials in the bathroom. She's smoking; she leaves me
alone." These revelations were especially scary for Elissa, as
her mother had told her to be silent on this issue: "My
mother told me to hide under the table at school and curse
you, but I'm not going to."*

*Elissa's teachers and the on-site therapist supported her
and addressed her ambivalence about sharing these details,
but they were not sure where else to turn. Elissa's mother's
drug use was already well documented, and child protective
services had been involved several times. When the school
social worker reported these revelations, the child protective
services worker replied that Elissa and her older sister were
not being harmed physically or left unattended for extended
periods; she would therefore take no immediate action.
Repeated efforts by the school to have caseworkers take a
more active role, including reporting to their supervisors,
were met with a limited response. In the end, it took more
than 3 years of continued substance abuse and neglect by
their mother before the girls were removed and placed with
a relative.*

Although child care centers recognize that the dilemmas facing the
protective and judicial systems are numerous and their task a monumental one, situations like this one are heartrending and demoralizing
for teachers and other staff members. Sometimes all mental health consultants can do is to lend an ear to educators' disappointment and distress. Clinicians may suggest other avenues of intervention, and help
the staff focus on their own task of helping children comprehend and
cope with their situations, while being careful to monitor and report
any further signs of deterioration or neglect. Consultants may also encourage early childhood programs to take more active roles in reaching out to caregivers suspected of abuse, especially if staff have given
up hope of making any headway or if their anger at a parent has pre-
vented them from trying.

Maintaining Connections with Parents Suspected of Abuse
Forging an alliance with parents suspected of abuse can be a daunting
task for even the best trained and most experienced educators and clinicians. Aside from facing anger or resistance from other staff, they may

be fearful that any intervention will compound an already abusive situation. They may worry about their own safety as well, fearing that a discussion of potential abuse with parents might lead not only to disavowals of the behavior but also to direct threats toward the staff member making the allegations or inquiring about reports made elsewhere. Without denying these possibilities, the consultant can participate in a discussion regarding ways the child care staff can reach out to parents while broaching their concerns in an honest and straightforward manner. These discussions may be a first step when considering whether to report abuse, but they are often just as important *after* reporting a case to protective services. Some child care programs have specific mandates about contacting parents before or after reporting, a decision that may also hinge upon who is making the report.

> *Three-year-old Warren was enrolled at the Andrews Child Care Center. He had some developmental delays, particularly in speech-language, but was otherwise doing well in class. One morning he came in with a gash on his leg and told his teachers that his father had hit him with an umbrella when he was slow getting dressed that morning. The incident was reviewed with the director, Ms. Marino, who called Mr. Wilson, Warren's father, and told him she must report this incident. Mr. Wilson was livid and complained that she knew him and could not possibly believe he would intentionally hurt his son. Despite the occasional outbursts of anger she had witnessed from Mr. Wilson, Ms. Marino agreed with him because she had observed that father and son were quite connected. She suggested that Mr. Wilson come in and discuss the situation with her. Dr. Bailey, the consulting psychologist who knew Warren from previously conducted testing and observations, would also be present in the meeting. Ms. Marino reiterated that she would still have to report the case to Child Protective Services and that it was their job to investigate what had occurred and what else should be done.*
>
> *Though hesitant, Mr. Wilson agreed, but he asked to meet with Dr. Bailey alone. The two men had developed a solid rapport in previous meetings. Mr. Wilson began, saying he did nothing wrong and repeating that he would not hurt his son. Dr. Bailey confirmed that he had seen much affection between Mr. Wilson and Warren but also explained that he had heard Warren's report from that morning and asked what happened. Slowly, Mr. Wilson described that the*

family had a difficult time the night before, with Warren's
younger sister awakening several times. In the morning, he
was alone with the two children after their mother went to
work. He described rushing to get the children ready, fearful
that they would miss their bus. Warren was taking his time
as he often did, and Mr. Wilson grew increasingly
exasperated. Finally, he admitted, "OK. I did hit him with
the damn umbrella, but I didn't mean to hurt him."

Dr. Bailey thanked Mr. Wilson for being honest and
suggested he do the same with the investigator from Child
Protective Services. He also suggested that Mr. Wilson come
in on a more regular basis to talk about his frustrations and
how to deal with his anger. Dr. Bailey assured Mr. Wilson
that his dilemma was not an uncommon one and told the
father that many parents have feelings of anger toward their
children, particularly when they are stressed. This was the
beginning of a series of meetings between them over the
next 2 years, during which Mr. Wilson revealed in much
more detail the extent of his rage and his problems
controlling his temper in a wide variety of situations. There
were additional inquiries by Child Protective Services during
this time and, though upset by them, Mr. Wilson understood
that they served a purpose and that he could use reminders
about how to handle his temper.

Although the center-based discussions in the wake of abuse
charges rarely resolve the immediate crisis completely, they can open
the door to an ongoing dialogue that can eventually lead to parents
gaining more control over their impulses and more awareness of their
tolerance for stress. In the short term, these meetings with the consultant and other staff members can also reaffirm the program's commitment to the family. Many parents worry that they will be isolated,
judged, or openly rejected by their children's school after charges are
reported, concerns that are usually not altogether unwarranted. They
may also fear that their own anger and ambivalence toward the child
care staff in the wake of an abuse investigation initiated by the school
will not be tolerated and that they either have to withdraw their children from the program or pretend that all is fine. Small, empathic over-
tures by staff to parents can generally improve relations enough that
the ties to the school are not severed. This is critical for the children in
abuse cases, who often endure much turmoil during the investigative
process (as well as feelings of guilt whether they revealed the abuse)

and can benefit greatly from the security, comfort, and routines of their preschools.

Observation and Assessment of Abuse and Neglect

Although most child mental health professionals receive training in child abuse and neglect and are mandated reporters, few have the expertise or inclination to conduct a formal investigation with young children. This is true of most early childhood consultants as well, who will often refer clear cases of sexual abuse to outside "validators" and report suspicions of physical and sexual abuse to the proper social services or oversight agency. Although the child care staff and mental health consultant are not charged with the task of investigation, they do have the advantage of knowing children over time and are equipped to make careful observations, assessing children's progress and development on a regular basis. Some preschool-age children quite conspicuously display marked changes in their behavior or emotions that suggest that something might be seriously amiss in their lives. For a child whose parent has a history of chronic mental illness, for example, the consultant may suspect that new behaviors might be tied to a deterioration in the parent's condition. This situation is illustrated in the following vignette.

> *Four-year-old Jill's mother had stopped taking her medication and was increasingly disorganized, disoriented, and unable to care for her daughter. A bright child, Jill's interest in learning had declined dramatically, and her sadness and malaise had became pronounced. Jill talked of her mother's increasingly bizarre behavior and her concern for her mother in a joint meeting with the teacher and the consulting psychologist. The school social worker was then able to contact Jill's mother and encourage her to resume her medication schedule. Sadly, in this case, the alliance could not be maintained. Jill was removed from the program 2 months later, as her mother again became inconsistent in her medication routine and dropped out of her psychiatrist's care. Child Protective Services were called in again at that point.*

Preschoolers are often much less articulate than Jill, and the consultant and teacher need to more carefully read the nonverbal communications in children's behavior:

> *During the spring of her prekindergarten year, 4-year-old Sandra became increasingly defiant and oppositional in her*

*Head Start class, without apparent provocation, and would
not respond when her teacher inquired about the cause of
this change. She had previously been compliant and
cooperative and engaged in most classroom activities. Her
behavior shifted around the time her father entered prison.
Ms. Cara, the consulting social worker, agreed to spend
some individual time with Sandra at the request of her
teacher and with Sandra's mother's consent. The child spoke
little during those sessions but played out much anger and
aggression. After several sessions, Sandra began to act out
sexual acts in graphic detail. Finally, feeling safe enough,
she revealed that her father had repeatedly sodomized her
and her siblings. Sandra's younger sister, who attended the
same center, later supported her revelations. Ms. Cara
helped Sandra work through her fear and anxiety regarding
her parents' reaction to this information. She also offered
reassurances regarding the investigative process and
accompanied Sandra when the police and Child Protective
Services interviewed her.*

The effectiveness of interventions with victims of abuse often
hinges on the rapport that they are able to develop and maintain with
the professionals who care for them. In Sandra's case, she already had
a well-established relationship with both her teacher and the consultant. Ms. Cara had a good sense of Sandra's typical affect and play
themes and agreed with the teacher that Sandra's behavior and demeanor had shifted dramatically and warranted further observation.
These joint appraisals are often critical in helping staff sort through the
myriad classroom behaviors that could potentially be linked to incidents of abuse or neglect.

At times, there are few visible changes in the behavior or affect of
children who are in abusive or neglectful situations. Some preschoolers are able to adopt a stoic approach and grow accustomed to the contained but fairly constant harsh treatment from their caregivers. Assessment of abuse can be particularly difficult in these cases, especially
in communities where family privacy and social acceptance is highly
valued. There are instances when seemingly well-adjusted children report family conflicts or punitive treatment, often in casual or jarring
ways. During the course of a developmental evaluation, a consulting
psychologist asked 4-year-old Tina to name three wishes. After a momentary hesitation, she replied: "I wish my mother would stop hitting
me and poking me with her fingernails." Had she not been scheduled
for this evaluation, which was unrelated to any emotional concerns, it

is unlikely that Tina would have had time alone with the consultant, and this behavior may not have been reported for some time. Mental health consultants and early childhood professionals are not meant to be detectives; nevertheless, such cases serve as reminders of the need to maintain appropriate levels of vigilance and objectivity when working with all young children, even when there are no clear signs of trouble in the classroom or at home.

Staff Vulnerability to Accusations of Abuse

Caring for young children brings inherent risks regarding the appropriateness of adults' verbal and physical interactions with them. Young children require a level of care and comfort that diminishes considerably by the time they enter elementary school but is essential to their feelings of well-being and safety in preschool. Most need help washing and toileting; some need extra hugs and comforting touches. Still others need stern reminders and occasional physical restraint. All of these activities present opportunities for learning and emotional development but they also present dilemmas regarding the potential for misinterpretation or misperception. They can be fraught with ambiguity and, without proper supervision, training, and due diligence, even well-intentioned child care staff and mental health professionals can run into trouble.

The best prevention is for early childhood programs to have clear rules and reminders as well as proper orientation for new staff. Concrete instruction in areas such as staffing (e.g., not leaving one teacher alone with children), bathroom time (e.g., keeping doors open, having more than one staff person present), and physical interventions (e.g., using proper restraint techniques in clear view of other staff members) can go a long way toward diffusing potential misunderstanding or misjudgment and minimizing ambiguity. If the consultant is unclear on any of these rules, chances are that other staff may be also, and asking for clarification from the director may point out areas of confusion that need to be addressed with all staff.

Even with these precautions, parental suspicions or charges of abuse may surface.

> Tony was a 3-year-old boy new to The Discovery Center, an on-site child care facility at his mother's company. He was pleasant and cooperative but was not yet toilet-trained, usually a prerequisite for entering this school. However, Tony's mother, Ms. Copeland, had offered to come to the center during her breaks and change his diapers, and the director agreed to this arrangement. Over time, the staff

agreed to change Tony occasionally, in part because of the inconvenience to his mother and her occasional unavailability.

Ms. Essex, the head teacher in Tony's class, was a long-time staff member at the center and well respected by the director, her fellow teachers, and parents. She took a particular liking to Tony and was determined that he catch up with the rest of the class. Tony was quite attached to her as well, and he spoke often of Ms. Essex at home.

Tony's school year began fairly smoothly but in October, Ms. Hedges, the director of Discovery, received an angry call from Tony's mother. Ms. Copeland reported that Tony mentioned that Ms. Essex had touched his penis. Ms. Hedges suggested that Ms. Copeland come to the center the next day to talk to her, as well as Ms. Essex, and the mother agreed. Ms. Essex did not deny that she may have touched Tony's penis in the course of wiping him but would have done so unintentionally and without further incident. Ms. Copeland was somewhat relieved by the school's lack of defensiveness and decided to keep her son in the school with the assurance that Ms. Essex would no longer change Tony's diapers.

Dr. Edison, the consulting psychologist, was informed by telephone of the meeting and, upon returning the following week, he spoke to Ms. Essex and Ms. Hedges. Dr. Edison assured Ms. Essex that, based on the information they told him, the situation seemed likely to resolve itself. He did suggest that Ms. Essex continue with the current precautions indefinitely for her own safety and peace of mind. Dr. Edison had also offered to meet with Tony's mother. However, Ms. Copeland's tone and questions implied that she was looking for Dr. Edison to corroborate her suspicions. She did not keep the two appointments they made to discuss the situation further.

Meanwhile, Tony had returned to class after being held out for 3 days. He seemed happy to be back, and his behavior and affect had not changed in any appreciable way. But a few days later, Ms. Copeland again removed Tony from the center and called the police to report Ms. Essex for suspicion of child abuse. The detectives assigned to the case informed Ms. Hedges that she would have to call Child Protective Services to have them begin an investigation of Ms. Essex.

*Two days later the police returned to interview Ms. Essex.
The two detectives interrogated her in a thorough and
somewhat grueling manner, asking for details about her
class, her contact with Tony, and her personal life. She was
extremely distressed by the interview and was saddened by
being temporarily removed from her class, a state mandate
in abuse cases. Although the police soon dropped their
investigation, she was disheartened to learn that Child
Protective Services would continue their inquiry for the
requisite 90-day period.*

*Ms. Essex was feeling desperate to talk, so she began to
meet with Dr. Edison regularly and to speak with him by
telephone between his weekly visits. Dr. Edison assured Ms.
Essex that she had his support and that of Ms. Hedges and
the administration. He listened to Ms. Essex recount her
feelings of betrayal by Tony's mother and her anxiety over
the investigation. Dr. Edison reviewed in detail the
regulations governing abuse investigations and the rationale
for doing complete inquests even where evidence was slight.
To some extent, he served as a foil to the investigators for
Ms. Essex, supportive where they were accusatory,
reassuring where they were suspicious.*

*Ms. Hedges authorized these meetings. As the director,
she recognized that this crisis took precedence over any
other business, and she too needed help in dealing with the
investigators and coping with her own stress. Ms. Hedges
confided in Dr. Edison regarding her own misgivings about
the process and her fears that she would be less resolute in
another such case if she were less confident in a teacher's
innocence. In addition, she conferred with him about a
letter sent home to parents discussing the situation and how
to protect the rights and privacy of the individuals involved
while responding to the curiosity and rumors that were
developing. They also talked of trying to turn the situation
into a positive one for Tony, hoping that the investigation
would relieve some of Ms. Copeland's anxiety and that
maybe he would return to the center. They agreed that in
time the center would fully regain its equilibrium and that
Ms. Essex and the other teachers would eventually feel more
relaxed and confident in their interactions with the children.*

In this crisis, the mental health consultant played a number or
roles. He first and foremost offered support and counsel to the accused

teacher and the director. He worked with them to maintain their focus and manage the stress of the reporting and investigative process. By his continued presence as a respected professional who valued his colleagues at the center, he helped counterbalance the instability and commotion that followed the report of abuse and provided a counterweight to the increased scrutiny of the outside investigators. He worked with the director to develop coping strategies for her staff, to help increase her own tolerance for the information emerging from the case, and to maintain her optimism that the situation would eventually resolve.

The consultant's work in this case was made easier by the lack of evidence supporting the charges and the continued physical and emotional well-being of the child. At other times, details of events are murkier and the prospect of genuine mistakes or misbehavior by teachers or other staff members is greater. A teacher may, for instance, become angry with an aggressive child and strike out at or pull him too hard. Less experienced teachers may not be clear about their own physical boundaries with children and may not set appropriate limits regarding displays of affection. Some teachers might unwittingly or by necessity be understaffed in their room, leading to more dangerous or out-of-control situations.

Each of these circumstances needs to be addressed individually by the director and other supervisory staff. Some might require simple reminders of program rules or further education regarding teacher limits or expectations. The consultant may take part in these discussions and help the director decide which situations require disciplinary action. An important variable is the intent involved. It is not uncommon for a young or inexperienced teacher, or a consultant for that matter, to be tested or provoked by children, especially those who have a history of difficult relationships with adults or intensive trauma. A brief response driven by anger, frustration, or helplessness will be more understandable in this context and more tolerable if the staff person is otherwise caring and responsive toward the children. However, if a pattern of inappropriate behavior develops or if one serious breach of professional conduct occurs, regardless of whether it is provoked, the director may have to decide if that staff person is up to the challenges of caring for young children. This becomes more critical in programs that serve a large proportion of children exposed to multiple traumas or those with special needs, where the work is inevitably more intense and more physically and emotionally demanding.

FAMILY INSTABILITY

Reports of violence and child abuse tend to put early childhood centers on immediate alert and often lead directly to school-based interventions or outreach to community services. Long-standing family problems or chronic instability tend not to draw such attention, and they may be overlooked by harried child care workers who are focused on their day-to-day activities or are responding to current crises in the center. Sometimes salient details of family history captured and noted on intake forms become lost over time, despite occasional indicators in a child's behavior that something might be amiss at home. The sheer volume of family stressors encountered in some programs—including poverty, housing problems, or parental absences—is so great that staff become inured to their impact on any one child.

The mental health consultant often has the advantage in these instances of asking for or hearing about family history for the first time. In some centers, the consultant may be the one who retains crucial information or reminds teachers of the connections between family stress and a child's behavior at school.

> Four-year-old Amy had been enrolled at her child care center for 5 months. Although she entered the program late and had brief separation struggles, she adapted well to the routines of her class. Amy's mother needed the center's services less during the summer months because she had finished a job training class and was not scheduled to begin full-time work until the fall. Therefore, Amy attended the center only sporadically during July and August.
>
> In September, Amy joined a new class with most of the same children but different teachers. Despite her familiarity with the center and her previous successes, she became extremely anxious at school, often crying inconsolably for extended periods. Amy's mother would drop her off on the way to work in what were usually uneventful exchanges, but Amy would begin crying soon afterward and would often be unable to join in any play or work activities with the other children for most of the day. Amy's teachers were sympathetic and supportive and tried a number of strategies to help her calm down, including walking with her, holding her hand, giving her extra hugs, and initiating contact with other children. However, they grew increasingly exasperated when none of these seemed to work consistently.
>
> In the third week of school, Ms. Peters, the director, informed the consultant, Dr. Rosen, that Amy was her main concern. Ms. Peters reported on Amy's increasing separation difficulties and also offered some brief details of Amy's history. She was an only child who was recently reunited

*with her mother after 2 years in foster care. Amy had been
removed from her parents after her father was accused of
physical abuse, including one instance in which he was
inebriated and dropped her accidentally, leaving her with a
broken leg. Amy's father was no longer in the home or in
consistent contact with the family. Amy's mother seemed
caring and connected to her but was apprehensive about
leaving her daughter in the care of others, especially now
that she was working 8 hours a day. Nonetheless, she did
openly review the history of their relationship upon intake at
the center, and she gave Ms. Peters permission to share
these details with Amy's teachers.*

*While observing Amy on the playground, Dr. Rosen spoke
to her teacher, Ms. Harris, about Amy's long absence from
her family. The teacher seemed surprised, having had only a
vague recollection of what Amy's home life was like from a
brief conversation with the center's social worker. Together,
Dr. Rosen and Ms. Harris reflected on this new information
and began to strategize about how to help Amy contain her
anxiety and maintain her new but fragile attachment to her
mother. They decided to try to establish closer contact with
Amy's mother, with whom Ms. Harris had already been
developing a healthy rapport. They talked of having Amy's
mother visit more regularly and for longer periods and of
suggesting that she shorten the length of Amy's days in the
center as much as the mother's schedule permitted. They
also talked about potential transitional objects that Amy
could bring from home, perhaps a photo of her mother, a
small toy, or a special bracelet. Perhaps most important, Ms.
Harris and her co-teachers seemed to gain a renewed sense
of commitment to Amy at a time when their patience and
tolerance was beginning to wear down.*

In this example, the key to the intervention strategy was recognizing the dilemma facing Amy and then brainstorming how to integrate
that knowledge into a plan of action in the classroom. Once the teacher
became aware of Amy's circumstances, she had clear ideas about how
to optimize opportunities to support Amy's connection to her mother
while in school. The consultant's main role was to be a bridge to the
knowledge about Amy's family history and home life, giving staff the
occasion to use this information to effect practical changes in their
teaching techniques and to sustain their commitment to the child.

Chronic and Severe Family Stress

Some family circumstances are more vexing and evoke more painful associations in child care staff, leaving them less prepared to incorporate
their knowledge in the classroom. Children who are homeless or living
in extreme poverty and others who are bereaved or living without
parental support because of chronic substance abuse, mental illness, in-
carceration, or abandonment face such severe challenges that many
staff cannot bear to hold on to this information. In some respects, this is
a natural response that can even have some benefits for these children.
When teachers focus primarily on their children's development and the
positive signs of growth and advancement in their classrooms, they can
avoid placing too much emphasis on the negative realities that can stigmatize children or lead to lowered expectations for success.

Yet these children inevitably bring their home lives with them to
school; ignoring their realities or painting a rosy picture of "normal"
family experiences can leave them feeling isolated and different. This
is not to suggest that children's painful memories or current travails
should dominate class discussions. Instead, they might be woven into
the fabric of the achievements and disappointments, the moments of
joy and despair that are part of any group's and any individual child's
experiences. For some children, the comfort and encouragement received in preschool is in striking contrast to the danger or deprivation
they endure in other environments. When adults fail to acknowledge
these discrepancies, they risk leaving the children with a division in
their perceptions and experiences that may be difficult to unify in any
coherent and meaningful way.

The mental health consultant may address these situations by first
reviewing the home lives of all the children with staff in regular team
meetings. For a child living in chronic stress, the team may reflect on
how this influences her behavior, emotions, and relationships in school
as well as try to recall if the child has referred to the situation in any direct or indirect manner. Some children appear particularly resilient in
light of reported family instability, and teachers sometimes gain a new
appreciation and respect for a child's achievement in overcoming the
challenges he faces. Others present a more enigmatic picture, sometimes appearing happy and focused, other times acting defiant and
angry. Upon further examination, these changes in behavior may be
closely related to disruptions in their home lives and the care a child receives as a result. This is not to suggest, of course, that early childhood
staff adopt a reductionist model in which each change in a child's behavior is quickly tied to a suspected parental lapse or new stressor. In
fact, the impact of trauma can exert itself more fully during periods of

relative calm when the child is no longer focused on an imminent threat or danger. Moreover, like all children, those who have experienced trauma react to the everyday stresses of childhood, which may not be connected to any major disturbance at home. Yet teachers might begin to note more carefully shifting moods or behaviors in certain children and to ask questions about the meaning of these discrepancies.

In addition to looking closely at family history or talking directly to parents, a teacher may also openly ask a child if she has noticed a recent or marked change in her behavior or demeanor. This approach is appropriate for all children, including those who do not have a history of family instability, but it may be especially pertinent when there is a well-documented history of chronic stress at home. Often children will give vague or marginal responses to such questions, to which a teacher might reply simply, "I just noticed you were upset," "I hope you feel better," or "Let me know if I can help." These phrases indicate that the teacher is recognizing a difference in a child's behavior, is accepting his mood, and is available to offer any possible assistance. They are not meant to be intrusive or demanding statements, and they all lie comfortably within most early childhood teachers' repertoire. In many instances, they are the first steps toward developing an alliance between the teacher and the child that may eventually lead to a more straightforward discussion of difficulties the child faces elsewhere.

Children sometimes describe an encounter with a parent from the previous evening or that morning that has left them feeling unsettled. They may need brief comfort, extra reassurance, and perhaps an offer to check in with their parents to see if everything is fine at home.

Four-year-old Todd, who usually came in beaming to his Head Start program, entered in a rage one morning and began hurling objects about the room. When the consulting social worker was called in to help contain him, he told her, "My mother was yelling at me today; she said, 'Get on the bus, you f____ midget.'" Todd's mother had a history of serious mental illness and, although lucid and caring at times, she could also be condescending and verbally abusive, and Todd's account rang true to previous interactions observed by staff. After sharing this exchange he calmed down considerably, and he quietly asked to sit next to his teacher during breakfast and circle time. The consultant called Todd's mother later that day. She was remorseful and apologetic and agreed to come in the next day to speak with Todd's teachers.

Children are often noticeably relieved when details of their family lives that they thought could only be met with astonishment or shame are received openly. Many young children have already experienced the value judgments and stigma in the larger culture regarding individuals struggling with substance abuse and mental illness, and these children may have been directly warned that discussing such issues will only be met with scorn. Yet a number of children who have been able to talk about family members affected by these problems learn that some of their peers share their experiences and that other children and adults are less critical than expected. Children have expressed similar relief in talking about family members who have been incarcerated, and they often volunteer more details when their revelations are met with interest. Some have talked of visiting jail and the fear and anxiety they felt upon entering as well as the anguish upon leaving a parent behind. Others have chosen to bring in letters they have received from relatives imprisoned in distant locales, sharing them with teachers or sometimes with friends. In all of these cases, the point is for children to be allowed to go at their own pace and to reveal as much or as little as they choose.

Sometimes before proceeding with group discussions, the teachers and the mental health consultant together review how much detail is appropriate for the class to hear, especially if stories contain graphic or unsettling details. It is also important to examine how the experience of telling can be helpful to the child. As noted in the previous discussions on violence, it is often the validation and acceptance the child experiences from other members of the group and the realization that others share his or her dilemma that provides comfort and solace. Children also appreciate that they can go on being full and active members of a class, enjoying the games, rituals, and learning activities of preschool, without worrying that they have a terrible secret that could undo or lessen their accomplishments in the eyes of others. In fact, sometimes a single revelation from a child that paints a clearer picture of his home life suffices in establishing what he requires from the adults in his school environment and clarifies the dilemmas he faces in trying to make sense of his experiences in different settings.

Some children carry to school the fear and danger they perceive in their home environment. In one Head Start program serving homeless families, the children would often describe fights among adults in the shelters, unsanitary conditions in public areas, drug dealing, and a constant police presence. Families were often awoken by fire alarms in the middle of the night, during which the children were forced to wait outside for several minutes in their nightclothes. Practice fire alarms in the school were extremely frightening for many of these children, recreating a small trauma in what was otherwise a safe and cozy environment. Staff worked to minimize these intrusions and also used these situations as opportunities for group discussions of the events children had witnessed and experienced. The teachers and the consulting psychologist sought to normalize these fears while helping the children develop coping strategies for the different situations they faced in the shelters. The educators and the consultant also acknowledged the tremendous stress these children endured due to the demand for constant vigilance on their part. The staff did not have easy answers, but they allowed and encouraged the children to bring their stories and experiences from the shelters into the center. This served to help the students develop more integration between the divergent environments they confronted during the day and at night.

SITUATIONAL CRISES

Fortunately, most young children do not face these extreme challenges to their own healthy development and their families' stability. Although the prospect of job loss and financial insecurity haunts many middle-income families, they do not face the same economic constraints and accompanying stresses as those living in poverty do, and they have more resources available for their young children's health care and education. Caregivers in all economic sectors who are able to meet the demands of their home and work lives and maintain their physical and emotional health are likely to provide a solid home environment for their children. Young children with adequate physical and mental capacities and strong relationships with their parents usually develop a sense of security and wonderment that they carry with them to preschool, where they have the freedom to develop their intellectual and physical curiosity.

Nevertheless, trauma can strike in even the most optimal settings. Disease and chronic illness are often random events, and sudden and unexpected deaths occur in any community. Great challenges can emerge at any point in the life span, from a toddler diagnosed with autism to an adolescent struggling with schizophrenia to a middle-age adult confronting alcoholism. Families enjoying financial success have seen their future turn quickly through downsizing or disability. Children living in what appear to be solid and contented families are often shocked by the news of their parents' pending separation or divorce. In many of these instances, it is the suddenness of events and the rapid changes they entail that often overwhelm even resilient and prepared families and may lead them to seek assistance for the first time (Kliman, 1978).

Families in crisis often turn to their immediate community, and many with young children turn to the early childhood program for support and direction. The specific request may be to help a child cope with a trauma, but often the call for assistance extends to the entire family and sometimes beyond. At times, crises occur in quick succession, affecting the entire child care community as well as the individual families.

> *Dr. Anderson was a consultant at the Waverly Nursery School, a small preschool in a suburban middle-class community. Within the space of one academic year, the school experienced an inordinate amount of trauma: a boy's older sibling drowned while on a fishing trip; a girl's father suddenly died of a heart attack; the mother of several young children was diagnosed with a serious form of cancer; and the father of a classroom teacher became critically ill and died, necessitating the absence of the teacher for several weeks.*

Although this community benefited from relative prosperity and stability, the series of tragedies strained both the individual families and the capacity of the program to respond. In each of these situations, the consultant discussed how to respond to the crisis with the families involved, the teachers, and administrative staff. In most cases, families and teachers wanted the consultant to help deal with the crisis both by checking in with the child who was directly affected and also by talking with the other preschoolers about what had happened. A long-term benefit of this difficult period was that the school staff grew in their ability to discuss and tolerate the painful life events that ordinarily occurred much less frequently in this community. By modeling an approach to trauma that entailed open discussion rather than avoidance, the consultant was able to work closely with teachers to support the children during times of crisis.

Separation and Divorce

Parental separation or divorce is not necessarily a traumatic experience for children, although it nearly always leads to significant and lasting changes in a child's life. Mental health consultants must be sensitive to the significance of each family's particular situation, and they should encourage the child care staff to refrain from making general assumptions about the impact of divorce or forming any preconceived notions or judgments regarding each parent's role or culpability in the situation. Some children are able to maintain solid relationships with both parents after a breakup, and many young children make successful transitions into reconstituted families. The preschool staff may need help in being open to a wide array of family relationships.

Nonetheless, young children clearly face particular developmental challenges in a divorce situation. Their drives toward independence and autonomy can be compromised by their anxiety over the potential loss of a parenting figure, and they may display varied symptoms of regression and a strong wish to remain dependent. Preschoolers are also coping with phase-specific attachments and alliances with each parent and may worry that their anger or rejection of a parent has directly led to the adults' separation. Research and clinical practice suggest that when a divorce is particularly acrimonious and parents are unable to contain their hostility, anger, and disappointment, the effect on young children can be serious (Hetherington, 1989; Wallerstein & Kelly, 1980).

Kevin Rogers had just turned 5 when his parents divorced, and everyone at his school was extremely concerned about him. An energetic and verbal child, Kevin had always been a handful at preschool. Rather than becoming more settled and manageable over time, Kevin's behavior grew increasingly chaotic, aggressive, and unpredictable. At times, he busily immersed himself in play, and he especially loved the block area, constructing impressive and complex structures. At other times, he would suddenly lash out at other children, shoving them or even spitting when he was angry.

Kevin's teacher, Ms. Carter, was aware of his strained family situation, and she had spoken several times to Kevin's parents about their son's behavior in the classroom. She was particularly concerned about Kevin's potential to injure another child seriously, but she liked Kevin and worried that he was gaining a reputation as a "bad kid." By the time Ms. Carter approached the consulting psychologist, Dr. Williams, she had grown quite frustrated by the Rogers, who seemed more concerned about blaming each other for their son's difficulties than addressing his problems in school. Each parent had given an angry litany of the other's mistakes and transgressions, and their venom was palpable. Ms. Carter also felt that Mrs. Rogers seemed angry at her; the mother coldly stated that she did not have the types of problems with Kevin at home that the teacher experienced at school.

Mr. Rogers, however, was friendlier and seemed to want the teacher to understand how difficult his ex-wife could be. Kevin's teacher began to feel that she was losing her sense of perspective; she worried that she was being manipulated by each parent and somehow would become embroiled in the Rogers' legal conflicts.

By the time Ms. Carter approached Dr. Williams about the situation, she was worn out by Kevin's demands and overwhelmed by the situation between his parents. Dr. Williams suggested that prior to developing any school-based interventions for Kevin, the team had to establish a more solid relationship with both of Kevin's parents. The consultant, the teacher, and the program director met several times with the Rogers, attempting to refocus their energy on Kevin's needs and appealing to each parent's real desire to do the best they could for their son. Despite the school's efforts, these meetings made little headway with the Rogers. By the time Kevin was ready to start kindergarten, his parents remained embroiled in a bitter legal struggle and were not consistently working together to help him. On the positive side, Kevin's teacher did learn to set limits with the Rogers by not engaging either one in discussions about the other and by focusing solely on Kevin's functioning in school. Kevin made a strong attachment to his teacher and had days without problems; however, he continued to become angry and easily frustrated and often got into physical fights with other children.

Similar to many situations in which parents are in conflict, the preschool staff in this example made few strides in their repeated attempts to get a divorced couple to cooperate and concentrate on their child's experience. They were frustrated by these failed efforts and angered that the child's escalating behaviors in school were not enough to unify his parents. In this case, the mental health consultant could only suggest a logical course of action as the best hope for change, knowing that the parents' discord and resistance to working together was likely a contributing factor to the child's acting-out behavior in school. Although this plan ultimately bore little fruit, meetings with the parents brought into bold relief the extent of the conflict that the child witnessed and endured. These discussions helped his teacher press on with a new appreciation for the constant stress and strife in the child's home life as well as the boy's unfulfilled wish to bring his parents together.

Failed experiences at building trust with caregivers are among the most difficult aspects of the work for most early childhood staff, especially for those who pride themselves on creating a community of families devoted to enriching the lives of young children. It is particularly painful when a child clearly needs the adults in her life to work closely together and the gathered parties all seem to want what is best for the child. These dilemmas faced by staff are of course reminiscent of the struggles children face regularly in homes where conflict is endemic. Solutions that appear close at hand are many times lost, and the children are often in a constant cycle of longing for resolution, hopefulness, disappointment, anger, and resentment. Even the best-equipped and most savvy clinicians and teachers can feel powerless watching this drama unfold. Yet witnessing these events gives preschool staff an opportunity to enter into these children's lives more fully and can help them acknowledge painful realities that many adults would prefer to ignore. For many children with parents in conflict, understanding and respect for their experiences are key to developing more genuine and trusting relationships, which may have a long-lasting impact on their emotional and interpersonal development.

Children Undergoing Medical Treatment

There are times when the traumas children face are minimized or misunderstood by adults, particularly if there is reasonable certainty that the child or family will survive intact. Such is often the case when a young child is hospitalized or requires surgery. Medical advances have made many childhood illnesses more manageable and nearly eradicated others, and what were once complicated surgical procedures are now fairly routine. Parents, of course, cling to the hopeful information they receive from medical providers and generally do their best to calm and reassure their children that things will turn out fine. Yet such well-intentioned words of comfort often do little to assuage children's fantasies and fears related to their illnesses and may gloss over the psychological consequences of medical procedures they endure.

Jake stood out to his teacher, Ms. Abero, from the first week of school. She noticed that he seemed wary of both children and adults and was reluctant to try most of the appealing activities she offered the children. At the same time, he conveyed a false bravado, gave other children little pushes as they stood on line, and bragged about how he could kill "all the monsters and bad guys." This astute teacher also observed Jake's anxiety whenever he had to use the bathroom, which he tended to avoid. After the first few days of school, Jake's behaviors intensified, and although he was clearly bright, he was unable to focus on any of the class activities.

Although Ms. Abero had wanted to give Jake a chance to settle in, she saw that things were getting worse rather than better. By the time she approached Dr. Richards, the consulting psychologist, during the end of the second week of school, Ms. Abero was annoyed by and angry at Jake's behavior. She asked Dr. Richards to observe and talk with Jake before they called Jake's mother, Ms. Griffin. After observing him, Dr. Richards approached Jake as the child sat alone at a table drawing ferocious-looking dragons. His first words to Dr. Richards were "Nobody can hurt me."

Dr. Richards encouraged Ms. Abero to call Jake's mother to express her concerns. When she spoke with Ms. Griffin, Ms. Abero was surprised to learn that Jake had undergone surgery to remove a benign tumor from his groin only 2 weeks before school had started. Ms. Griffin had intended to call Ms. Abero but was busy at work and at home and also felt that Jake was doing fine. However, she added that her son had been in a lot of pain following the surgery, and he seemed angry with her for "letting" the doctors hurt him. Jake's father, who had minimal contact with his son, had not called or visited Jake for more than 6 months, including the period prior to and after his surgery.

Ms. Abero, who was caught off-balance by all of this news, suddenly felt more sympathy for Jake's behavior. She asked Jake's mother if Dr. Richards could contact her to talk more about Jake's development, and Ms. Griffin agreed to meet with both of them several days later. They discussed Jake's obvious anxiety about the surgery and the fact that the procedure was performed near his genitals—an area of great significance to a 4-year-old boy—which probably intensified his distress. On top of that, his father's indifference during this traumatic experience was deeply hurtful.

The school meeting resulted in several interventions. Jake was included in Dr. Richards' small school-based social skills group for children who needed help with peer interactions. Ms. Griffin also began to think that therapy might help Jake work through the aftermath of the surgery as well as the issue of his father's absence. Ms. Abero seemed energized in her ability to think of ways to help Jake feel more comfortable in school. With renewed patience and using the insights she had gained in this meeting, she slowly

*developed a stronger relationship with Jake and began to
gain his trust.*

Here the consultant had the opportunity to bring together a caring
teacher and a concerned parent to help a child cope with a major psychological assault on his body image. The child was clearly left fearful
and angry after his surgery but, up to that point, he had only been able
to act out these fears through aggressive play and fantasies. Knowing
the details of Jake's medical procedures gave his teacher a new perspective on the child's behavior as well as hope that she could form a bond
with him and that he could eventually participate more fully in classroom activities. The child's mother also welcomed the chance to hear
more about his behavior, and, feeling supported in the school context,
she considered getting her son additional assistance outside of school.

Illness in the Family

Most preschool children worry a good deal about their own body integrity and the health and well-being of their family members. Many
need continued reassurance that minor illnesses and injuries affecting
their loved ones are not serious and that they can generally count on
the health and safety of their caregivers. When a family member faces
a more serious illness, many parents and child care workers are per-
plexed at how much they should tell a child regarding potential risks
and understandably want to balance any negative news with reasons
for optimism. At times, remaining positive in the face of medical uncertainty is a monumental challenge, and undue optimism is not necessarily in the best interest of the young child. Reviewing the details of
the illness with the children may also not be the focus in a family that
has shifted to crisis mode and is primarily concentrating on the treatment of the affected individual. Perhaps even the adults are overcome
with their own grief and anxiety.

*When the consulting social worker, Ms. Green, heard Mrs.
Westin's voice on the telephone, she immediately knew that
something was wrong. Mrs. Westin's children, Julie and Lee,
attended the preschool, and she was a frequent volunteer
who had helped parents encountering the special education
process for the first time. During the telephone call, Ms.
Green could barely understand Mrs. Westin, who cried,
"You have to help me! I was just diagnosed with cancer. I
don't know what I'm going to tell the kids. You have to help
my children!"*

*A previously healthy woman, Mrs. Westin had just
learned that she had a serious though treatable form of
cancer and would need surgery imminently. At the moment
she called Ms. Green, Mrs. Westin's greatest concern was
for her children. The Westin's were a stable family:
Although her children had some developmental language
delays, life had gone fairly smoothly for them, and Mrs.
Westin considered herself lucky. Suddenly this stability was
shattered and she was terrified. After talking for several
minutes, Ms. Westin became calmer and seemed comforted
by Ms. Green's promises to inform the children's teachers
and the school director about the situation and, if needed, to
be available for the children during school.*

*The next week, Ms. Green called Mrs. Westin, who by
this time was feeling much less panicked, more hopeful, and
also quite embarrassed about her outburst on the telephone.
Her surgery had been postponed for several weeks, Mrs.
Westin's friends and family had been supportive and
available, and she was feeling more optimistic that she
would survive and the family would cope. She still
expressed a great deal of concern about the effects of her
illness on the children and asked for a referral to an outside
therapist, someone who could help her children if the need
arose. She added that although Julie did not want to speak
with Ms. Green right now, she seemed relieved that Ms.
Green knew about her mother's illness. Although the future
was still shaky, the immediate crisis was less frightening to
Mrs. Westin and her family, and they seemed comforted by
the responses of Ms. Green and the school staff.*

In this example, the mental health consultant did not have firsthand interactions with the children whose mother had become ill but
instead helped the school create an atmosphere of support for the family. The consultant's main function in this situation was to listen, to
communicate promptly with other staff, to provide a referral, and to
follow up with the family. Her work was simplified due to the family's
many strengths. The mother had a strong network to help her through
a time of crisis and she was comfortable asking for assistance, both
from the school directly and from a therapist whom the social worker
recommended. The family's basic sense of optimism and hope sustained them even though their predictable routines and expectations
for the future had been dramatically altered.

Death in the Family

Anxieties and fears about death are common in preschoolers, especially as they become more aware of their own vulnerability. Young children are also unable to maintain consistency in separating their own thoughts and fantasies about death and destruction from real events. They worry that their angry thoughts will magically pose a threat to ones they love and are often consumed by guilt when those close to them suffer serious accidents or injury. When there is a death in a family, often the young children are the most confused and overwhelmed, and they cannot understand the facts about the cause of death or grasp its finality. Although one step removed, the young child's peers will inevitably share some of the same anxieties and need assistance in coming to terms with the situation.

> For days, 5-year-old Jeffrey had been talking excitedly at circle time about the imminent birth of his baby brother. The whole class awaited the happy news; most of the children had seen Jeffrey's mother, who was obviously pregnant, drop him off at school. Jeffrey's aunt worked in the office, so the staff also felt part of the family's joyful anticipation. It came as a great surprise when Jeffrey's aunt called the school one morning to report that the baby had been stillborn, without any apparent cause of death.
>
> The family was, of course, in shock, and the school staff also reacted strongly. Jeffrey's teacher sought out the consultant, Dr. Stein, and together they made a plan of action that included having a school representative telephone the family to discuss how they wanted the school to respond. Jeffrey's parents wanted his classmates to be told what happened before his return to school, so Dr. Stein scheduled a time to talk with the class. He visited the classroom within 2 days of the baby's death. Most of the children already knew about the tragedy and had begun forming their own often distorted explanations for what had happened. One child stated that the baby had died because its mother smoked, and another child guessed, mistakenly, that the umbilical cord had strangled the baby. Working through their ideas, fantasies, and feelings about the baby's death was an important preventive step in terms of mitigating rumors, guilt, and misinformation that could be potentially hurtful to Jeffrey and others.

As is often the case, many of the children in the class could identify with Jeffrey's loss and quickly related it to their own experiences. The children offered their own memories of deceased relatives and pets. Although allowing the children to express their own experiences of loss was helpful, Dr. Stein also believed it was important to contain their anxiety. He reassured the children about their own safety and reminded them that the baby's death was a rare occurrence. Dr. Stein then turned the conversation to how the children thought Jeffrey might feel when he returned to school and what they might do to help him. At this point, Dr. Stein more actively involved Jeffrey's teacher, asking her for reactions to the children's suggestions and ideas about how and when to facilitate them. A range of feelings and ideas emerged, reflecting the ability of individual children to tolerate and understand the situation. For instance, one girl said, "Don't say anything to him. It will make him feel sad." Another child suggested, "Give him a party?" Finally, as a group, they decided they would make a card for Jeffrey expressing their sad feelings at his loss and reassuring him that they were still his friends.

Dr. Stein also offered to see Jeffrey once or twice individually as a way to support him after he returned to school. Both Jeffrey and his family eagerly accepted, and their openness was likely due, in part, to the fact that Dr. Stein was a familiar face in the preschool. He had been in Jeffrey's class numerous times for various reasons, had often passed the class in the hallways, and had been observed taking other children out of the classroom.

Dr. Stein listened as Jeffrey described the details of the story. Jeffrey also expressed some shame in returning to a group that had only recently been anxiously anticipating exciting news from him. Dr. Stein told Jeffrey that these concerns were unfounded, and the clinician referred to the card the class had made with its words of encouragement and support. When Jeffrey expressed misgivings about returning to school, Dr. Stein assured him that it was normal to have mixed feelings about being away from his family and to sometimes have a hard time concentrating. He was aware that some of Jeffrey's ambivalence and shame might be related to expected feelings of jealousy he felt toward the unborn baby. Dr. Stein also reminded Jeffrey that his sad feelings might last for a while, that they might come and go,

*and that he should not feel he must hide them. He offered to
check in with Jeffrey for the next several weeks, and the boy
gladly agreed to this plan.*

In this example, the goal of the mental health consultant was not
only to address the needs of the child and his family but also to ascertain how this trauma affected the larger preschool community. By engaging the child's classmates, he was able to calm some of their anxiety, address their related fantasies, and correct misinformation they
had received. He also took these opportunities to draw the group together so that they might be another support for their classmate when
he returned to school. In his individual work with the grieving child,
the psychologist mentioned the support of both the class and Jeffrey's
teacher, thereby reassuring the boy that his school was a welcoming
and nurturing place where he need not hide his pain or pretend that all
was well. The therapist also gave Jeffrey license to be happy and joyful
and assured the child that he need not conform to any expectable pattern of mourning.

Community Disaster

Most references to trauma in early childhood refer to singular events or
chronic circumstances affecting a particular child and family. Yet there
are times when an entire community is affected by a catastrophic event,
whether man made or natural. Reports of hurricanes, floods, earth-
quakes, and other natural disasters have stressed the psychological impact of these events on children and families that can persist long after
the devastation has passed and the restoration process has concluded.
Incidents of school violence have shattered the calm and anonymity of
some suburban and rural communities and have led many residents to
question long-held beliefs and values.

Although it is common practice to dispatch crisis response teams
to schools and communities affected by disaster, there is often much
more confusion about how to handle public traumatic events with very
young children. There is a general misperception both in families and
in preschools that these children are not aware of what has occurred
around them. For example, a child care director assured a consulting
psychologist that no child in her program had been affected by a local
murder-suicide, despite the fact that the shooting occurred at midday,
500 yards from the center. All of the children were evacuated hurriedly
through a rear exit of the building during a police siege on the gun-
man's house. The incident was widely reported in local newspapers
and on the evening news. Yet an offer to provide assistance was met
with a respectful decline of any psychological intervention in the school
and a report that "none of our children knew anything about it."

Young children pose more of a quandary because they often do not speak directly about their fears or worries related to recent events. They may, however, play out these concerns and frequently need help from adults to articulate what they are experiencing.

> Ms. Garcia was the consulting social worker at an urban preschool program serving mainly Latino families. She returned to the school after a weekend to discover that a major fire had occurred in a neighborhood social hall, killing several dozen people. Many of the mothers were lingering outside the classroom, discussing the tragic event. Although none of their immediate family members were affected, quite a few parents did know a neighbor or an acquaintance who had lost a loved one in the blaze. Ms. Garcia suggested that the teachers invite the parents to the classroom for a discussion with their children about this traumatic event. In the meeting, the parents stood together at the edge of the room while the children raced around them in a noisy and tumultuous manner. As the teachers sought to engage the adults and children as a group, she observed that the mothers welcomed the opportunity to talk to each other but were hesitant to express themselves in front of the children. One mother disclosed her understandable concern that direct discussion of the fire would be too frightening for the children, suggesting that they were "too young to understand." Another stated her fear that the group's expressions of sadness would overwhelm the children. The parent group generally agreed that the children were not even aware that this terrible tragedy had occurred and wished to protect them from the trauma.
>
> While Ms. Garcia listened to this discussion, she continued to observe the children's behavior, which was becoming increasingly boisterous. She wondered aloud whether the children were not in fact demonstrating to the adults that they had some level of awareness of this event. She suggested that even if they did not consciously know the specifics of the fire, they were affected by the emotional response of parents and neighbors and were, on some level, struggling with this traumatic event as well. At that moment, 3-year-old Louis ran up to Ms. Garcia and bluntly stated, "Mommy's crying." The parent group then began to acknowledge the ways their children were exposed to this tragedy, reporting various incidents that were indicative of

some degree of stress in the children. The consultant told the parents that it would be helpful for the children to verbalize their thoughts and put words to feelings in the presence of their parents and teachers, who could provide understanding and reassurance.

The teachers and Ms. Garcia unified the group, with most children finding their way into the lap of an adult. At that point, Ms. Garcia supported the parents as they discussed the fire and their feelings about it in simple, straightforward language. She encouraged the children to share their feelings directly and helped them find the words, suggesting that while the fire itself was frightening, it was also "scary to see grown-ups so sad." The group leaders closed by telling the students that although a terrible thing did happen and many people were hurt, the grown-ups present would work hard to protect the children. When the discussion broke into free play, a number of children spontaneously began to play "fire truck"; they ran around making siren noises. Ms. Garcia then informed the parents that this was an expected play enactment of the recent trauma and encouraged the parents to join in, helping the children confront the fire and, if it felt right, finding the hoses to extinguish it as well.

In this situation, parents had legitimate concerns that the details of the traumatic event would overwhelm or confuse the children, but they came to see that saying nothing would likely exacerbate the children's worries. With a small amount of coaxing from the teacher and the consultant, the parents were able to discuss the incident in concrete terms the children could understand. They also could see that it was the children's fears for their own and their families' safety, in addition to concern for their parents' emotional vulnerability, that were more troubling than the actual event.

The desire to protect young children from painful real-life experiences, although usually well intended, can often have the opposite effect. Children left alone with their own fears and fantasies can create catastrophic and foreboding images that go beyond an immediate disaster, leaving them anxious and insecure about the future. This is not to imply, of course, that preschoolers need to know the event's graphic details. They are entitled, however, to a reasonable and, if possible, causal explanation: "A fire started in the basement from a candle. Many people were inside, and there were not enough doors so some people could not get out. The firemen tried to save them." This material should not be given in isolation; it needs to be included in overall discussions about the magnitude of the tragedy and people's feelings about it. The adults should also address the children's anxiety about safety and include specific examples of the ways in which they are kept safe, such as fire extinguishers, fire alarms, telephone calls to 911, and the presence of supervising adults. Young children often need permission from adults to express their fears and misgivings, and they typically welcome the opportunity afforded them by adults who are clear and direct regarding their own emotional reactions. Parents and other caregivers are then able to offer reassurance that they are still capable of and firmly committed to protecting and caring for their children.

THE IMPACT OF TRAUMA ON EARLY CHILDHOOD PROFESSIONALS

Although they often focus on ameliorating the effects of trauma on young children and their families, teachers, social workers, administrators, and mental health consultants must also contend with the deleterious effects of exposure to trauma. Professionals who work with families affected by violence, abuse, and other intense stressors usually have to find a balance between maintaining an empathic engagement and being overwhelmed by their clients' stories. Most clinicians rely heavily on their training, supervision with colleagues, and their own self-protective instincts to help them manage their anxiety and to continue to function effectively in their roles.

Yet reports of burn-out and high stress among clinicians working with multiply stressed families are widespread. Lyon (1993) identified a series of symptoms of "secondary" PTSD in clinical staff with ongoing exposure to trauma. She described the "toxic" nature of this work and a feeling among workers of being contaminated by the stories they hear. Lyon also observed that many clinicians become isolated and alienated from those who do not share their experiences. Some staff overidentify with their clients, lose distance from their work, and become consumed with rescue fantasies. Professionals who regularly confront severe violence and trauma frequently find themselves wrestling with existential dilemmas about the prevalence of good or evil in the world, and they can come to question the nature of humanity.

Teachers and child care workers, who traditionally have less training, experience, and support in coping with these issues, are even more vulnerable to the risks inherent in working with victims of trauma. Some assume that a constant barrage of crises or traumatic material should be borne with confidence and self-assurance and that seeking help or admitting to feeling overwhelmed would be unprofessional or a sign of weakness. Others attempt to shut out any reports of child trauma or family distress. Teachers may choose to avoid the children's revelations about their home lives, feeling that such information is outside the realm of their competencies and not appropriate in the classroom. Yet traumatic family events are hard to ignore, and, as previously noted, preschool is often an opportune environment for interventions with young children and their families.

Programs that do attempt to help young children cope with trauma must also make provisions for staff. As discussed in Chapter 4, formal support groups can help teachers see that their colleagues are struggling with the same dilemmas and give them a chance to speak of their own frustrations and stress. For some staff, smaller team meetings or informal gatherings can serve a similar purpose. In either case, staff members need to feel safe to talk about their fear, anger, distress, and sense of helplessness. Sometimes finding reasons to laugh can help early childhood workers withstand what can seem like surreal or absurd situations. Such discussions tend to release some of the tensions in staff, particularly if they realize that there are no repercussions from speaking honestly about how the work affects them. Meetings may also offer a place where staff can relate their own histories and experiences and how particular stories and traumatic situations resonate with and affect them. This mutual support can help teachers and administrative staff maintain a strong investment in the families without becoming consumed by their distress.

Mental health consultants can participate in these discussions and sometimes model for other staff members by talking about their own feelings and reactions to trauma. Clinicians not only have the opportunity in these moments to dispel the notion that they are distant or neutral, but they can also join with staff more fully when they acknowledge their own anxieties, misgivings, and feelings of limitation. Retaining and managing painful stories and crisis situations can be a monumental task for preschool administrators and staff. By agreeing to share this responsibility and helping with strategies for intervention, the mental health consultant can sometimes lighten the school's burden, even if not physically present for parts of the work week. The collaborative model can enhance a child care program's resilience, as it encourages all the professionals to rely on each other for both concrete advice and emotional support when confronted by trauma.

Joint appraisals of crisis situations can also help both the clinical and educational staff develop more realistic expectations for themselves and the families they serve. Major traumas cannot be undone quickly, and, for some children and families, the early childhood center may simply be one consistent and secure place amid perpetual turmoil. Maintaining focus and sticking to the task of providing a nurturing educational and social environment is often the best and only course of action. Recognizing where and how to intervene, and when not to, is a continuous process that requires diligence, creativity, and humility. If they are to address crisis situations effectively, the professionals involved have to develop a sense of teamwork, respect for families, and a willingness to recognize that many crises have no immediate solutions.

Ultimately, the way a program responds to difficult or tragic circumstances will depend in large part on how it defines its overall mission. Some solid preschools choose to focus primarily on children's academic and social development, having relatively little contact with families. Others see working with families as central to their goals. Certain programs, often in underserved neighborhoods, define their role more broadly, and they are typically a focal point for various kinds of family and community events as well as for interventions in times of crisis. In early childhood programs that accept this challenge, teachers, administrators, and mental health consultants are asked to do more and to be more available. Many welcome this opportunity to join with other early childhood professionals who share their values and sense of purpose, and they are eager to accept the invitation to become active and integral members of the community.

Reflections
and Implications

chapter nine

Maintaining
an Effective Collaboration

The success of collaborative efforts between mental health professionals and early childhood educators will depend largely on their ability
to develop a shared set of goals and assumptions about their work with
young children. Preschools that emphasize early academics and skill
development may be less receptive to a partnership that includes an
emotion-centered curriculum and the integration of children's home
and school experiences. Likewise, clinicians with narrow definitions of
therapeutic interventions may not be prepared to provide broader, less
formal early intervention services in child care centers. Fledgling early
childhood programs still struggling to establish basic care and educational services may need to be on firmer ground before they enter into
a collaborative relationship. Sometimes the collaborators make the difficult decision to discontinue services because of an inability to develop
a shared agenda.

ONGOING ASSESSMENT

This assessment of "goodness of fit" is an ongoing process, one that should be revisited from time to time even in well-functioning partnerships. Typically, consultants meet with staff to review the effectiveness of their joint efforts across several dimensions and to assess if new needs have arisen in the center. Clinicians may speak with administrators about observations regarding staff communication and development and inquire if they see movement toward overall program goals. With teachers, consultants may discuss gains in being able to handle emotionally charged material and difficult behaviors in the classroom as well as the teachers' levels of stress and job satisfaction. Social work staff may help consultants determine if planned inroads with parents and the larger community have been successful or if outreach strategies need to be redesigned.

A less objective but no less important assessment involves looking at the current state of the relationship between the mental health consultant and the staff of the school. The strength of this partnership is the key to the effectiveness of the collaboration; it is the best prognostic indicator of future success in efforts to expand or enhance the collaboration. The willingness to persevere together, to respect each other, and to communicate openly about differences are all critical elements in the development of a healthy working relationship between mental health professionals and early childhood educators. Yet evaluating the partnership and what it means to both parties is no easy task. Often it is only during periods of absence or after a consultant has left a program that a center acutely senses the value of cross-disciplinary exchanges. Similarly, when consultants are reassigned to more traditional clinical positions, they often feel a void and long for the communal spirit, informality, and commitment of early childhood workers. Sometimes the relationship continues to be an ambiguous one, and its value remains unclear to one or both participants.

> In one child care center, the mental health consultant,
> Dr. Kelly, was growing increasingly frustrated by her
> seeming inability to form connections with the teachers,
> many of whom had been at the center for more than 20
> years. The director assured her on several occasions that she
> was making an impact, but Dr. Kelly was not persuaded.
> The consultant attended a staff workshop one afternoon
> during which the staff held their traditional lottery for door
> prizes. One teacher, Ms. Hayes, who had been particularly
> resistant to meetings with the consultant, spoke to the

director in front of the group: She wanted to be certain that
Dr. Kelly had a ticket for the drawing. Then Ms. Hayes
turned to the clinician and said quietly, "After all, you're
one of us."

It may take a year or two, but in time strong collaborative relationships become easier to recognize, both internally and externally.
They are characterized by trust and mutual respect. Such partnerships
also tend to galvanize both parties, increasing their investment in the
work, sense of competence, and satisfaction.

Many mental health professionals welcome the range of activities
and the opportunities that are available in early childhood centers for
connecting with children, parents, and families. The extent to which
they take advantage of these situations and are encouraged to do so are
other important factors in determining the vitality of the partnership.
This work offers new challenges and exciting alternatives to the other
tasks undertaken by mental health practitioners. For example, consultants may offer new services to programs such as support groups for
staff (described in Chapter 4), drop-in times for parents (Chapter 5),
and a "feelings circle time" for children (Chapter 6). Such interventions
usually emerge over time from discussions with staff and administrators. They involve conducting a mutual needs assessment and, in some
cases, a rethinking of how to apply the consultant's abilities on site. In
other centers, however, relatively few new ideas and strategies will
evolve. This lack of new initiatives might force the participants to look
more closely at the overall impact of the collaboration and the vigor of
the relationship.

In addition to opportunities for creative planning and innovation,
the consulting role presents numerous possibilities for working with
young children in their natural environments. Successful consultants
are ones who take advantage of the freedom to move about the
preschool and enjoy working with children and teachers in the classroom, on the playground, and in the gymnasium. They also welcome
the chance to greet parents at drop-off or pick-up times or to meet with
them in informal gatherings in the cafeteria or lounge. Consultants
who join in school celebrations of birthdays, holidays, and graduation,
as well as those who express genuine interest in learning about local
customs and ethnic rituals, tend to be accepted in a way that offers
them a far wider berth in designing and planning interventions for
families. Clinicians who limit their efforts to problems with individual
children and prefer one-to-one interventions outside of the classroom
are not as likely to take advantage of the potential for other kinds of
personal contacts in the school. They are also not apt to have as broad

an effect as those who strive to develop rapport with staff, enhance the skills of teachers, and present new ideas and strategies to parents.

The consultant's sense of joy in his work deserves special attention. Although the job can be a difficult and stressful one, early childhood consultants report that they feel a great deal of professional and personal satisfaction when things are going well. For clinicians trained to deal with psychopathology, trauma, and family disturbances, working outside of a private office or clinic and fostering healthy development in children can be a liberating and exciting endeavor. Some welcome the chance to use their clinical judgment in planning their day, free from administrative constraints or from the burden of having to account for their time through billable sessions with individual clients. The chance for "wellness visits" with children, families, or entire classrooms can feel like a special privilege, and close-up observations of how young children grow and change over time, with or without special interventions, can be particularly rewarding. Some consultants, perhaps feeling pressed to act quickly or to be "useful," lose sight of these opportunities and dismiss the importance of acknowledging where programs are already functioning well and championing those on site who are responsible for these successes.

Despite the challenges, frustrations, and limited resources in many early childhood programs, the level of commitment and caring of staff members is inspiring. Many preschool teachers, even those without formal training in child development, are blessed with patience and perseverance that allows them to carry on when confronted with increasing numbers of children with challenging behaviors and difficult life circumstances. Each program seems to have at least one staff member who best epitomizes the tradition of the firm but caring preschool teacher, who has a special place in her heart for each of her charges. Many early childhood educators approach their work with good humor and playfulness and welcome other professionals to join with them on the journeys they take with children. Mental health consultants may struggle with how to help transfer these teachers' skills and gifts to their less enthusiastic colleagues. Yet sometimes the consultants just have to stop and marvel at the performance of their fellow teaching professionals.

THE SCHOOL'S POINT OF VIEW

To this point in this book, the ongoing assessment process has been described primarily from the point of view of mental health consultants and how they approach this work. Preschool staff, particularly the administrators, frequently voice similar themes when describing the components of a healthy collaboration. In their view, developing a strong relationship and having agreed-on goals are essential for beginning a successful partnership, and the consultant's ability to engage children, parents, and teachers in a range of activities largely determines its ongoing viability. Many directors report that they have had at least one experience with a mental health agency in which goals were not reconciled, mainly because the proposed partner had a predefined agenda and did not consider the center's specific needs. They differed at times over what evaluation and treatment services should be provided and how research protocols should be employed, but the primary complaints revolved around clinicians' lack of respect for classroom staff. One child care director suggested that both parties need to be patient and "respect the evolution" of the relationship. She was referring to her gradual understanding that the consultant could not readily "fix" children and that she instead needed to use this time to review administrative and staff communication issues as well as to reduce her own stress level. None of these were on her mind when she entered into the relationship 2 years earlier.

The need for support in sharing the responsibility of working with young children and families has been documented repeatedly in informal surveys with directors and teachers. In addition to their own needs for support, many directors point to the mental health concerns of their staff, both in combating job stress and in helping them manage their roles within their own families. The chance to offer families support when they drop off children and visit the classroom is also cited as a key ingredient of the collaboration. Some administrators commented that this kind of availability is especially helpful for reluctant parents, who are hesitant to seek mental health services. In many centers, knowing that there is someone on site to whom they can speak in confidence and at their convenience seems to lessen families' resistance to considering additional kinds of help for their children.

Preschool administrators also cite the immediacy and the comprehensive nature of the services when asked to describe what works well in these partnerships. Some express frustration in seeking services by referral to outside providers or local school districts, which tends to be a time-consuming process that is bogged down by administrative demands. They often are more at ease with consultants who can proceed quickly with an evaluation in the center. One program director also noted that in these evaluations, the consultant has the advantage of working with and assessing a child at many levels, both individually and in his family and classroom contexts. Although they often want more information and are sometimes frustrated by the limits of confidentiality, many teachers and directors are pleased that they receive more immediate feedback on the course of evaluations and on-site treatment interventions.

DEVELOPING INSTITUTIONAL
SUPPORT FOR THE COLLABORATIVE MODEL

Both early childhood educators and mental health professionals have stressed the need for comprehensive and well-funded collaborations that reflect the shared commitment of their institutions. Some early childhood directors have been particularly successful in drawing attention to the mental health needs of their children, families, and staff and have convinced their oversight agencies to support these linkages. In many communities across the United States, Head Start teachers and staff have actively sought to develop partnerships with local mental health providers. In the more successful collaborations between mental health and early childhood agencies, the partners share a similar vision of early intervention services, a commitment to families, an investment in their communities, and a willingness to pool resources to support their joint endeavor.

Even when the collaborators have a healthy working relationship, developing consistent funding sources can be a monumental challenge. However, many foundations and individuals have responded to the notion of preventive, community-based services for young children. Some corporate philanthropists have found this model appealing and consistent with their growing concerns about child care for their own employees and for the larger community. In 1998, Head Start changed its program mandates nationwide to include on-site mental health services and, in some cases, has been willing to fund demonstration programs, including the consultation model described in this book. Other federal sources of support are also available; grants from the U.S. Department of Housing and Urban Development have also supported early childhood mental health consultation.

If the mental health and early childhood agencies are successful in securing funds, and are able to provide technical and administrative as well as financial support to the collaboration, the clinicians and educators are far more likely to form solid connections and to work as a team. Grant-funded programs that do not have to rely on a fee-for-service model put less pressure on the mental health consultants to focus exclusively on children with serious delays or disturbances and allow the relationship to develop beyond the confines of a traditional medical model. Representatives from mental health and other agencies may make a host of promises about possible clinical and research partnerships that eventually fail because the realities of providing and receiving payment for services tend to dominate their agendas, leaving little time for more collaborative endeavors.

Just as consultants need this freedom, early childhood staff members require time to develop the relationship and take advantage of the consultation. If program administrators view mental health training as a priority, they are far more likely to give teachers and other staff chances to attend meetings and workshops with the clinician. A director's openness to and acceptance of the consultant sets a tone that can help teachers be less defensive or protective about their individual classrooms. In some instances, directors are confused about clinicians' presence because they inherited the consultation or were persuaded by their oversight agency to collaborate. These partnerships are commonly fraught with more tension and take longer to develop into working relationships; teachers in these programs are given neither the time to meet with the consultant nor the blessing of their supervisors to formulate joint techniques. Even in preschools where mental health consultation is viewed as a much-needed service, there are problems translating this commitment into curriculum development and classroom interventions. A lack of regular staff meeting times and coverage issues, particularly in child care, may hinder the consultant's efforts to join forces with the early childhood staff. However, over time, these relationships are usually fruitful, especially if consultants can meet with directors and other administrators to discuss these obstacles and ways of overcoming them.

Yet in some areas of the United States, both rural and urban, the concept of establishing such institutional partnerships may be at best a remote possibility. Many small child care centers are unaffiliated with a larger umbrella organization and have few resources to contract with local providers. Some regions have few mental health centers that promote services for young children or extend their services readily into the community. In these cases, developing an affiliation with a single mental health provider may be the best alternative. The main factors for establishing successful partnerships are similar in these instances, but the relationships may experience different challenges. Out of necessity, private providers may have to contract for their clinical services and limit their consultation time to the assessments or therapies for which they are hired. Even if services are offered on a pro bono basis, the clinician may not bring the right qualifications to the early childhood center. Such was the case in the early 1990s when the American Psychological Association put out a call for its members to volunteer in Head Start centers. Many psychologists offered their time, but a number of them had little clinical experience with young children. Others came to the centers expecting to conduct a few brief sessions with children or families each week, so they were not prepared to forge ongoing relationships with the teaching or administrative staff. This initiative was well intentioned but it ultimately failed because of inadequate consideration of the needs of the early childhood programs.

In developing collaborations with either mental health agencies or private practitioners, educators have to feel that they can help set the agenda for their joint efforts. Although they may welcome the clinical expertise of mental health professionals, child care directors and staff need to see evidence that their ideas on child development and education are respected and that consultants appreciate the relationships the program has developed with families and the larger community. Again, this comes down to fostering trust and spending substantial time together. Being on staff at a reputable mental health agency or academic child study center does not guarantee success as a consultant for any one clinician, even if the agency and the early childhood program have an established and healthy partnership. Some excellent therapists are not well suited to this role because they have trouble translating their theoretical understanding and clinical acumen to a broader, less academic setting. Ultimately, as in any consulting relationship, both parties need to feel comfortable assessing whether there is an adequate match in their goals and expectations, and they must have the freedom to suggest changes in—or, if necessary, terminate—the relationship.

PROFESSIONAL DEVELOPMENT
FOR EARLY CHILDHOOD CONSULTANTS

It is evident, then, that successful consultants must have certain clinical and collaborative skills before entering this role, including a solid command of child development, an understanding of family systems, and a familiarity with the goals of early childhood education. Yet even clinicians with this background continually require support and supervision, especially when working with more fragile child care systems and centers having high incidences of trauma.

Supervision

Supervision will generally focus on several overlapping areas. Not unlike most clinical situations, the sessions will include material on assessments of individual children and reports regarding ongoing therapeutic interventions, but it will also include a broader review of how the child functions in the classroom and other settings. Thorough consulting supervision includes a systems evaluation or an appraisal of a child's interactions with her family and child care providers. Some aggressive young children, for instance, are exploiting real or perceived weaknesses in their teaching team, and the supervisor may help the consultant address the behavior by working to strengthen the team. Supervision should also address the relationship among consultants, teachers, and preschool administrators as well as the need for staff support and potential areas of conflict. This assessment will influence the timing and pace of interventions and help determine when new strategies or approaches can be tested. Finally, consultants should be prepared to discuss personal dilemmas encountered in the work and how they manage issues of autonomy and isolation, the role's inherent ambiguities, and their own responses to trauma.

Teamwork and Peer Support

In addition to supervision, it is useful to develop a mechanism for team support for consultants. Consultant group members might meet regularly to discuss work regarding individual children and families, staff development and training topics, crisis intervention strategies, and general program issues in their respective sites. These meetings also help counteract a feeling of isolation in being the only mental health clinician in a child care center, and it can be reassuring when consultants hear that other consultants are encountering similar challenges. This kind of professional support is critical even for experienced clinicians who welcome the freedom and flexibility of their roles and are well versed in the dynamics of early childhood centers. These group meetings can also help clinicians who are struggling to maintain their professional boundaries while becoming more steeped in the communities they serve. The familiarity, friendliness, and community activism of numerous child care centers are greatly appealing to many who do this work, and the idea of joining the staff on their mission is compelling. Although consultants in early childhood programs have much flexibility in this regard and can enjoy the benefits of community-based work, they also have to maintain some degree of independence to maintain their effectiveness. Sometimes the consultants feel torn between providing more services to the center and meeting their responsibilities at their own agencies, and the group can also address these struggles over divided loyalties.

Additional opportunities for professional training and development can be encouraged among members of the consulting team. Many clinicians attend lectures and workshops on various child development topics, such as emotion-centered curriculums for young children, assessment and early intervention strategies, and family systems therapies and brief treatments for children. A group of clinicians from one agency may prepare case examples of successful consulting strategies for directors, social workers, and educational supervisors from the collaborating programs. They may also provide training to school districts on establishing collaborations, supporting staff, and managing aggressive and violent behaviors in the classroom. Some clinicians may choose to meet with other professional groups to discuss this work in the context of larger developments in the fields of early childhood education and mental health as well as recent changes in welfare and workfare legislation.

IMPLICATIONS FOR POLICY

This book aims to elucidate opportunities for early intervention and prevention in early childhood programs that combine the strengths of educators and mental health professionals. By expanding preschool curricula to include a fuller range of emotional experiences and family dynamics, early childhood professionals can guide young children through day-to-day stresses as well as periods of upheaval. Championing this expanded model may seem to increase the considerable burden already shouldered by many early childhood educators. However, by most accounts, the needs of young children in child care have grown considerably, and this book's main purpose is to suggest ways of devising and implementing cross-disciplinary strategies to meet these new expectations. Nonetheless, support from other professionals and joint intervention planning may not always sufficiently aid early childhood educators in adapting to this role. Even dedicated teachers and those willing to try different techniques may find themselves in settings that are less conducive to these changes; some centers would require fundamental shifts in philosophy and the distribution of resources to accomplish the goals set forth in these pages.

Professional Status

Until the professional status and compensation for early childhood educators becomes commensurate to the tasks that they perform and the stresses they endure, providing quality early intervention programs on a wide scale will remain an elusive goal. This is particularly true in underserved and disadvantaged areas where teachers and other staff members are often asked to do the most with the least support, training, and pay. Collaborations with other professionals are of course critical to these programs, but they may fall short of expectations if the frontline staff are overwhelmed by the degree of distress they encounter and do not feel that the financial and emotional support they receive is anywhere near adequate. Paying people fast-food wages for the demanding and critical task of providing nurturing and stimulating care for young children is nothing short of demeaning. In many centers, this limited compensation leads to high turnover, frequent absenteeism, lessened job satisfaction, or underqualified personnel.

Publicly funded programs have heretofore had a checkered record at best in this regard. Although the federal Head Start program makes a strong effort to recruit teachers from the community and to provide a diverse work force with solid academic credentials, its pay scales lag significantly behind those of private early childhood programs and do not reflect the cost-of-living differentials in various regions of the United States. Many state licensing boards give little direction regarding salaries for child care workers, who often are paid at or just beyond minimum wage. Prekindergarten programs that are part of local school districts often offer more reasonable teacher salaries, but the pay in many instances remains below that of their peers in elementary and high schools.

There are also fewer opportunities for professional advancement in many early childhood programs. In some cases, the pay differential between head teachers and assistants is marginal and provides little incentive for junior staff to receive further training or college degrees. Successful teachers often feel hampered by the limited resources of their centers, and many feel torn between continuing to do the work they most enjoy and to which they are committed or seeking more money in the private sector. In some publicly funded centers, the best teachers are asked to take on administrative or supervisory roles, decreasing their classroom time without sufficient thought to who might replace them. Ironically, success in the classroom can limit teachers' direct work with children, and many find their new tasks much less rewarding.

Although they generally receive more compensation, mental health professionals who choose to work with young children face some of the same dilemmas. Until the 1990s, few mental health dollars were aimed at early intervention or prevention. Many child psychiatry departments still do not serve children younger than the age of 6 and their training programs do not usually offer many opportunities for clinical work with this age group. Some insurance companies do not provide mental health coverage for young children. Similar to other health professions and education, the younger the target population, the lower the status in the fields of psychology, psychiatry, and social work. Community-based interventions and partnerships are considered the best practices in many segments of the child mental health community, but many clinicians, academics, and researchers have chosen to avoid this arena. For some, it provides too many variables that confound their abilities to study in straightforward terms the effect of interventions. Practitioners often bypass direct community-based service because of the loss of control it implies, and many do not relish negotiating foreign terrain when trained primarily to work in an office environment in which they retain a good deal of authority. Some dedicated child therapists do not pursue community-based work because administrators who determine levels of advancement, pay, or academic rank may not recognize it as a significant contribution to their organization's overall goals.

Shifts in Early Childhood
Education and Mental Health Funding

Despite these challenges, the forces that have thus far limited the appeal of early childhood work appear to be weakening. Some states, such as New York, have begun actively pursuing the notion of a universal prekindergarten that is publicly funded, administered by local school districts, and staffed with certified teachers. Reports on the importance of early intervention and the successful development of private pre-schools have earned early childhood educators a new respect and prominence in many communities. Competition from corporate child care centers and other providers has forced some publicly funded centers to examine the career benefits and compensation they provide staff.

Clinicians and researchers who work with young children are witnessing a similar shift in emphasis in mental health policy and funding. Early intervention and prevention are among the most common buzz-words in the field, and collaboration and community-based interventions no longer have the stigma of being less rigorous or less professional work. Partly to enhance their future work options, trainees in psychology and social work are looking for opportunities to work in these settings. Many academic medical centers have established child study centers that focus on brain development in young children and the impact of healthy and detrimental environments on cognitive and emotional functioning. Some researchers have begun specifically studying the consequences of the mental health environment of early childhood classrooms (Kaplan, 1998). Others have created new means of assessments (Feil, Severson, & Walker, 1998) and school-based interventions with families (McDonald, Billingham, Conrad, Morgan, & Payton, 1997) that have particular relevance for preschools serving increasing numbers of challenging children and families in distress. Some of these efforts are receiving additional federal support from government agencies, including the National Institute of Mental Health; the Administration for Children, Youth, and Families, and the Department of Education.

Valuing Early Childhood

Few argue that children should receive quality care and should be educated and socialized to the larger society's rules and expectations, and that the adults who provide for them should be trained to meet these needs. Something gets lost, however, in many new educational initiatives or well-intentioned research and clinical efforts. Academics who study early childhood do not always appreciate what these young children really have to offer. Even early childhood workers trained to look beyond deficit or delay models often lose sight of the innovation, the curiosity, and the wonderment of the preschool child. Early childhood is often called the "magic years," and Piaget has taught respect for young children's cognitive skills; yet, on a day-to-day basis, it is easy to miss the incredible leaps and bounds that children are continually making. Even as child therapists, developmental psychologists, and early childhood educators, we sometimes forget the value of play and the young child's expertise in creating imaginative worlds filled with possibility.

Overlooking children's playfulness, creativity, and imagination is not surprising, however, in a society that does not recognize these as lasting accomplishments. Play in preschool children is tolerated and encouraged to the extent that it bolsters other forms of cognitive development, but with the understanding that, by a certain age—one that appears to be constantly lowering—they will turn to more productive and rational endeavors. Similarly, young children's clear expressions of the need to be nurtured and cared for, and their ability to honestly describe a wide range of feelings and experiences without reservation, make them an anomaly in our culture. The gifts and talents of young children are not acknowledged fully by most adults, who equate success with strength, self-reliance, and seriousness. Although society has become more fluid and individuals are allowed a wider breadth of expression and emotions, young children still stand in stark contrast to the adults around them who are, of course, in charge.

This limited appreciation for young children can be transferred to early childhood caregivers, the best of whom are similarly playful, imaginative, and fun-loving. It is the ability to engage in interactive play that often differentiates teachers and therapists who are well suited to working with preschoolers from those who are not. There is a tendency to denigrate this work by those who see it as "just playing with kids" or, worse, as babysitting—as if the children are passive and unresponsive and only need to be supervised. Those of us who have enjoyed the guilty pleasures of running around a playground with young children, joining in their pretend play, or sharing a meal with them while on the job as "professionals" can understand this criticism. We also sometimes question the value of our presence and wonder how we are using all that we have learned about child development, needing to explain away or validate our reasons for "indulging" in play with the children.

Until those of us working in early childhood environments succeed in combating these perceptions, real change in the value society places on interventions for young children will not take root in any systematic way. The longer we do this work, the more we describe our goals in simple terms and state that our aim is to allow preschoolers to play or to be children. We believe that if we join with educators to talk with children about their feelings, relieve some of their worries, and get them through difficult times, their development can proceed along a natural course of discovery and learning. The consultant's task is to support teachers, families, and caregivers so that they can encourage children along this course or get back on track if they have been temporarily de-railed. Working together in this way offers hope to children that they can meet and overcome many of the obstacles and challenges they will face by turning to trusted adults, expressing their concerns, and seeking comfort and support from their peers and their families. In our view, there can be no loftier goal or more lasting achievement.

References

Aber, J.L., & Allen, J.P. (1987). Effects of maltreatment on children's socioemotional development: An attachment theory perspective. *Developmental Psychology, 23,* 406–414.

Achenbach, T.M. (1991). *Child Behavior Checklist.* Burlington: University of Vermont, Department of Psychiatry.

Alpert, J.L. (1982). *Psychological consultation in educational settings.* San Francisco: Jossey-Bass.

Carter, S.L., Osofsky, J.D., & Hann, D.M. (1991). Speaking for the baby: A therapeutic intervention with adolescent mothers and their infants. *Infant Mental Health Journal, 12*(4), 291–301.

Christenson, S.L. (1995). Supporting home–school collaboration. In A. Thomas & J. Grimes (Eds.), *Best practices in school psychology III* (pp. 253–267). Washington, DC: National Association of School Psychologists.

Cohen, P., Provet, A., & Jones, M. (1996). The prevalence of emotional and behavioral disorders in childhood and adolescence. In B. Levin & J. Petrila (Eds.), *Mental health services: A public health perspective* (pp. 193–209). New York: Oxford University Press.

Conners, C.K. (1997). *Conners' Rating Scales (CRS)–Revised.* North Tonawanda, NY: Multi-Health Systems.

Cowen, E.L., Hightower, A.D., Pedro-Carroll, J.L., Work, W.C., Wyman, P.A., & Haffey, W.G. (1996). *School-based prevention for children at risk: The primary mental health project.* Washington, DC: American Psychological Association.

Craig, S.E. (1992, September). The educational needs of children living with violence. *Phi Delta Kappan,* 67–71.

Dion, M.D., Braver, S.L., Wolchick, S.A., & Sandler, I.W. (1997). Alcohol abuse and psychopathic deviance in noncustodial parents as predictors of child-support payments and visitation. *American Journal of Orthopsychiatry, 67,* 70–79.

Donahue, P.J. (1996). The treatment of homeless children and families: Integrating mental health services into a Head Start model. In A. Zelman (Ed.), *Early intervention with high-risk children* (pp. 151–170). Northvale, NJ: Jason Aronson.

Dubow, E.F., Roecker, C.E., & D'Imperio, R. (1997). Mental health. In R.T. Ammerman & M. Hershon (Eds.), *Handbook of prevention and treatment with children and adolescents: Intervention in the real world context* (pp. 259–286). New York: John Wiley & Sons.

Edlefson, M., & Baird, M. (1994). Making it work: Preventive mental health care for disadvantaged preschoolers. *Social Work, 39*(5), 566–572.

Faber, A., & Mazlish, E. (1980). *How to talk so kids will listen: Group workshop kit.* New York: Avon Books.

Fantuzzo, J., Coolahan, K.C., & Weiss, A.D. (1995). Resiliency partnership-directed intervention: Enhancing the social competencies of preschool victims of physical abuse by developing peer resources and community strengths. In D. Cicchetti & S.L. Toth (Eds.), *Rochester symposium on developmental psychopathology: Vol. 8. Developmental perspectives on trauma: Theory, research, and intervention* (pp. 463–489). Rochester, NY: University of Rochester Press.

Feil, E.G., Severson, H.H., & Walker, H.M. (1998). Screening for emotional and behavioral delays: The Early Screening Project. *Journal of Early Intervention, 21*(3), 252–266.

Goldman, R.K., Botkin, M.J., Tokunaga, H., & Kuklinski, M. (1997). Teacher consultation: Impact on teachers' effectiveness and students' cognitive competence and achievement. *American Journal of Orthopsychiatry, 67*, 374–384.

Greenspan, S.I. (1992). *Infancy and early childhood: The practice of clinical assessment and intervention with emotional and developmental challenges.* Madison, CT: International Universities Press.

Gridley, B., Mucha, L., & Hatfield, B. (1995). Preschool screening. In A. Thomas & J. Grimes (Eds.), *Best practices in school psychology III* (pp. 213–225). Washington, DC: National Association of School Psychologists.

Griffith, D.R., Azuma, S.D., & Chasnoff, I.J. (1994). Three-year outcome of children prenatally exposed to drugs. *Journal of the Academy of Child and Adolescent Psychiatry, 33*, 20–27.

Groves, B., Zuckerman, B., Marans S., & Cohen, D. (1993). Silent victims: Children who witness violence. *Journal of the American Medical Association, 269*, 262–264.

Gutkin, T.B., & Curtis, M.J. (1990). School-based consultation: Theory, techniques and research. In T.B. Gutkin & C.R. Reynolds (Eds.), *The handbook of school psychology* (2nd ed., 577–611). New York: John Wiley & Sons.

Harry, B. (1992). Developing cultural self-awareness: The first step in values clarification for early interventionists. *Topics in Early Childhood Special Education, 12*(3), 333–350.

Hetherington, E.M. (1989). Coping with family transitions: Winners, losers and survivors. *Child Development, 60*, 1–14.

Hintze, J.M., & Shapiro, E.S. (1995). Systematic observation of classroom behavior. In A. Thomas & J. Grimes (Eds.), *Best practices in school psychology III* (pp. 651–660). Washington, DC: National Association of School Psychologists.

Howarth, M. (1989, November). Rediscovering the power of fairy tales: They help children understand their lives. *Young Children*, 58–65.

Hyson, M.C. (1994). *The emotional development of young children: Building an emotion-centered curriculum.* New York: Teachers College Press.

Jaffe, P., Wilson S., & Wolfe, D. (1988). Specific assessment and intervention strategies for children exposed to wife battering: Preliminary empirical investigations. *Canadian Journal of Community Mental Health, 7*, 157–163.

Kaplan, M.D. (1998). *A quality start: Assessing the mental health of Head Start classrooms.* New Haven, CT: Yale Child Study Center.

Kliman, A.S. (1978). *Crisis: Psychological first-aid for recovery and growth.* Austin, TX: Holt, Rinehart & Winston.

Knitzer, J. (1993). Children's mental health policy: Challenging the future. *Journal of Emotional and Behavioral Disorders, 1*, 8–16.

Knitzer, J. (1995). *Project Safe Haven: Developing and testing best practices for Head Start children, families and staff exposed to violence.* New York: National Center for Children in Poverty.

Knitzer, J. (1996). Meeting the mental health needs of young children and their families. In B.A. Stroul (Ed.), *Children's mental health: Creating systems of care in a changing society* (pp. 553–572). Baltimore: Paul H. Brookes Publishing Co.

Knitzer, J. (in press). Early childhood mental health services: Through a policy and systems perspective. In J.P. Shonkoff & S.J. Meisels (Eds.), *Handbook of early childhood intervention* (2nd ed.). New York: Cambridge University Press.

Koplow, L. (1996). *Unsmiling faces: How preschools can heal.* New York: Teachers College Press.

Lewis, C.C. (1995). *Educating hearts and minds: Reflections on Japanese preschool and elementary education.* Cambridge, UK: Cambridge University Press.

Lieberman, A.F., & Pawl, J.H. (1993). Infant–parent psychotherapy. In C. Zeanah (Ed.), *Handbook of infant mental health* (pp. 427–442). New York: The Guilford Press.

Lopez, T., Balter, N., Howard, S., Stewart, R., & Zelman, A.B. (1996). Cornerstone: A therapeutic nursery for severely disadvantaged children. In A. Zelman (Ed.), *Early intervention with high-risk children* (pp. 23–64). Northvale, NJ: Jason Aronson.

Lynch, E.W., & Hanson, M.J. (Eds.). (1998). *Developing cross-cultural competence: A guide for working with children and their families* (2nd ed.). Baltimore: Paul H. Brookes Publishing Co.

Lyon, E. (1993). Hospital staff reactions to accounts by survivors of child abuse. *American Journal of Orthopsychiatry, 63*(3), 410–416.

Lyons, P., & Rittner, B. (1998). The construction of the crack babies phenomenon as a social problem. *American Journal of Orthopsychiatry, 68,* 313–332.

McDonald, L., Billingham, S., Conrad, T., Morgan, A., O., N., & Payton, E. (1997, March–April). Families and schools together (FAST): Integrating community development with clinical strategies. *Families in Society: The Journal of Contemporary Human Services,* 140–154.

National Center for Children in Poverty. (1998). *Five million children.* New York: Author.

Osofsky, J.D. (1995). The effects of exposure to violence on young children. *American Psychologist, 50,* 782–788.

Osofsky, J.D., & Fenichel, E. (Eds.). (1994). *Hurt, healing, hope: Caring for infants and toddlers in violent environments.* Arlington, VA: ZERO TO THREE: National Center for Infants, Toddlers, and Families.

Parry, A. (1993, September). Children surviving in a violent world: "Choosing non-violence." *Young Children,* 13–15.

Preator, K., & McAllister, J. (1995). Assessing infants and toddlers. In A. Thomas & J. Grimes (Eds.), *Best practices in school psychology III* (pp. 775–788). Washington, DC: National Association of School Psychologists.

Pynoos, R.S., & Eth, S. (1986). Witness to violence: The child interview. *Journal of the American Academy of Child Psychiatry, 25,* 306–319.

Reynolds, C.R., & Kamphaus, R.W. (1992). *Behavior Assessment System for Children* [Manual]. Circle Pines, MN: American Guidance Service.

Ross, V.M. (1988). *Helping parents help their kids.* Arlington, VA: National School Public Relations Association.

Rutter, M. (1979). Protective factors in children's responses to stress and disadvantage. In M.W. Kent & J.E. Rolf (Eds.), *Social competence in children* (pp. 49–74). Hanover, NH: University Press of New England.

Rutter, M., & Quintin, D. (1977). Psychiatric disorder: Ecological factors and concepts in causation. In M. McGurk (Ed.), *Ecological factors in human development* (pp. 173–187). New York: North Holland.

Samalin, N. (1988). Running parent education groups: Goals and techniques. *Family Resource Coalition Report, 3,* 18.

Scarr, S. (1998). American child care today. *American Psychologist, 53*(2), 95–108.

Simons, M. (1997, December 31). Childcare sacred as France cuts back welfare state. *The New York Times,* pp. A1, A8.

Terr, L. (1991). Childhood traumas: An outline and overview. *American Journal of Psychiatry, 148*(1), 10–20.

Tobias, L.T. (1990). *Psychological consulting to management: A clinician's perspective.* Levittown, PA: Brunner/Mazel Publishing.

Wallerstein, J.S., & Kelly, J.B. (1980). *Surviving the break-up: How children and parents cope with divorce.* New York: Basic Books.

Werner, E. (1989). High-risk children in young adulthood: A longitudinal study from birth to 32 years. *American Journal of Orthopsychiatry, 59,* 72–81.

Yoshikawa, Y., & Knitzer, J. (1997). *Lessons from the field: Head Start mental health strategies to meet changing needs.* New York: National Center for Children in Poverty.

ZERO TO THREE: National Center for Infants, Toddlers, and Families. (1994a). *Caring for infants and toddlers in violent environments: Hurt, healing, and hope.* Arlington, VA: Author.

ZERO TO THREE: National Center for Infants, Toddlers, and Families. (1994b). *Diagnostic classification of mental health and developmental disorders of infancy and early childhood.* Arlington, VA: Author.

Zigler, E.F., Finn-Stevenson, M., & Stern, B.M. (1997). Supporting children and families in the schools: The school of the 21st century. *American Journal of Orthopsychiatry, 67,* 396–407.

Appendix

Early Childhood Consultation: Intake Assessment

Physical Setting

What is the physical state of the neighborhood?

What is the physical state of the building? Is it welcoming to children?

Where do staff members meet? Does the site have a lounge or cafeteria? Is it welcoming to staff?

Is there a parent room or other open space for families?

How are the classrooms organized?

Is there an appropriate balance among organization, safety, and open exploration of materials?

Are the classrooms well lit with age-appropriate materials in good condition?

Is there a good variety of gross and fine motor activities, books, and creative art supplies?

Are toys within children's reach?

Community

What is the relationship between the center and the community? How has the center been viewed historically?

What is the economic status of the community?

What is the ethnic makeup of the community? Are there many recent immigrants to the area?

Mental Health Consultation in Early Childhood, by Paul J. Donahue, Beth Falk, and Anne Gersony Provet ©2000 Paul H. Brookes Publishing Co., Baltimore

Is the community urban, suburban, or rural?

Are program staff drawn from the community?

Are there differences in language and culture between staff and the community? If so, how are these differences handled?

How does the center interact with other agencies (e.g., child protective services, department of social services, foster care, mental health clinics, preschool special education services) and other early child care providers?

Approach to the Consultant

What is the history of mental health consultation at the center?

What has been the experience of staff with other agency partners and professional collaborations?

Staff

What is the level of experience, education, and training of teachers and administrative staff?

What is the ethnic composition of the staff?

What is the socioeconomic status of the staff?

What alliances and conflicts exist among the staff?

What is the general approach to collaboration? Is there a well-developed team approach, or do individuals function primarily independently?

How regularly does the staff meet?

What is the hierarchical and supervisory structure of the program?

What administrative supports are available?

What needs have been identified by staff as the most pressing?

Mental Health Consultation in Early Childhood, by Paul J. Donahue, Beth Falk, and Anne Gersony Provet ©2000 Paul H. Brookes Publishing Co., Baltimore

Approach to Children

What is the general approach to structure in the classroom? (How is classroom time structured and managed? What is the daily routine within the classroom?)

What is the role of play in the classroom? Are creativity and free play encouraged?

Is the program oriented more toward individual or group experience?

Is the attainment of early academic skills emphasized?

Are children encouraged to be independent thinkers?

To what extent are children expected to conform to strict behavior codes?

How are discipline and problem behaviors handled?

What is the usual approach to withdrawn or fearful behaviors?

How are separation difficulties handled?

What types of assessment are used in the classroom?

Approach to Children with Special Needs

Are children with special needs identified in a timely manner?

Are children with special needs included in the program?

What is the referral process when special needs have been identified?

What is the program's approach to on-site services? Does the center tend to facilitate on-site services or to encourage alternative placements? Is the center comfortable recommending evaluation for alternative placement, or is this seen as a program failure?

Mental Health Consultation in Early Childhood, by Paul J. Donahue, Beth Falk, and Anne Gersony Provet ©2000 Paul H. Brookes Publishing Co., Baltimore

What is the attitude of the program toward outside
specialists who provide on-site services? Is there a
cooperative spirit or resentment toward the
interruption?

Where are services provided?

What resources are available to staff working with
children who have physical disabilities?

What resources are available to staff working with
children presenting problem behaviors?

Approach to Families

How are families involved in the day-to-day running of
the program? Do families serve as school volunteers?

How are families encouraged to participate in program
activities?

How is communication between the center and
families handled?

Are parent conferences held regularly?

Are parent workshops or support groups available to
families through the program?

What type of contact do various staff members
(e.g., teachers, administrative staff, program
directors, social workers) have with families? How
do teachers typically interact with families?

Overall Formulation

What are the strengths and weaknesses of the
program?

What is the emotional atmosphere of the program?

What stresses do families face?

What stresses do staff (teachers and administrators) face?

Mental Health Consultation in Early Childhood, by Paul J. Donahue, Beth Falk, and
Anne Gersony Provet ©2000 Paul H. Brookes Publishing Co., Baltimore

How are these stresses interrelated?

How well established is the program? Does it have solid ties to the community?

What central themes emerge in the assessment?

Initial Plan of Intervention

What are the short-term aims of the consultation?

What are the long-term goals of the consultation?

Is there mutual agreement regarding these objectives?

What potential challenges to collaboration have been identified? Is there an openness to the collaboration?

Where does the consultant need to establish alliances and build rapport?

What will be the initial points of intervention?

Are there any crises that need immediate attention?

Mental Health Consultation in Early Childhood, by Paul J. Donahue, Beth Falk, and Anne Gersony Provet ©2000 Paul H. Brookes Publishing Co., Baltimore

Staff Development Workshop Topics

Promoting self-esteem in the classroom

The social and emotional development of young
children

Dealing with temper tantrums and other oppositional
behaviors

Understanding diversity: Social values and cultural
differences

Talking and playing: Communicating with preschoolers
and understanding their symbolic play

The sexual development of young children

The psychological problems of young children and
their families: How to identify and manage behavior
and emotional concerns

Working with trauma and crises in the classroom

Language development in young children

Handling aggression in the classroom

Classroom structure and behavior management

Working with parents and families

Mental health services: When and how to use them

Mental Health Consultation in Early Childhood, by Paul J. Donahue, Beth Falk, and
Anne Gersony Provet ©2000 Paul H. Brookes Publishing Co., Baltimore

Topics for Parent Workshops

The following are topics related to raising young children. Please mark any that you would like to discuss during our parent workshop series.

_____ Setting rules, limits, and consequences

_____ Dealing with my own and/or my children's anger

_____ Sibling rivalry and jealousy

_____ Disagreements between me and my spouse or my relatives about childrearing

_____ My fatigue, stress, and impatience

_____ Television arguments and rules

_____ Being a single parent

_____ Difficulty leaving my child with a baby sitter or relative

_____ Conflicts about food and eating

_____ Sleep problems

_____ Dealing with my child's fears

_____ Talking about sexual issues with young children

_____ Toilet training

Mental Health Consultation in Early Childhood, by Paul J. Donahue, Beth Falk, and Anne Gersony Provet ©2000 Paul H. Brookes Publishing Co., Baltimore

Sample Topic Letter for Parent Workshops

Dear Parents,

We have received your input regarding parent workshops and want to thank you for your participation and suggestions.

The following list represents the most requested topics, and many of your other concerns will be incorporated into these topics.

We are looking forward to meeting with you at these workshops. All workshops will be held from 5:00–6:00 P.M.

1. When it's Time to Say No   November 17, 1999
    Helping Parents Provide
    Positive Discipline and
    Set Limits for Children

2. Play with Me   December 15, 1999
    Activities to Do at Home
    with Your Child

3. The Balancing Act   January 26, 2000
    When There Aren't Enough
    Hours in the Day

4. Mr. Mom and Ms. Dad   February 23, 2000
    Managing the Stress
    and Problems of
    Single Parenting

5. TV in the Home: Friend or Foe?   March 16, 2000

6. Sibling Rivalry/Sibling Love   April 20, 2000

7. Sexuality in Young Children   May 7, 2000

Mental Health Consultation in Early Childhood, by Paul J. Donahue, Beth Falk, and Anne Gersony Provet ©2000 Paul H. Brookes Publishing Co., Baltimore

---

SAMPLE FLIER
ANNOUNCING PARENT MEETING

YOU ARE INVITED TO A
PARENT WORKSHOP

THE TOPIC: HELPING CHILDREN
GET ALONG WITH SIBLINGS AND FRIENDS

WHEN: FRIDAY, JANUARY 24, 1999
9:30–10:30 A.M.

THE WORKSHOP WILL BE LED BY OUR
CHILD PSYCHOLOGIST, REBECCA THOMPSON,
AND OUR FAMILY WORKER, MERCEDES PEREZ.

ENJOY REFRESHMENTS
AND THE COMPANY OF OTHER PARENTS.

Mental Health Consultation in Early Childhood, by Paul J. Donahue, Beth Falk, and Anne Gersony Provet ©2000 Paul H. Brookes Publishing Co., Baltimore

**SAMPLE CERTIFICATE OF
ACHIEVEMENT FOR PARENTS**

CERTIFICATE OF ACHIEVEMENT

AWARDED TO

_____

ON

_____

THIS CERTIFICATE IS GIVEN TO YOU IN
RECOGNITION OF YOUR ATTENDANCE
AT PARENT WORKSHOPS

GIVEN AT _____.
YOU HAVE DEMONSTRATED THE
WILLINGNESS TO LEARN AND
TO HELP OTHERS TO BECOME BETTER PARENTS.

_____   _____
Workshop Leader   Program Director

Mental Health Consultation in Early Childhood, by Paul J. Donahue, Beth Falk, and
Anne Gersony Provet ©2000 Paul H. Brookes Publishing Co., Baltimore

SAMPLE PERMISSION LETTER
FOR PARTICIPATION IN
SCHOOL-BASED GROUP

I give permission for my child, _____,
who attends the Cedar Community Center, to
participate in a group led by Dr. Steven Vincent.

Dr. Vincent will run a small playgroup to enhance
the children's social skills and overall emotional
development. This group will meet once a week.

_____

Signature of Parent/Guardian

_____

Date

Mental Health Consultation in Early Childhood, by Paul J. Donahue, Beth Falk, and
Anne Gersony Provet ©2000 Paul H. Brookes Publishing Co., Baltimore

Index

Page numbers followed by "f" indicate figures.